Century 21 City

Century 21 City

Seattle's Fifty Year Journey from
World's Fair to World Stage

Michael Luis

Fairweather Publishing
Medina, Washington

Library of Congress Control Number: 2012946656

ISBN: 978-0-9847882-1-7

For further information, contact:

Fairweather Publishing
P.O. Box 15
Medina, WA 98039
425-453-5123

www.centurytwentyonecity.com

Contents

Note to Readers

I am not giving too much of the story away to indicate that Seattle owes a great deal of its success to innovation and the willingness of individuals to experiment with new technologies and business models. In that spirit, this book is being published with a set of tools available to authors and readers only in the past few years.

Two production and distribution technologies in particular—electronic books and print-on-demand manufacturing—provide an unprecedented opportunity for authors to do something very important: correct mistakes. There is no warehouse with boxes of copies of *Century 21 City* waiting for distribution. Rather, the book exists as electronic files that can be updated at any time.

So, if you find things that need correcting—typos, data problems or demonstrable factual errors—let me know and I will incorporate corrections into the files.

If you disagree with some interpretation or analysis, I would certainly like to hear your point of view, but I cannot guarantee that your take on events will make it into future editions.

Please send your notes and comments, along with any back-up data I will need, to: corrections@centurytwentyonecity.com.

Introduction

One morning in late October, 1992, when I was working at the Greater Seattle Chamber of Commerce, I walked by the President's office and saw inside a huge blow up of a cover of *Fortune* magazine, with the headline "Best Cities for Business." In the cover photo, with blue sky and the Seattle skyline in the background, stood Frank Shrontz, CEO of Boeing, Bill Gates, CEO of Microsoft, Minoru Arakawa, CEO of Nintendo of North America, and, seated in front of them, Seattle Mayor Norm Rice. I had glimpsed the holy grail for a public affairs staffer at a chamber of commerce. *Best City for Business*!

The photo itself says some interesting things, though. To begin with, the businesses represented are fully globalized companies: they scour the world for customers, for talent, for inputs, for partners. They also depend on very high levels of brainpower. These firms recruit absolutely the best technical talent, that they lure to Seattle with pictures like this one.

Another thing to notice about the photo: although the background shows Seattle and the photo was taken on a Seattle fireboat with Seattle's mayor sitting front and center, all three of the firms represented have their headquarters outside of the Seattle city limits. So while we do not have a very good term to use as a substitute, "best cities" is a bit misleading. As in all modern metropolises, Seattle sits in the center of a much larger regional economy. And while the Seattle brand is powerful,

Mayor Rice needed to work with many city, county and special district governments to create an environment in which these businesses could thrive.

The editors of Fortune were probably unaware that Mayor Rice and about 75 business, government and civic leaders from the Seattle area had returned just a few months earlier from the region's first International Study Mission, to Amsterdam, Rotterdam and Stuttgart. As my colleague Bill Stafford and I assembled the agenda for that trip we began to build it around a central theme: the emerging reality that metropolitan regions compete as independent actors in the global economy. The purpose of the trip was to learn how these three very globalized cities were meeting that challenge and to establish relationships with them as we built our own global metropolitan network. At dinner on the last night of that trip, when Mayor Rice shared the podium with Stuttgart's remarkable Mayor, Manfred Rommel, son of the German general from World War II, we began to see that metropolitan leaders could make connections and play very unique roles in the evolution of the global economy.

As I write, the world still struggles to emerge from the worst economic downturn since the Great Depression, and the economic discussion centers around national and international policies that, depending on your point of view, will bring us out of this mess, or make it worse. But macro-economic policymaking will not determine the standards of living for most people around the world over the long term. Employment opportunities, earning levels and economic security are increasingly determined at the metropolitan level. We need to recognize that within the developed world we will find more economic variation among metro areas within a country than we will find variation among countries.

Fifty years ago, Seattle made its big splash on the world scene by hosting the Century 21 Exhibition. Since then, the region has enjoyed a high level of success in building a competitive economy and has become an even more attractive place to live. I hope that current, former and future residents of the Seattle area will enjoy learning how that happened and gain insights that will help us chart the region's future. I also hope that readers from other regions who are looking beyond the current situation and building their economies for the long term will draw useful lessons from Seattle's story.

Scholars and popular writers who study cities often do so through the lens of a particular discipline. Urban economists and geographers ask why people settle in certain areas and why businesses locate where they do. Urban planners seek the most efficient and pleasing arrangement of the built environment. Political scientists and sociologists examine how diverse populations live together in close proximity and how power is arranged and services provided. Historians trace all these forces over time. Social scientists often study many cities to identify patterns of behavior and activity within narrow disciplines. This book, in contrast, looks at a single city through a variety of lenses. My goal, in addition to telling a story that I hope you find interesting and compelling, is to provide a case study that applies current thinking from a several social science disciplines to one metropolitan area.

You will, no doubt, figure out that I like Seattle and its surrounding areas (especially the small suburban city where I grew up and currently reside). And since the late 1980s I have been a participant in, or a close observer of, many of the developments that both led to and resulted from Seattle's evolution over the past 25 years. So be forewarned that I will have a hard time being totally objective when it comes to analyzing the economic or political landscape.

You will also figure out that I generally approve of the way that the Seattle area has changed since the 1950s. If you listen around town you will easily find many people who do not approve of the region's growth and what they see as the loss of a unique, less aggressive atmosphere. I too miss some of the low-key quirkiness that has faded from Seattle, but I do know this: an economy, like a bicycle, must keep moving forward or it falls over. I have had the privilege of studying metropolitan areas across the country and abroad and have yet to find one that could make time stand still. Whether we like it or not, technology and global connectivity compel change, and our challenge is to embrace the change we need while clinging tightly to the things in our community that we cherish and keep us rooted here.

The rise from obscurity

To understand why my jaw dropped so far at the sight of that Fortune magazine cover, let me take you back a few years.

Scrap plywood was plentiful at construction sites in our suburban Seattle neighborhood in the 1960s, and an older neighbor kid was allowed to use his dad's saber saw to cut out models of the hydroplanes that raced on Lake Washington. We painted the models like our favorite boats—the Miss Bardahl, the Miss Thriftway, the Atlas Van Lines—and towed them behind our bikes, doing our best imitation of the roar of the old World War II Allison and Rolls Royce airplane engines that powered the Thunderboats and that we could hear from across the lake.[1] In a town with no major league stadium sports (the hapless, one-season Seattle Pilots being the exception) the annual unlimited hydroplane races were the most anticipated event of the year. In the 1960s Seattle was a big small town.

We got used to the obscurity of our dank little corner of the map. Although the commercial jet age was born in Seattle and the city had embraced modernism in some important ways, we always had a sense that the rest of the country saw us stuck somewhere back in the frontier. Hollywood did not help matters when, in 1967, it came out with *Here Come the Brides*, set in Seattle of the 1860s. Based loosely on the story of the Mercer girls, it featured a crusty sea captain, a saloon-keeper-with-a-heart-of-gold and a lot of men with axes and women with bustles. On a camping trip in Canada I remember meeting some kids from the East who were not clear that the show had been set one hundred years prior.

As we got a bit older many of us found out just exactly what the nation's literary elite thought of Seattle. In *Catcher in the Rye* our hero, Holden, wanders into the Lavender Room and sits down with three young women visiting New York. Although good dancers, he concludes that they are "three real morons." They are, of course, from Seattle. The scene leaves no doubt that they lack any of the sophistication that Holden prized, with their city of origin meant to emphasize that point.

Now, fast forward a few decades. The producers of a *Cheers* spinoff need a city in which to locate their new sitcom featuring the overeducated, snobbish Dr. Frasier Crane. Dr. Crane had no back-story, so the writers could choose any city for the hometown where he would join his equally snobbish brother and their ex-cop father. The city had to seem a credible place for the brothers' elitist lifestyle, and the writers chose Seattle. Frasier Crane's elegant condominium was followed by Tom

Hanks' swanky houseboat in *Sleepless in Seattle*, the charmingly dingy apartments of *Singles*, Mike Doonesbury's room-with-a-view and the ultra-cool loft where the teens of *iCarley* film their webcast. Whether it was the Seattle hospital on *Grey's Anatomy* or Austin Powers' nemesis Dr. Evil living under the Space Needle, Seattle had acquired an attractive image that Salinger obviously did not see in 1950.

Seattle's rise from cultural obscurity reflected its economic rise, which is the story in this book. In the 1960s, Seattle had, in many ways, become a Boeing company town. It seemed that every other kid's mom or dad worked at the Lazy B. Much of the remainder of the economy remained rooted in the traditional natural resource and port-related businesses that had dominated the regional economy for its first hundred years. The tallest building in Seattle was the Smith Tower, a terra cotta gem built in 1914 that anchored an otherwise unimpressive skyline. To the north of downtown the Space Needle stood as a symbol of hope, but otherwise just a nice place for a view or a special occasion dinner in the restaurant.

Since then the metropolitan economy of Seattle has added a mix of technology-based industries, business services and life sciences research activities that complement a still-large Boeing presence and highly competitive ports. A crowded skyline now dwarfs the Smith Tower, and an impressive skyline has arisen across Lake Washington, in Bellevue. Incomes in the region now rank among the highest in the nation, and individuals and families come from all over the country and the world to live here—in spite of the weather, which has not evolved at all.

The fact that the world has "discovered" Seattle, both culturally and economically, does not sit well with many residents, both natives and recent arrivals. Long-time Seattle Post Intelligencer columnist Emmet Watson founded the "Lesser Seattle" movement to point out the folly of chasing growth and fame. Seattle has always labored under a sort of civic cognitive dissonance, being at the same time a city of hard charging capitalists and a city of laid back environmentalists, edgy artists and dreamers. The latter have, it seems, been fighting a losing battle, but they rise up periodically to thwart some ambitious civic undertaking or another and keep the hubris in check.

A note about geography and names

This book has "Seattle" in its title. It is, of course, about far more than the city of 600,000 people on the shores of Puget Sound. Only about one out of six people in the greater Seattle region live within the city limits of Seattle, yet Seattle has the brand name that means something. Say "Puget Sound Region" anywhere outside of Washington State and you may or may not elicit a glimmer of recognition. But say "Seattle" and Americans and many people in other countries will know what you are referring to. So at the risk of offending my friends and neighbors who are in that 5/6 of the population outside of Seattle's city limits, I will often refer to the entire region simply as Seattle.

This is no trivial matter, as you can imagine. Each of the 79 cities in the area is unique, and the larger cities, especially Tacoma, have strong historic identities. But I have no alternative that really works in the printed word. So, if I refer to Greater Seattle, the Seattle area, Puget Sound, or simply Seattle, I am referring to the region. I will always be clear if I am referring to the city of Seattle itself.

Now, on to the geography. The Seattle region can be described in several levels.

King County. 2012 population: 1.96 million This is Washington's largest County, with a little less than one third of the county population living within the city limits of Seattle. The rest of the urbanized area can be neatly divided into two sections. East King County cities include Bellevue, Redmond, Kirkland and Issaquah, which are home to a large part of the region's technology industry. South King County cities include Kent, Auburn, Federal Way and Renton, and the area hosts a large share of the region's manufacturing and distribution businesses, including the Renton plant where Boeing builds the 737. Most of the historical discussion in the book centers on King County.

Seattle-Bellevue-Everett Metropolitan Division. 2012 population 2.68 million. This includes King County and Snohomish County, to the north. Snohomish County has its county seat in Everett, which is host to the world's largest building – the massive plant where Boeing builds the 747, 767, 777 and 787. South Snohomish County also houses tens of thousands of people who commute into King County, and the two counties are considered a single housing market.

Seattle-Bellevue-Tacoma Metropolitan Statistical Area. 2012 population 3.49 million. This is the basic Census designated metro area, and consists of King, Snohomish and Pierce counties. Pierce County, which includes Tacoma, has strong historic and economic identity of its own, and is host to major port and manufacturing facilities, as well as Joint Base Lewis McChord. The area from Everett to Lakewood, south of Tacoma, is continuously urbanized. Much of the regional economic data in this book will cover the three counties.

Puget Sound Regional Council planning area. Population 3.74 million. For purposes of growth and economic development planning, the Puget Sound Regional Council includes the three counties in the metro area, plus Kitsap County, across Puget Sound. Kitsap is the smallest of the four counties and is dominated by several large Navy installations.

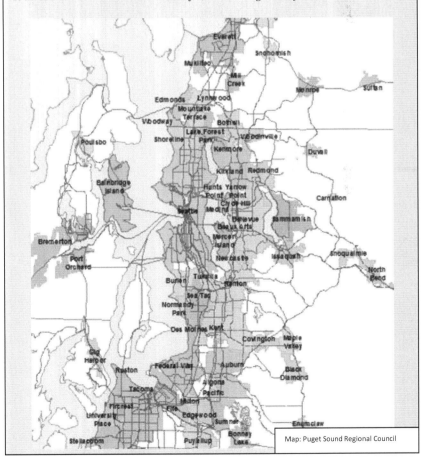

Map: Puget Sound Regional Council

Does Seattle's story matter?

Or, more to the point, does it matter to anyone outside of Western Washington? I think so. To begin with, there is a basic curiosity. In 1994, a time when Seattle's star was rising rapidly, I attended a convention of chamber of commerce staff in Fort Worth: the only time in my life I have felt like a rock star. My colleagues from around the country knew all about what was happening in Seattle and more than a few of them asked me if I could find them a job there. In May, 1996, Newsweek ran a cover story with the headline "Is Everyone Moving to Seattle?" Deserved or not, Seattle has developed a reputation as a place where interesting things happen, so it seems useful to tell a more complete story.

My own interest, though, is in exploring just what drives the economic progress of cities, and having watched Seattle's story unfold I can begin to draw some conclusions, some of which you might find counterintuitive. Cities, states, provinces and nations around the world go to great effort and spend huge amounts of money on investments and programs designed to advance regional economies, and, unfortunately, much of this effort and spending produces disappointing results. Unpacking Seattle's success to see what factors made the biggest contribution to it will, I hope, make a useful contribution to the larger questions of regional development.

I vividly recall a session at the Seattle Chamber of Commerce Leadership Conference—an annual gathering of 250 public and private leaders from the region, described in Chapter 7—that took place in the fall of 1991 in Spokane. The session, titled "The Region on Trial," consisted of a mock trial of political and civic leaders who had been indicted for failure to address economic needs. Distinguished University of Washington political science professor Hubert Locke sat as presiding judge and various experts appeared as prosecutors and witnesses. The assembled conferees served as the jury, and at the end of the trial pronounced the region "Guilty! Guilty! Guilty!" on all counts. And, indeed, the charges included a long and depressing list of failures, from education funding to traffic congestion. Well, within a few months, Nirvana's *Nevermind* bumped Michael Jackson off the top of the charts, Microsoft shipped Windows 3.1 and began its domination of the software world, Boeing began production of the 777, Starbucks went public and Seattle entered its greatest period of growth and wealth creation since the Klondike Gold Rush.[2]

I tell this story not to poke fun at a well-crafted and serious conference agenda, but to point out that the ingredients of success may not always be the ones we intuitively latch onto. The prosecutors accurately described our failings, but the regional economy was rapidly moving forward in spite of the fact that we had not dealt with any of these failings in a meaningful way. Clearly, other factors were driving the Seattle economy. The conference agenda reflected a very traditional approach to economic thinking, and that approach proved less than relevant. So, if we can figure out what the conference agenda missed, and what allowed Seattle to burst out of the pack in the 1990s, Seattle's story will prove useful. The Region on Trial will come up again later in the book.

We begin in Chapter 1 by stepping back and looking at some of the current thinking about how cities and metropolitan areas work. Social scientists who concern themselves with urban areas have made huge strides in recent decades and their work will provide a context to better understand Seattle's experiences.

Chapter 2 provides an overview of the Seattle area economy and some of the metrics and indicators showing that the region is, on balance, economically successful. We'll talk about the price of that success, in terms of the trade-offs that accompany growth, such as high housing costs and traffic congestion.

Chapter 3 traces the chronology of Seattle's economic story. We'll swing briefly back to the beginnings in the 1850s and move quickly up to the beginning of our period, with the Century 21 Exhibition in 1962. From there we'll move through the various boom and bust cycles, bringing us to 2012.

In Chapter 4 we'll look back over that chronology of fifty years to distill out the important trends that have shaped the economy, outlining the significant ways the region has changed, and the ways it has not changed.

Next, in Chapter 5 we'll examine the key contextual drivers of the economy and how they have evolved over the past fifty years. This will include tangibles such as infrastructure and education, as well as the tax and regulatory environment. We will also have a look at less tangible, but very important quality of life and cultural factors.

Chapter 6 flips the view around to examine the major industries that underpin the economy and how they have evolved. This will include aerospace, which is still the largest employer, as well as port and trade activities, software and the life sciences.

With a handle on the basics of the economy and how it has evolved, we turn in Chapter 7 to the question of leadership. The relationship of local government to economic success has never been entirely clear, and it becomes more difficult with the diffusion of industries and population across the metropolitan area.

Chapter 8 begins to wrap up by drawing out some key lessons from Seattle's fifty year history. I will describe why I think Seattle has succeeded and why the region's many limitations and failings have not inhibited that success. I will also lay out some conclusions that observers from other region's might find interesting.

Finally, in Chapter 9 we look forward to assess how Seattle fits within the context of global economic growth and change. What opportunities can the region take advantage of, given its unique capabilities and constraints?

A sense of place

Throughout these chapters you will find a consistent theme: the central importance of geography. Seattle's history is built around the challenge of creating a vital and growing economy in a remote part of the country.

Not too long ago we got used to hearing confident predictions of the diminishing role of place and the death of distance. While transportation and communications have certainly speeded up, Seattle remains a unique place, with a unique set of opportunities and challenges, as does every other metropolitan region around the world.

If you are reading this book as a current or former resident of the Seattle area, I hope you will see how the region's location both in the upper-left-hand-corner of the U.S. map and in a key spot on the Pacific Ocean have shaped its history. I hope you will think about how trees, fish, rain, mountains and water have contributed to the trajectory of Seattle's evolution from a resource-based economy to a diversified technology and commercial center. And I hope you will think about why so many people have become rooted here, through good times and bad.

For those of you reading this book to add to your understanding of metropolitan geography, think if it as a sort of trick mirror that will give you unexpected reflections of your own unique region. On the city visits that Seattle area leaders have taken for thirty years, they do not often return with specific models to copy, but they always bring back a fresh perspective on Seattle, having learned how another city addresses issues that all regions share. I hope this book will provide similar fresh perspectives.

Chapter 1

Metropolitan Regions in the Twenty-first Century

Our study of Seattle begins by stepping back and examining what it means to be a metropolitan region in the twenty-first century. Metro regions have become the basic unit of economic geography, but because they have not become a unit of political geography, we often struggle to understand them: you will never see a metropolitan economic region outlined on a map.

The trajectory of Seattle's economic growth is unique, but the power of that uniqueness has diminished, and the region finds itself competing for investment and talent with other regions across the nation and the world. If Seattle is to serve as a case study of the challenges facing metro areas, it helps to understand the context within which the they operate.

A century of study

The study of cities has gone through a distinct set of cycles over the past hundred years. Early twentieth century cities were pretty foul places, in general, with all manner of pollutants in the air and underfoot, so early thinkers like Frank Lloyd Wright and Le Corbusier concentrated on ways to get people out of cities into the healthier countryside. The "garden city" movement started in England and became influential in the U.S., through concepts like Wright's Broadacre City and successful early suburban developments around the country.[1]

But by mid-century the backlash had started: the paint was not dry at the first Levittown before fierce criticism arose, with writers like William Whyte, David Riesman and Jane Jacobs fulminating about the new social patterns that were showing up in soulless suburbs and rhapsodizing about the wonders of old city centers and older ways of life.[2]

By this time, however, a combination of industrial and societal change had made those old city centers challenging places, and scholars shifted again to focus on the myriad social and economic problems facing residents of declining inner cities. In many ways, the growing field of "urban studies" was less about the geography or economics of cities themselves than about the impact of these huge changes that happened to be taking place within cities and suburbs.

The "urban crisis" began to dominate thinking about central cities, with persistent poverty, housing discrimination, racial tension, rioting, school desegregation and all manner of social dislocation dominating the discussion of city life. The prevailing view of suburbs shifted as well. Outlying areas were seen not just as unattractive, bland, socially empty places, as the 1950s critics observed, but were now seen as the destination of "white flight" and, therefore, complicit in the crisis. The political and social divide between central city and suburb had hardened.

By the 1980s things had started to shift yet again. Across campus in the urban planning schools, concern with the fate of cities and disappointment in the evolution of suburbs gave rise to the "new urbanism." Although intended to address the future of metropolitan areas, the new urbanism had its most prominent debut, with an alarming lack of irony, in exurban places like Kentlands, Maryland and remote villages like Seaside, Florida.[3]

Meanwhile, interesting things had started to happen over in the economics department: the burgeoning of the distinct field of urban economics. The same tools that define markets for goods and services could help figure out why people live where they live, why people move and why businesses set up shop where they do. Over the past twenty years or so, urban economists have made great progress in understanding the dynamics of cities. Meanwhile, their colleagues in the political science department have made similar progress unraveling the power structures of urban areas.

Starting in the 1980s, some sharp observers began to recognize that the sprawling metropolitan area, with multiple cities surrounding a central city, was here to stay. And more importantly, these same observers recognized a pattern in which metropolitan economies become interdependent with one another, and at the same time, increasingly divorced from the national economy.[4]

The most encouraging outcome of this latest wave of scholarship has been the emergence of a new perspective: cities are the solution, not the problem.[5] Until not very long ago, the persistent view of cities was of dysfunction: the challenge before the nation was to ameliorate urban pathologies, whether the crisis of the inner cities, the anomie of the suburbs or the environmental degradation brought on by urbanization itself. Now we are seeing acknowledgement that, in a globalized, post-agrarian world, cities provide the greatest opportunity for human betterment, a notion made clear by the continued migration of people to urban areas everywhere on the planet. Moreover, the city-suburb conflict has eased, and we now can look at the metropolitan region as a more or less organic whole.

This renewed appreciation for cities and metropolitan regions has begun to generate new activities. For example, the Brookings Institution, which long concentrated on federal policy, launched its Metropolitan Policy Program in the late 1990s. In a statement in November, 2011, Program director Bruce Katz summed up Brookings' new thinking about cities:

> This "next economy" will, no doubt, require aggressive federal policies to realize the potential of our broad and diverse economy. Yet federal policies are no longer sufficient. More and more, global trends and commerce reflect energy and innovation at the local—and especially the metropolitan—level. Cities are the locus of the forces and assets that power trade: innovative firms, talented workers, supportive public and private institutions, and modern infrastructure.[6]

The ideas in this chapter provide some context for understanding what it means to be a globally competitive metropolitan area in the twenty-first century. For metro regions, and the cities, suburbs and exurbs that comprise them, the game has changed dramatically over the fifty years covered in this book, with much of that change happening in the past generation. Success starts with understanding the playing field and the new rules.

An urbanized world

America has become an urban nation, with two thirds of the population living in metropolitan areas of over a half million people and 85 percent of the population in cities with over 100,000 people. This is part of a long-term trend that has seen farm populations shrink from 36 percent of the population in 1900 to a mere two percent today.[7] As farm populations shrank, so too did the small towns that served farming areas: fewer people working on farms meant fewer families shopping in local stores and sending children to local schools.

Over the past hundred years, massive increases in the efficiency of agriculture have meant that farms can no longer support a large number of people. We have all benefitted from this. In 1948 Americans spent 24 percent of their income on food, and today they spend just eight percent.[8] Rural poverty, while not eradicated, has become far less pervasive: the rural poverty rate has fallen from 35 percent in 1959 to 16 percent today, the same as the poverty rate in metropolitan areas.[9] The Walker Evans images of hardscrabble farmers in the 1930s depict a social scourge that has declined significantly. Today's farmers are more likely to be middle class and upper middle class businesspeople running highly mechanized operations that serve global markets.

As we have learned to eat well (maybe too well) with fewer people growing food, the action has shifted to cities, with the most impressive growth taking place in metropolitan regions between a half million and five million people. Of the places designated by the Census Bureau as "metropolitan areas," those with populations under 500,000 and those over 5 million in 2010 had grown an average of 24 percent over the previous twenty years, while those with populations between a half million and five million people had grown by 28 percent. From 1990 to 2010 the three largest regions, New York, Los Angeles and Chicago, together grew only 13 percent, while the combined population of four big Sunbelt regions, Dallas, Houston, Atlanta and Phoenix, doubled in size.[10]

When it comes to cities, in a whole variety of ways, bigger is better. Bigger cities tend to be more productive than smaller ones, allowing residents to earn more money. Bigger cities use less energy per person and fewer natural resources.[11] Larger cities offer more opportunities for people to find just the right place to put their talents to work and thereby maximize their own potential. In his book *The Triumph of the City*, economist Edward Glaeser decries the regulatory burdens that keep the biggest cities from getting even bigger.

Globally, the shift into cities has an added environmental benefit: lower birth rates.[12] Farmers in the agricultural areas of developing countries view larger families as economically productive: children are an asset that will yield returns in terms of farm labor. In contrast, in urban life children become an economic liability. While they bring delight to our lives, children do not produce much of economic value while we are raising them, and we take a gamble that they will produce grandchildren to bounce on our knees and will provide comfort in our old age. Thus, as populations in developing countries continue to urbanize, people are choosing to have smaller families, easing world population growth.

The trend of increasing urbanization will continue, both in the U.S. and globally—in early 2012 China became more than half urban.[13] Rural areas simply cannot support many people, and small towns struggle to offer the economic and cultural opportunities that young people seek. We can count on cities, especially the larger ones, to absorb nearly all future growth in the developed world and a very large share in the developing world.

Metro areas in the world economy

Cites and their surrounding metro areas began to grow in earnest during the industrial revolution, and for most of the time since then the fates of cities in the U.S. have been closely tied to national geography and markets. Industries were driven by agricultural activity, sources of raw materials and by transportation links and tended to grow up in clusters. Product and service markets were predominantly domestic. The role of national policy actually increased in the post-World War II decades, as federal regulation of labor and capital markets shaped how businesses evolved, and booming markets within the U.S. absorbed most of what business could produce.

Then, starting somewhere around the 1970s that began to change. Industries in Europe and Japan had finished rebuilding from World War II and competed vigorously around the world. Multinational firms began to focus their investment activities on specific metro areas, and global industrial centers began to emerge. New York and London became world financial centers, Los Angeles became the global leader in entertainment, Paris and Milan became global leaders in fashion. Gradually it became clear that metro areas could have a distinct role in the global economy beyond their role in their national economy.

In her 1982 book *Cities and the Wealth of Nations*, Jane Jacobs noted the disjuncture between national macro-economic policy making (which she viewed as a dangerous failure) and regional economies that operate on more micro-economic terms.[14] Gradually, a new way of viewing metropolitan regions emerged. It seemed that the city-states of the Italian Renaissance were making a re-appearance, with individual metro areas stretching beyond national boundaries to operate within a globally integrated economy. Federal and state governments provide crucial underpinnings of education and infrastructure, as well as the legal and regulatory environment, but success within those contexts would be determined at the metropolitan level.

Neal Peirce identified this trend in his 1993 book *Citistates*. Since then, scholars have advanced the idea that metropolitan regions form networks across the globe, as with the Seattle-Stuttgart story in the introduction. Columbia University sociologist Saskia Sassen developed the "Global City" framework, William Barnes and Larry Ledebur introduced the concept of a global "common market" of metropolitan regions, and UCLA geographer Allen Scott writes about the "global mosaic of regional economies." These global metropolitan networks overlay, but certainly do not obviate, the traditional international system of nation states.[15]

In his bestseller *The World is Flat,* journalist Thomas Friedman says that technology has accelerated the integration of the global economy and has spread opportunity around the world.[16] Author Richard Florida countered that the world is not flat, but rather "spiky," with individual metro areas capturing disproportionate shares of investment, talent and economic activity.[17] The fact that metro areas have experienced such varying levels of success suggests that Florida's assessment is closer to reality, and that economic activity is concentrating in distinct areas around the world. A truly flat world would have mechanisms to achieve equilibrium outcomes, but as we will see next, significant imbalances persist among regions. The question, then, is how an individual metro area can become one of the success stories.

Measuring metropolitan success

While metropolitan regions have become the center of the economic action, and larger cities have mostly done better than smaller ones, there is great disparity in the success of cities within any one country. Among metro areas in the U.S., annual per capita GDP in 2010 ranged from over $100,000 in San Jose to $17,000 in McAllen, Texas, and inflation-adjusted GDP growth rates in metro areas from 2000 to 2010 ranged from minus 20 percent to nearly 100 percent[18]. Educational attainment in those metro areas ranges from 11 percent with at least a bachelor's degree to 57 percent.[19] In July, 2012 unemployment in the nation's metro areas ranged from 2.5 percent in Bismarck, North Dakota to 31.2 percent in Yuma, Arizona.[20]

A 2012 paper by economists Peter Ganong and Daniel Shoag noted that from 1880 to 1980, income levels in metro areas tended to converge, as technologies, industries and people moved around. By the 1980s, however, that trend had reversed, with some areas becoming noticeably wealthier than others. Ironically, the world has become less flat as communications technologies have spread.[21]

City and regional leaders recognize the disparities in various metrics across metro areas and look for ways to improve economic performance. After all, governments have a lot to gain by metro area growth, since they depend on growth-related taxes to support services. Development, especially commercial development, expands the property tax base. A new office building rising out of a parking lot brings a nice new slice of property tax while making very few demands on schools, public safety, roads, parks and libraries and other local services. Local governments in most states have some way to tax businesses and most have local sales taxes collected by retailers.

It is not just governments that like expanding communities. About 70 percent of any economy consists of locally-produced goods and services.

The real estate industry, both development and brokerage, thrives in a growing economy. Banks, retailers, utilities and service businesses all get more customers.

All of this to say that the old "small is beautiful" ethos[22] does not have many adherents among the leaders of metropolitan America: too many people gain directly from success of cities. But the search for success has become far more complicated in the past generation, as metro areas emerge from the shadows of national and state affairs to take their own unique place in the global economy.

Urban economic stress and the search for new models

Beginning with the oil shocks of the 1970s and continuing through the wrenching industrial restructuring of the 1980s, metropolitan areas around the country began to experience instability and rising unemployment. Metro areas, particularly those of the mid-Atlantic and upper Midwest, had grown organically as industries expanded, starting in the nineteenth century and accelerating after World War II. These large cities often specialized in particular industry clusters, ranging from the Detroit area with its massive auto assembly plants and Pittsburgh with its steel mills to smaller metro areas such as Akron, which specialized in tires, and Grand Rapids, a center of furniture building. As long as the overall economy expanded and foreign producers were still rebuilding from the War, these cities could grow and prosper.

But as the industries in these cities matured, not having been destroyed by war, they found it increasingly difficult to compete with the newly rebuilt industries of Europe and Japan. In addition, aggressive industrial policies in developing countries created huge new basic industries such as steel and cement. The crisis in American industry came to a head in the 1980s, a decade that saw manufacturing employment fall from 23 percent of the workforce in 1979 to 17 percent by 1990.[23] In 1970 imports accounted for 14 percent of autos sold in the U.S, and by 1981 that had grown to 25 percent,[24] creating pressure for "voluntary" import quotas on Japanese cars. As industries restructured and fought for survival, the metropolitan areas that housed them also fought for survival. Once it became clear that the old industries, even if they survived, would never return to the employment levels of the past, leaders in these cities began to look for new economic models that could replace the lost jobs.

The first place to look was the computer and information technologies industries that had taken off at about the same time that basic industries began to struggle. And although much of the activity centered on Boston's Route 128 corridor, the heaviest growth and entrepreneurial activity could be seen on the other coast. Sometime in the mid-1980s word started leaking outside the technology community that something unique was happening among the apricot orchards of the Santa Clara Valley between San Francisco and San Jose. The area had long had a strong presence of defense contractors, and the Stanford University engineering department was among the best in the world. But it was the development of the first semiconductors and integrated circuits, and the emergence of the Fairchild Semiconductor company in 1959 that launched what became known as Silicon Valley.[25]

This sprawling, sunny valley would end up creating more wealth in a shorter time than any urban area in history. And in doing so it created entirely new ways of doing business and managing talent.

The new model proved irresistible. Leaders from around the country and around the world (Seattle included) flocked to Palo Alto, Cupertino and other formerly sleepy towns to examine this hotbed of technology and business creation in hopes of bottling the formula. Over the years we would see Silicon Forest, Silicon Beach, Silicon Wadi, Silicon Fen, Silicon Prairie and even a vowel-less Welsh version, Cwm Silicon. An observer of the phenomenon found 79 places around the world with Silicon in their names.[26] With or without a silicon moniker, economic developers put in place many of the elements that seemed to make Silicon Valley tick, including facilities modeled on Stanford Research Park. Many years later, though, Silicon Valley remains unique, and it is not clear that there can ever be two of them—the draw of the original is just too strong. As University of Washington historian Margaret O'Mara has pointed out, the "city of knowledge" model that Silicon Valley exemplifies, has deep roots in the Cold War-era and cannot be replicated by fiat.[27]

The search for a new model of metropolitan economic development would continue, with biotechnology and the life sciences as the next big target. Rising spending on healthcare and the seemingly limitless potential for new life-saving or life enhancing drugs made this sector the big promise of the 1990s. While the computer industry generates a limited number of high value products, the human body and the many things that can go wrong with it offers vast opportunities for product development. It seemed that any place with a decent medical research institution could get into the bio-medical game. Again, research facilities were built, venture funds started and bright futures promised. But converting university research into new biomedical products, and developing job-creating industries around those products turns out to be more difficult than originally thought. Economic strategists greatly underestimated the scientific risks and regulatory hurdles of biomedicine, and a second model for rescuing metropolitan America ended up delivering far less than hoped.

The third great wave of economic development is now upon us: clean technologies. Just as the promise of biomedical research and product development was rooted in rising healthcare expenditures, the promise of clean technology is driven by the need to head off climate change by transforming the way we use energy and other resources. And like biomedicine, the numbers appear massive. The jury is still out on this latest economic development phase, but it is unlikely that very many metro areas will see the big payoff, and those with an existing lead in energy industries, like Houston, will have a head start.

Some metro areas have found success with information technologies and life sciences and some will, no doubt, create vibrant clean tech sectors. But a clustering pattern of industries and, more importantly, talent, tends to result in concentration of activities in just a few areas. No single model or industry will provide the answer to all metro areas in search of new, future-oriented economic activity.

The mid-size dilemma

The Census Bureau currently identifies 367 places in the country as "metropolitan areas" for statistical purposes. Most of these are relatively small places, with only one hundred having populations over 500,000 and only thirty with populations over two million.[28] The country can have a lot of smaller metropolitan areas, but by a curious pattern known as Zipf's Law, we can have only one New York City, one Los Angeles, and one Chicago. No nation on earth has two equal-sized cities in its largest ranks, and these large cities follow a mathematical pattern that seems to keep them from ever being the same size.[29] But when we get down to the middle ranks, many metro areas have similar populations and similar purposes: Richmond is about the same size as Oklahoma City and both serve as regional commercial centers.

If we go back to the global city-state idea discussed above, and think of metropolitan regions operating in a global context, there seems to be a group of regions that are smaller than the major world capitals, but are large enough to be caught up in the global economic stew. Some, such as Amsterdam, Dublin or Stockholm are capitals of smaller countries. Others, such as Munich, Barcelona, Vancouver, Melbourne or Fukuoka, are secondary cities in larger countries. Seattle falls into this category, having over three million people, but living in the shadows of Los Angeles and the San Francisco Bay area.

These mid-sized regions, with between two and four million people, find themselves in a challenging position in the firmament of global city-states. They require a constant influx of new business activity in order to remain fresh and competitive, yet may not be large enough to attract top talent and major firms. These cities face a challenge similar to that faced by mid-sized firms in today's business environment. Small firms can position themselves as nimble, specialized boutique operations, and large firms can offer a full menu of services through globally integrated operations, while firms in the middle can do neither. For better or worse, the Seattle area finds itself in this middle ground.

Spatial equilibrium: no free lunch

As much as I like living in Seattle I know that it is far from perfect. In fact, lots of people happily move away from the region every year. After all, Seattle has high housing costs, traffic congestion, an undersized higher education system and a pervasive gloom that can send even the natives fleeing to Mexico in mid-February. Seattle, like every other place, has its pluses and minuses.

Highly mobile Americans move around looking for places where, for their particular preferences, the pluses outweigh the minuses. This movement is constant: according to IRS tax records, between 2009 and

2010, about 9,500 people moved from California to King County, and about 9,100 people moved from King County to California. So although King County gained a net of 400 Californians, we cannot ignore the fact that 9,100 people prefer sunshine to overcast.[30]

This dynamic drives a great deal of work among urban economists who try to figure out why people live where they live. Much of their work is based on what is known as the Rosen-Roback model which demonstrates what most of us know: there is no free lunch.[31] All cities have advantages and disadvantages that balance each other out such that all cities are, in the end, equally desirable. Really, you ask? How can a depressed old mill town be as desirable as Honolulu? Well, the basic formula looks like this:[32]

$$W + Q - C = U$$

W stands for wages, which is an indication of productivity and earning power of the industries in a city. **Q** stands for quality of life, which involves natural and man-made amenities as well as things like traffic congestion and air quality, all of which determine the degree to which a region is a nice place in which to live. **C** stands for the cost of living, which is dominated by housing costs, but also includes the cost of local services. **U** stands for the overall "utility" of a city, and—here's the kicker—**U** *is the same everywhere.* In other words, places with high wages tend to have high costs, and in the quality of life measure, attractive amenities are often offset by bad traffic. Conversely, places with low wages and amenities tend to be inexpensive, less congested places to live. We can imagine other combinations of these elements. For example, resort towns tend to have low wages, high amenities, high costs and easy commutes. Old industrial cities still have high wages but fewer amenities, balanced by lower costs and uncongested freeways. A place like San Francisco scores high across the board, with high wages and quality of life balanced by very high housing and service costs.

This equilibrium is never static, however. The pieces keep moving and resettling. For example, if a new, high paying industry moves into a city, that city will likely experience an influx of people going to work there who will bid up housing prices, crowd the streets and strain the local amenities, all of which offsets the economic good fortune. Conversely, a city where a major factory closes will see a lowering of housing costs, lighter traffic and more available amenities. The equilibrium is maintained over time through migration, as people move around the country. And in choosing a new place to live, migrants, by definition, accept the trade-offs. A move to Manhattan means high earning potential and the excitement of a world cultural capital, but it also means brutally expensive housing.

Couldn't communities manipulate these factors, such that an attractive area need not have high costs? After all, bubbles notwithstanding, housing does respond to the laws of supply and demand, and a prospering region could pump up housing production to keep prices down. Perhaps, but the model still holds, since a combination of a strong economy and lower housing costs will attract low wage industries, driving down average wages. This is the pattern in the big Sunbelt cities, such as Phoenix and Atlanta, where nice weather and low housing costs attract a large workforce that, in turn, attracts lower wage employers that would never be able to operate in San Francisco, New York or Boston.

Within a metropolitan area it's all about choice

The movement of people around the country involves a relatively small percentage of the population, and people change cities far less often as they age. Within metropolitan areas, however, people move around a lot. In relocating from one neighborhood to another, households make choices, and those choices play a role in shaping the evolution of regions. Metropolitan areas are not homogenous places at all, but collections of independent cities and neighborhoods, each with its own distinct characteristics. In even a moderate sized metro area, individuals and families can choose among several cities, school districts and neighborhoods that meet their budgets and reflects their own values and needs.

An economist named Charles Tiebout noticed this process back in the 1950s, as booming suburban communities challenged the central role of big cities. Originally, Tiebout wanted to know how local governments arrive at the right level of taxes and services, and in thinking about this distinct problem, he came upon a general idea that forms a central underpinning of urban geography. The Tiebout Hypothesis states that within a fragmented metropolitan area with many jurisdictions, households will shop around and choose a city that offers the level of taxes and services they think appropriate.[33] Some households will opt to pay high taxes and receive premium services while others will opt for low taxes and minimal services. And as households sort themselves into these cities and towns, each individual place becomes more homogenous internally, while the individual towns becomes very different from one another. This pattern, once established, can persist for generations.

As metropolitan areas expanded and underwent dramatic changes in the post-War era, it became clear that Tiebout's observation applied to more than just taxes and spending. Land use patterns, in particular, vary from city to city, with some places insisting on large lots and limited commercial zoning, while others allow for a variety of housing types and encourage commercial areas. In recent years some cities and towns have embraced the new urbanist or "smart growth" concepts of pedestrian-oriented mixed use development while others have stuck with more traditional suburban patterns.

Because the residents of individual cities and towns share a common outlook on what they think their city ought to be—taxes, services, land use, etc.—they elect leaders who share those values and who will enact policies to perpetuate them. Few people get themselves elected to local government or appointed to a planning commission in order to promote change, and if they do, they rarely succeed. As Tiebout famously noted, most people who do not like the direction of their town respond by voting with their feet: it is far easier to move to a new, more agreeable town than to change the one you are in.

In his 2009 book, *The Big Sort*, Bill Bishop takes Tiebout one step further, suggesting that people choose places to live based not just on their preferences for community features and taxes, but in order to be near people with similar overall political and social views. And Bishop notes that liberals like to live closer together and conservatives prefer their homes more spread out, which may help explain the political split we usually see between central cities and their surrounding exurbs.[34]

Residents of a metropolitan area face a second choice: the trade-off of housing costs and commutes. Another of the fundamental theories of urban economics, the Alonso-Muth-Mills model, says that in a metropolitan area the cost of housing plus the cost of commuting will be the same everywhere.[35] In other words, the monthly mortgage payment plus monthly commute costs will be the same for two identical houses in comparable neighborhoods, one close to a job center and one far away. The distant house will cost less to purchase, but the owner will spend more in commuting expenses. Looked at another way, a buyer can get "more house for the money" in outlying areas, but will face a more difficult commute to get there. The owner of the old overpriced bungalow in the close-in neighborhood will have her feet up and a drink in hand long before the owner of a similarly-priced McMansion gets to his gated exurban community.

Consumer city

The second element of the spatial equilibrium formula, Q for quality of life, has become an increasingly important factor in urban development. When facing choices about where to live and pursue a career, individuals have options that may be equally compelling from an employment perspective, so the decision of where to live will come down to the attractiveness of the place. Economists have recognized that cities themselves are "consumer" products.[36] The package of amenities that a city offers is a critical factor in its ability to differentiate itself from the competition and attract high skill people.

The trick is to figure out what that package of amenities can and should be. For Honolulu or San Diego it is not too difficult: delightful weather, beaches, surfing. Areas with fewer natural endowments need to look a bit harder, but they can choose from a long menu. Cultural assets are important to a large segment of the well-educated, sophisticated target audience, and cities can foster those. And although we tend to think of Richard Florida's Bohemian districts as essential, we cannot forget that those young hipsters will eventually grow into young parents who will seek out family friendly features.

Cities that may not be obvious choices for young, mobile, talented people can devise ways to position themselves in appealing ways. Des Moines, Iowa, is a very successful mid-sized metro area that labors under an image of Mid-Western blandness. Rather than try to turn itself into something else, Des Moines has built on that basic image and positioned itself as the antithesis of the hard-charging coastal city, a place where a person can have a satisfying career and still have the time and money to enjoy life outside of work.[37]

Superstar city and housing prices

Consumer City has consequences: the potential for superstardom. As the pattern of wide disparities in housing prices around the country accelerated in the past thirty years, economists began to notice, and concluded that economic success in a region will result in some combination of population growth and housing cost increases. The degree to which an economically dynamic region becomes larger, or just more expensive will depend on the ease of building houses. The cost of land and the process of permitting homes varies widely, and developers will have an easier time putting in subdivisions in some places than others (building apartments and condominiums is less difficult in most places). This explains why some very dynamic areas like Dallas, Atlanta or Phoenix grew rapidly but had flat housing prices prior to the bubble, while other dynamic areas like San Francisco and Boston have experienced slower growth and had expensive housing prices well before the bubble.

In a 2006 paper, economists Joseph Gyourko, Christopher Mayer and Todd Sinai coined the term "superstar cites" to describe those places that have strong economies, high incomes, restrictive housing regulations and high housing prices.[38] Their roster of superstar cities offers few surprises: coastal California, the New York-Boston corridor. One of their key conclusions does, however, give pause: the feedback loop reinforces, rather than self-corrects the pattern. We might think that a place with high prices would eventually lose residents to lower priced areas where employers could pay lower wages, but that does not happen with superstar regions. These places have unique industries that pay very high wages to people with very high skills, and as these industries grow they attract even more of these high value employees who can afford high housing prices. As long as the high value industries keep growing, and new employees flock to work for them, housing prices can stay high. This results in the divergence in incomes that Ganong and Shoag identified.

The problem with superstar regions, and a key concern in a place like Seattle, is that their high price structure drives out mid-range employers like manufacturers. The superstar city process can leave a regional economy with very high skilled employees and the people who mow their lawns. The question is, where does the Seattle region fit on the superstar scale? The good news is that the region still has a strong manufacturing base and other industries such as ports that provide middle-income jobs. Housing price trends will have a large influence on whether many of these industries remain in the area.

Metropolitan politics—a different animal

Let's look at one last piece of theory before we dive into the Seattle story: the political points of view that color how cities develop. We will get into more specifics of who is in charge of cities in Chapter 7, but as long as we are on the topic of choice, we need to understand just how different politics are in cities. Anyone who has spent time on a civic initiative or development project knows that the standard division of liberal-conservative does not describe local politics very well. We need some way to reconcile some odd behaviors: ardent business Republicans, who distrust large government, will often lead campaigns to purchase open space or to increase school levies, while liberal activists may oppose government-sponsored redevelopment projects that will create jobs and expand the tax base.

Sociologists recognized this categorization problem and came up with a new, more applicable continuum on which to evaluate voters.[39] At one end are the "cosmopolitans" who perceive that they will benefit from expansion of the local economy and improvements in local education and services. The cosmopolitan businessperson may distrust the federal government but knows that her employees will come out of the local schools and, therefore, has a stake in the quality of those schools. A cosmopolitan may be indifferent to major league sports but knows the value of national exposure and knows that businesspeople like to entertain in luxury boxes at ballgames. The cosmopolitan knows that public amenities contribute to the quality of life that attracts highly talented people and will happily pay for them.

The "locals" at the other end of the spectrum do not perceive that they benefit from an expanded regional economy, and may, in fact, feel that economic expansion will harm them. Many people are perfectly secure in their jobs irrespective of how well the local economy does, so big projects just mean higher taxes and economic growth means higher housing costs, more traffic and bigger crowds. The local will support things they personally enjoy—a local who is a baseball fan will support a new ballpark—but will shy away from projects that they will not use. Locals are not necessarily lower income, as the description may imply, but can also include wealthy retirees and individuals from "old money" who see little benefit in local growth.

The cosmopolitan-local cleavage is well known, but is often described as the "downtown" versus the "neighborhoods." This is not entirely inaccurate, since the typical community council will attract active members from among those closer to the local end of the spectrum. "Populism" does not quite describe locals, however, since at least in Seattle, organized labor and much of the non-profit community can be both populist and cosmopolitan at the same time.

I bring up this last bit of social theory because cities like Seattle depend on strategic investments that need local funding but will not benefit most residents directly. At the same time, locals provide a helpful check on rampant development and a voice for the essential character of a the region. Managing a healthy cosmopolitan-local tension is a crucial part of regional leadership.

Why does this matter?

To repeat: although barrels of ink and petabytes of data are expended daily analyzing national and international macroeconomic policy, the metropolitan area has become the basic unit of economic geography. The opportunities available to individuals in the developed world will be a function of the city they live in as much as the country they are citizens of. The distribution of economic activity among cities is not even or equitable. The rich get richer, the smart get smarter and the globally connected expand that connectivity. Seattle has enjoyed a great deal of success in the past decades, but will need to work hard to keep the momentum going.

Probably the most widely-read book on urban economics in recent years is Richard Florida's *Rise of the Creative Class*.[40] Academics and critics had a field day disputing his methods and findings, but Florida did get one thing right: metropolitan areas are becoming the aggregators of talent, taking over that role from big business. In the past, large companies would recruit young talent and deploy those people wherever the company's needs dictated. A person would stay with the same company their entire career, moving jobs and homes as often as required. IBM stood for "I've been moved," and the standard line from your buddy with the moving van outside his house was "my dad got transferred." Today, once individuals have settled in a city, they increasingly have the choice to shift companies in order to stay in the same city, rather than stay with the same company and shift cities.

Talent is fluid, and the most skilled individuals act as free agents, finding the firms that best suit them at a point in time, and moving down the street when it makes sense. Cities that can grab and hold onto that fluid talent and not let it leak out will succeed. It is not nearly as simple as Florida implied—build funky Bohemian districts that appeal to the high value creative types—but the data are clear: smart cities win.

One of the most widely-read books in recent years on global economic trends has been Thomas Friedman's *The World is Flat*.[41] As with Florida's book, critics had major issues with some of Friedman's findings and conclusions, but again, he has a valid underlying idea: economic success depends on global connectivity. With markets for capital, technology, products and services nearly wide open, and with markets for labor becoming increasingly open, no region can hope to prosper without being part of a web of connections that spreads across the globe. Some of those connections will be formal, but most will be informal, as, for example, when a foreign student at a local university goes back to her country but stays in touch with her former colleagues. Connected cities win.

Now, let's see how the Seattle area stacks up as an example of a twenty-first century metropolitan area.

Chapter 2

New York Alki—Are We There Yet?

W hen the first adventurous band of settlers arrived in Seattle in 1851, they christened their new home "New York Alki", alki being a Salish Indian word that translates roughly as "one of these days." Had Arthur Denny and his fellow optimists known about Zipf's law they would have perhaps been less ambitious, knowing that there could only ever be one New York City. Nonetheless, they had big plans for their new town, envisioning a major metropolis serving a booming Northwest. Like other settlers of the West they saw only possibility in the open spaces, tall trees, clear waters and fertile valleys. One-hundred-sixty years later it seems fair to ask how close we have come to realizing the vision of the original founders.

Seattle did not, of course, become a commercial center on the order of New York City. It never even surpassed the great nineteenth-century West Coast city, San Francisco, which built its famous row houses with Seattle timber. Even San Francisco, which became the largest city in the West during the California Gold Rush, was eclipsed by Los Angeles, which emerged as the second largest metro area in the country, taking the number two position in the Zipf order of things. And although it grew substantially in the twentieth-century, Seattle was eventually overtaken in the West by Phoenix and stays only slightly ahead of San Diego and Denver. Seattle is now the 15th largest metro area in the country, the same rank it held in 1990 and 2000.[1] So, no, Seattle has not lived up to the hope of creating one of the nation's giant metropolises. But in many respects it has more than lived up to the dreams of the Denny Party, and is certainly among the most dynamic regions of the country, having come a very long way since the Century 21 Exhibition.

If we keep in mind the spatial equilibrium idea from Chapter 1, and the principle that all regions are, on balance, equally advantaged, can we describe Seattle as more successful than other places? By definition, countervailing downsides not only accompany success, they result from it. Nonetheless, I think that when it comes to the things most people care about—job opportunities, high earnings, an attractive quality of life, a promising future—Seattle has been among the most successful metropolitan areas in the U.S. over the past fifty years. This chapter sets out to explain what Seattle's version of success looks like.

The pluses

Population growth and in-migration

Population growth provides the first indicator of success. The country as a whole grows by a little less than one percent per year, so to be considered at all healthy, a region needs to grow at least that fast. Growing slower than the nation means some combination of a low birth rate, a high death rate and net outmigration, all three being discouraging signs of metropolitan vitality.

Since 1960 the combined population of the King, Pierce and Snohomish counties has grown from 1.4 million to 3.5 million people, or 150 percent.[2] This translates into an average annual growth rate of 1.8 percent per year. Over that same time period Washington State has grown 136 percent, and the nation has grown 68 percent. As might be expected of a temperate coastal region, the Seattle area has outpaced the nation, growing over twice as fast. At the same time, however, the region has not kept pace with some of the big Sunbelt metro areas, which include not only Phoenix, but also Dallas, Atlanta and Houston.[3] Considering the dynamics of population shifts in the U.S. over the past fifty years, however, Seattle's performance has been impressive.

Population growth has two components, natural growth and migration, and we'll begin with the former. Natural growth, defined as births minus deaths, is the easiest part of the equation to track, since public health records do not miss many of these vital events. Absent wars or plagues, the death rate remains fairly consistent, dropping slightly as life expectancies lengthen. The crude death rate (deaths as a percentage of the total population) is about 0.8 percent nationally, and about 0.7 percent in the Seattle area.[4] Births vary much more, and birth rates will shift depending on demographic composition (more young adults mean more children, some immigrant groups have more children) and where we are in the waves of births that cycle through the population. These birth patterns have an impact on the economy as job markets need to absorb each wave of new entrants, and as we will see, some of these waves have come at inconvenient times in the business cycle.

The Baby Boom of the 1950s and early 1960s produced a huge wave of births, but came to an abrupt end in the mid-1960s, when cultural and other factors led to the Baby Bust, or "birth dearth" of the late 1960s and 1970s (GenX). Things bounced back in the 1980s when the Boomers themselves got into the baby business and created the Baby Boom Echo generation, the largest in history (GenY, or the Millennials). That ended as the Dearth generation hit its own prime child bearing years: the missing children of the 1960s and 1970s became the missing parents of the 1990s and early 2000s. And now the cycle has picked up again, as the Echo generation starts to have children.

With all of these birth cycles, the natural rate of population growth has been a bit lumpy over the past fifty years, ranging in the Seattle area from a high of 1.45 percent in 1961 to a low of 0.47 percent in 1973 and averaging 0.82 percent per year over fifty years.[5] Some of the big lumps, notably the tail end of the Baby Boom and the Echo generation both came into the job market during severe recessions, compounding unemployment problems.

As interesting as we might find those swings in birth rates, migration has had an even larger impact on regional demographics. At the metropolitan level, total population growth is determined by the natural rate plus the rate of net in-migration—people moving into the region minus people moving out. And when it comes to migration, Seattle has a very compelling story.

From its founding in the 1850s Seattle grew steadily, but only as fast as the basic timber, fishing and trade economy of the Puget Sound region could support. After gold was found in the Klondike in 1896 and in Nome, Alaska in 1898, tens of thousands of gold-seekers from around the world flocked to Seattle on their way to the Yukon and Alaska. After their adventures, many of those miners—very few of whom came back with any gold—settled in Seattle, my grandparents among them. The Alaska-Yukon trade and growing Pacific Rim trade had created huge economic opportunities, and the population within the city limits of Seattle ballooned from 43,000 in 1890 to 237,000 in 1910.[6]

Then things calmed down as the region began to feel the limitations of the trade and resource-based economy. A shipbuilding boom during World War I drew a large number of people to Seattle in the mid-teens, but growth slowed substantially in the 1920s, while the region spent the decade absorbing those wartime workers into the peacetime economy. With no new industries growing up in the region, and with the Great Depression, which slowed movement everywhere, migrants had little reason to move to Seattle.

By 1940 the city population was only up to 368,000. From 1920 to 1940 the region grew at just about the national rate, indicating very low levels of net in-migration. The next surge of population growth began with World War II and the buildup of the armaments industry in the Seattle area. Boeing employed 50,000 workers by 1944. The shipyards of the Duwamish and Houghton began cranking out vessels for the Navy, and Pacific Car and Foundry stopped building railroad cars and started building tanks. All of this activity required a workforce, and tens of thousands of people migrated to Seattle, including its first large population of African Americans. In all, the Puget Sound region, including Kitsap County added about 375,000 people from 1940 to 1950.[7]

Following World War II most of the new migrants stayed. After some hiccups, Boeing successfully shifted production to the new Cold War jet aircraft and, by the late 1950s, to civilian jetliners, cementing the region's position in the aircraft business. And whereas resource-based industries could hire mostly unskilled labor, the new industries needed far more top flight engineering and business talent than could be found at the University of Washington. Thus began the pattern of talent migration that continues to this day.

Data on migration is difficult to come by, especially at the local level going back fifty years. We do know that from 1960 to 2010 net in-migration to Washington State accounted for about 55 percent of total population growth, and with slow growth in the rural areas of the state we can assume that most of that in-migration was headed toward the Seattle area.[8]

We do have more detail on migration at the local level for recent years, courtesy of the Internal Revenue Service which tracks address changes on tax returns. According to this data, from 2009 to 2010, about 40,000 people moved into King County from other states and about 38,000 people moved from King County to other states, for a net flow of about 2,000 people (data for other counties in the region is badly distorted due to shifts in military personnel). In that year about 20 percent of the total in-migrants to the state came from California. But since far fewer Washingtonians moved to California, that state had a disproportionate impact on growth.[9]

The persistence of in-migration in spite of the region's poor weather makes Seattle unique in the bigger national picture of population flows. Studies show that climate is the single biggest factor in people's decision of where to migrate. More specifically, the average daily high temperature in the month of January correlates closely with net in-migration.[10] The Seattle and Portland, Oregon, metro areas are the exception to this general rule. People move here even though they know that January will be chilly, dark and damp (Seattle) or plagued by ice storms (Portland). This distinguishes Seattle's migration pattern from that of the Sunbelt cities of the West: people come here specifically to take advantage of economic opportunity. This shows up strikingly in the migration data from the recession years of 2007 to 2010, in which migration to warm places like Arizona, Nevada and Florida fell dramatically while migration to Washington remained steady.

A strong pattern of in-migration is not just a vote of confidence in the economy, but also a source of future income growth. While our literature is full of migrants who were running away from something (Huck Finn not wanting to be "sivilized") or escaping desperate circumstances (the Joads) most migrants today, as we will talk about later, are people any community would welcome.

Global connections

The two most commonly heard memes about the economy of Washington State and the Seattle area are: (a) we are the most trade-dependent place in the country; and (b) one out of every three jobs in the state is related to international trade. Both of these claims are generally true, depending on how one measures trade flows. But in any case, the area has always served as a hub for international business activity and a home to large immigrant populations.

Global connectivity goes back to the earliest days of the city. The ports of Puget Sound are the closest on the West Coast to all ports in East Asia, and when the transcontinental railroads got to Seattle in 1893, the ports became a favored gateway to Asia. The arrival of the *Miki Maru* in 1896 signaled the beginning scheduled steamship service between Seattle and Asia. For decades, Seattle was the largest port on the West Coast, and although the massive destination markets of Southern California have made the Los Angeles/Long Beach ports larger, Seattle and Tacoma remain important ports for products moving to Chicago and beyond.

Boeing is the nation's largest exporter, and it assembles commercial aircraft for export in factories in the Seattle area: the outlook of the entire region shifts when 85,000 people work for a company so heavily focused outside the U.S. Microsoft and other IT firms started at a time when they were "born global." In the past firms would get their business established in domestic markets before attacking overseas markets. Technology firms cannot afford to do this and design their products and marketing strategies for foreign sales from the beginning. Microsoft now books about two thirds of its sales outside the U.S., and Amazon's overseas operations generate about 45 percent of its revenues.

Perhaps the most visible sign of the region's globalization comes from the quest for technical talent. A large share of Microsoft's workforce in the Puget Sound area was born outside the U.S., and many other technology firms have similar overseas talent attraction strategies. This shows up in the region's demographics: in the cities of Bellevue and Redmond, which have high concentrations of technology firms, 31 percent of the population is foreign born, as is nearly half of the population between 25 and 44 years old.[11] I am not surprised anymore to look around in the park or the shopping mall and realize I am the only white guy in the area.

The rapidly expanding field of global health has added yet another element of connectivity in the Seattle area. The decision by the Bill and Melinda Gates Foundation to concentrate its tens of billions of dollars on global health has caused the existing research "industry" to expand rapidly. The result is a wide ranging exchange of researchers and policymakers from around the world. Global health has greatly increased the region's connections to areas that might not be on the business radar screen.

Talent

Just as an individual's talents will determine their earning power, the aggregate level of talent in the workforce will determine the overall productivity of a metropolitan area. This obvious point immediately raises the question of how to measure talent: the census does not ask for your IQ. Imperfect as it may be, the most common way to measure talent is simply through data on educational attainment. A simple syllogism: (a) talented people get paid more than less talented people; (b) well educated people get paid more than less educated people; therefore (c) more educated people are more talented. And in fact, the rate of holding of college degrees correlates closely with per capital annual wages and per capital GDP in a metro area. The correlation is not perfect, but this is the best we've got.

According to the 2010 American Community Survey, 37 percent of adults over age 25 in the Seattle metro area have completed a bachelor's degree, and of those, 13 percent have an additional advanced or professional degree. This places the Seattle metro area as the 10th best educated metro area with more than a half million adults, if measuring bachelor's degree-holding, and the 16th best if measuring advanced degree holding. The large metro areas that clearly have Seattle beat in the education department are Washington D.C., San Francisco, San Jose and Boston. Seattle is just slightly behind Minneapolis and Denver.[12]

We can joke about the barista with the PhD in Chinese literature, but education attainment really does have consequences. In 2010, a person with a bachelor's degree in the Seattle area earned 160 percent more

than a high school drop-out, 73 percent more than a high school graduate and 44 percent more than a person who had attended college but not
completed a bachelor's degree. A graduate or professional degree
increases those premiums to 224 percent, 116 percent and 80 percent,
respectively.[13] As the economic advantages of education continue to
grow, the regions that have high levels of attainment will further out-
pace those with lower levels.

Now comes the tough part—Seattle has achieved this high level of
educational attainment not by growing its own talent, but by importing
it from elsewhere. When it comes to opportunities to earn a bachelor's
degree within the state, Washington's record is dismal. The state ranks
44th out of 50 states in the per capita number of seats in four-year institutions for the population age 18 to 22.[14] In part this is because the state
long ago made a very large commitment to its community college system, which ranks among the largest in the country. But the state still
does not offer community college graduates enough upper division seats
to transfer into, and the rate of successful completion of a four-year degree by community college students is lower than the completion rate of
those who start at a four-year institution.

If we simply look at the rate of production of bachelor's degrees in the
state, compared to the number of 22-year-olds, Washington ranks 36th
out of fifty states. In 2008, public and private institutions in Washington
granted 33.2 bachelor's degrees for every 100 22-year-olds, compared to
44.3 in Minnesota and 42.1 in Colorado.[15] This is a poor showing for a
place that prides itself on education. Put crudely, but honestly, we do not
seem to have any difficulty shortchanging our own young people and
then embracing those who have received excellent educations courtesy of
parents and taxpayers in other states.

Having delivered that screed, we do know that even if Washington
were to dramatically increase the size of its higher education system, it
still would not have the capacity to produce the talent that the state
needs. World class organizations like Boeing, Microsoft, Amazon and the
Gates Foundation require world class talent, and although they would
like to find it in their backyards they know that the best people are
found scattered all over the world. This is not a new phenomenon: soccer
became very popular in the Seattle area in the 1960s in part because we
were coached by Scottish engineers working at Boeing.

According to the American Community Survey, of the adults who moved to the Seattle area from other states from 2008 to 2010, 52 percent had a bachelor's degree, and of those, 22 percent also had a graduate or professional degree. Of the adults who moved to the Seattle area from other countries during that time, 53 percent had a bachelor's degree, and of those, 19 percent also had a graduate or professional degree. This explains how the region's overall education attainment levels have climbed so impressively in spite of the state's undersized higher education system. Of course some of these well-educated in-migrants are local natives who went elsewhere for their education and some early work experience (the figures are for adults over 25 years old) and returned. But that simply reinforces the point that the state lacks education opportunities.[16]

The need to attract talented people brings up the limitations inherent in Seattle's status as a second-tier city, noted in Chapter 1. The footloose young, college educated people who tend to migrate may find bigger places more attractive. Basic agglomeration economics demonstrates that the more people doing the same thing in close proximity the more productive everyone will be. One hundred years ago Alfred Marshall famously noted that where an industry is concentrated, knowledge of that industry is "in the air."[17] Whether at professional societies or chatting in the stands at a kids' basketball game, we all learn things from people in our fields, and in other fields as well. And the more of them around us, the more we learn, and the more productive we become.

Another reason bigger places attract more talented people is that they offer better prospects for career mobility. If Richard Florida is right and cities serve as the aggregators of talent, the cities with the most choices of places to work will have the greatest success. We expect that individuals will change employers from time to time, so a young person will look to settle in a place where they will have lots of employers to choose from should they need to move on. An aspiring book editor will move to New York City knowing that if things do not work out at one publishing house he can look for a new job at dozens of other houses. A programmer moves to Silicon Valley knowing that if the start-up she is working at fails, she can use her talents in hundreds of other firms.

A second tier city like Seattle faces both of these problems. Although they are easing —software and perhaps life sciences research seem to be reaching critical mass—Seattle still must compete with the major centers for all of its large industries except aerospace. Can we lure enough IT professionals who might otherwise head to Silicon Valley? Can we recruit biologists who might head to Boston? Can we recruit people to the media and entertainment industries who would go to Los Angeles, or energy scientists who would head to Houston? We talk about the Mount Rainier factor, and the attraction of the region's natural beauty and quality of life, and these are really important. But if highly skilled people perceive a move to Seattle as a sub-optimal long term career decision, our strategy of relying on imported talent is at risk.

Productivity and earnings

After reading the section on spatial equilibrium you may have adopted a jaded view of productivity and wages. After all, a person living in a high amenity place where jobs pay well faces a high cost of living. Why would anyone live in such as place if real wages—wages adjusted for the cost of housing and local services—are no better than anywhere else? Good question, and the fact is that many people don't want to live in such places. In a high wage, high cost area like Seattle, the *net* inflow of people masks a substantial outflow. In 2009, for example, 1,600 people moved from the Seattle area to Dallas-Fort Worth and 600 moved to Atlanta, both affordable cities with good economic prospects.[18]

But set aside the individual perspective and look at the bigger picture of productivity and wages. Industries that have a good chance of growing and sticking around for a while tend to have high productivity and high wages. Employers generally do not want to pay any more than they have to, so if employees are paid well it means they are worth it; they produce a lot of value for the enterprise and their skills and talents are scarce. Jobs pay well in New York City or San Jose not because it is expensive to live there, but because workers there produce a lot of value and employers pay them accordingly.

Another reason employers of highly skilled people pay them well and provide generous benefits is because they cannot easily replace such people, even with individuals of equal talent. In complex operations employees acquire what is known as "tacit" knowledge, the intangible know-how that keeps things running. Long time employees know what has been tried before and can guide new efforts around the minefields that newer employees cannot see. Employers will pay a premium just to make sure the institutional knowledge does not walk out the door.

Nowhere is this more evident than at the Boeing Company's operations in the Seattle area. Assembling commercial aircraft is perhaps the most complex industrial operation in the world—millions of parts, each of which must be tracked, zero tolerance for defects, and a relentless production schedule. While Boeing has always outsourced parts and airframe sections, it took a big chance with the 787 in outsourcing the design and construction of very large sub-assemblies. This effort to save money and lower risk did the exact opposite, as Boeing's partners around the world failed to perform. Meanwhile Boeing's highly trained Puget Sound workforce, steeped for generations in the aircraft business, continued to produce other airplane models with high productivity and high profitability for the firm. In the fall of 2011 the company reached a long-term agreement with the machinist union that keeps wages high and provides long-term job stability. Boeing management had learned its lesson, and we learned that high wages and job security are both a sign of long-term industrial competitiveness and contribute to it.

And, indeed, productivity and wages are very high in the Seattle area. In 2010 the gross domestic product per job—the basic measure of productivity—of the Seattle metro area was about $132,000 per year, compared to an average of $111,000 in all metro areas. This placed Seattle 14th among all metro areas and 9th among metro areas with over a million people. The San Jose-Silicon Valley area is the standout for productivity, with a per job GDP of $186,000. San Francisco, New York, Houston, Washington D.C., Los Angeles and Charlotte fill out the rest of the top slots for productivity among the large metro areas.[19]

Productivity is a function of the effectiveness of both capital and labor, and wages (both hourly and salaried pay) reflect the slice of the production pie that goes to employees. Wages in the Seattle area are relatively high. In 2010 the average employee in the Seattle area earned about $56,500 per year, versus a national metro area average of about $49,000 per year. Seattle ranked eighth among all metro areas and sixth among metro areas over a million people. Again, the leaders on this metric among the large metro areas were the Silicon Valley-San Francisco region, followed by Washington D.C., New York and Boston.[20]

The story of Seattle becomes most impressive when we put average wage figures together with the growth figures described above. Typically we would expect an inverse relationship between average wages and population growth. The nice weather and inexpensive housing of the big Sunbelt metro areas attract many less skilled people who, in turn, attract lower productivity employers, all of which bring average wages down. Conversely, businesses will not set up low-wage operations in San Francisco or New York City, so those areas tend to grow more slowly and have higher average wages. Seattle has managed to achieve both strong population growth and high wages. Only one metro area, Washington D.C., exceeds Seattle in both average 2010 wages and average population growth from 1990 to 2010.[21]

There is no question that the software industry drives the region's high average wages. Removing software from the wage picture brings the region back to the national average. But that would be the case in any high wage city: imagine calculating average wages after removing financial services from the New York City economy, or information technology from San Jose, entertainment from Los Angeles or energy from Houston.

Industry leadership

Eight companies listed in the *Fortune* 500 have their headquarters in the Seattle area. And although Boeing moved its corporate headquarters to Chicago in 2001, the most promising half of the company, Boeing Commercial Airplanes, is still headquartered in the Seattle area and if a separate company would rank around eighty-five on the *Fortune* 500. The remarkable thing, though, is how many of these firms are global leaders in their industry and major economic and cultural trendsetters. Consider that in the Seattle area you will find:

Boeing Commercial, the nation's only remaining builder of large commercial aircraft, and one half of a global duopoly. Air travel is growing at a blistering pace around the world and half of all new passengers will fly on planes assembled in the Seattle area.

The dominant maker of computer software. For as far back as I can remember pundits and industry experts have been predicting the demise of Microsoft, but year after year it grows by double digits, reports huge profits and moves into every available piece of real estate in East King County.

Costco, the firm that taught people to walk out of the warehouse with far more stuff than they ever imagined when they walked in. Costco made the critical discovery that even upscale shoppers like to save money and that they could marry discounts with top quality merchandise.

The once simple bookseller, Amazon, which some see as taking over a big part of the internet, through its aggressive pursuit of technology services. Amazon was one of the few pure-play internet retailers that thrived after the dot-com bust, and has leveraged that position into annual sales growth averaging 30 percent.

Starbucks, the firm that taught people to spend four dollars on a paper cup of coffee with milk, but more importantly introduced to the nation and much of the world a new institution: the nicely appointed shop where anyone is welcome to sit all day, meet with friends or colleagues, work, or just stare out the window.

The region is also home to firms such as Nordstrom and Alaska Airlines that have redefined customer service, and Paccar, whose Kenworth and Peterbilt trucks are the premium brands of the freight industry.

A common feature of these firms is that they don't compete primarily on price, even Costco and Amazon. When McDonalds and Dunkin Donuts announced their intentions to go head-to-head with Starbucks by offering high quality coffee at a lower price we could hear an audible snicker from Starbucks headquarters: those guys missed the entire point. It's not just the coffee, it's the "experience," and as Starbucks CEO Howard Schultz noted, no one is going to make a special date with a friend for a cup of coffee at Dunkin Donuts.[22] The Seattle brand identity depends on the perception of quality and yes, more than a little snobbery. Starbucks has mastered the trick of making that quality and snobbery available to everyone without diluting it: a Starbucks outlet in an exurban strip mall has exactly the same coffee, décor and perky service as one on Michigan Avenue, and is probably more profitable.

In addition to leading their industries today, these companies should have staying power in the global economy. By trading on intangibles, like customer service and the "experience" they insulate themselves from much of the competition. Moreover, one of the things that all of these businesses have in common is high cost of entry for their industry. Being established and profitable, they can spend money to maintain their leadership position. Microsoft Research, the company's internal basic research arm, spends billions of dollars each year on a staff of hundreds of top scientists in nine laboratories around the world, making it larger than any university computer science department.

The flip side of the presence of these large world-leading firms is the danger of industrial monoculture. Diversification has been the watchword in economic development in the Seattle area for the past fifty years, but only in the past 25 years has Boeing's influence noticeably lessened. It is still the largest employer by far, but now supports about 20 percent of the economy versus 50 percent in the 1960s. The rise of Amazon as a major IT service provider has diluted Microsoft's dominance of software employment, and the establishment of engineering arms of Google, Yahoo, Adobe and Facebook in the Seattle area has helped the biodiversity of the IT ecosystem.

Although not a business in the strict sense, a section on industry leaders located in Seattle would be incomplete without mentioning the Bill and Melinda Gates Foundation, the world's largest charitable enterprise. By distributing massive amounts of money and by taking very different approaches to global health problems, the Gates Foundation has turned the once-comfortable world of international aid on its collective head. Regionally, the Gates Foundation's presence has strengthened the life sciences cluster overall, and the global health research sector in particular. Seattle now ranks as the most important center for global health after Geneva, and some believe it will soon surpass the Swiss city in importance.

Cultural leadership

This book began with a reflection on the transformation of Seattle from a cultural backwater to a place with recognizable cachet. But in many ways Seattle's cultural leadership reflects perception and does not signal a disproportionally large presence of cultural activities. We need to con-

centrate more on the semiotics: the *idea* of Seattle. The region symboliz-
es a certain lifestyle and image that cultural packagers find useful, even
if the products originate in Los Angeles and are filmed in Vancouver. In
his 2004 book *Selling Seattle*, British academic James Lyons says that:

> *The 1990s saw [Seattle] establish a new prominence within American
> popular culture: the location for a succession of headline grabbing
> events; the site for the genesis of new trends and developments; the
> subject of an increased number of magazine profiles; and the signified
> setting for a notable number of novels, motion pictures, television
> shows and documentaries.[23]*

Lyons claims that in the 1980s the signature urban areas of the country,
notably New York City and Los Angeles, were wracked by violence and
disorder, part of a larger decline of city life in America. Seattle, on the
other hand, represented a fresh start, a place that appeared untouched
by the pathologies so evident in other cities. This is a plausible thesis,
but does not account for grunge, which was rooted, like Punk or Bruce
Springsteen songs, in urban distress: shuttered timber mills, layoffs at
Boeing, fishing fleets rotting at the piers. Nonetheless, in the Seattle of
the mid-1980s the nation did find a screen onto which it could project an
attractive image.

That screen was not completely blank, however. Very real things
were going on in Seattle that shaped its image. Something authentic had
to be projected, and in reality Seattle did offer a unique combination of
cutting edge business, natural beauty and the possibility of a laid back
lifestyle. And although few outside the region keep score, we natives
know of the large number of just plain weird things that keep Seattle
from drowning in blandness: we have given the world a remarkable
array of cultural oddments, from Mary Kay LeTourneau to Amanda
Knox, DB Cooper to the Barefoot Bandit. *Twin Peaks* could only have
taken place in the Snoqualmie Valley.

Although it has never developed a large cultural industry based on
its attractive image, the Seattle brand does serve an important purpose
in helping attract talented people to the region. Seattle's chief competitors for talent, places like New York City, Los Angeles, San Francisco,
Boston and Chicago all have established cultural leadership, and Seattle's higher profile helps level the playing field.

Quality of life

This is our ace-in-the-hole, now, isn't it? We may be remote, a bit provincial and boring and very badly dressed, but you are never more than a few minutes away from the wonderful outdoor recreation opportunity of your choosing. When the clouds clear up and The Mountain is out (people really do say that) there are few lovelier places, and the delights are available pretty much to all. Even after fifty years here I still get a charge out of coming over a rise and seeing a sunset over Lake Washington and the Olympic Mountains.

All well and good for you, you might say, but what about those who don't give a rip about mountains and sunsets? Isn't that quality of life stuff pretty subjective? Well, yes, it is maddeningly ill-defined and subjective. In 2009 I worked on some research about talent migration that involved ten regions around the world similar to Seattle. We wanted to know what sorts of quality of life factors mattered to highly mobile and talented people. So, we commissioned a survey of our target group in each of the ten cities, asking survey respondents to rate the importance of a wide range of natural, social and built factors that, cumulatively, could measure the quality of life. I distinctly recall hearing back from our pollster, Stu Elway, that never in his thirty-five years of polling had he seen such flat, undifferentiated responses. No single factor stood out above any other, with all variation stuck firmly within the margin of error.

So how can we say that Seattle has an enviable quality of life if we don't know what people envy? It turns out that we can look for an answer in our old friend the spatial equilibrium formula: $W + Q - C = U$. Utility remains constant and because we have data that measure wages and the cost of living, we can derive a value for amenities by solving for that one remaining variable—it's just a more complicated version of what you did in eighth grade algebra. Researchers have done this—known as capitalizing amenity values—and published results that show the value of the quality of life package for metropolitan areas in the U.S. This process estimates what sacrifices people are willing to make in terms of low wages and high housing and service costs in order to live in a nice place. Or, conversely, it measures what inducements people need in terms of high wages and low costs to live willingly in a less pleasant place.

In a 2008 study by University of Michigan economist David Albouy, the Seattle metro area ranks sixth in quality of life among metro areas with over a half million people.[24] Honolulu leads the way in that study, by a considerable margin, followed by San Francisco, San Diego, Sarasota and Los Angeles. Again, note that all the leaders enjoy decent winter weather, the one amenity that looms large in the decision processes of those thinking of where to move. In a study of the impact of weather on migration patterns, Jordan Rappaport, of the Kansas City Fed, put Seattle's weather in a category that actually encourages out-migration, indicating that Seattle must have other amenity factors so superior that they can overcome the weather negative[25]. In a 2008 amenity capitalization study by Yong Chen and Stuart Rosenthal, the Seattle area ranked 15th in quality of life among metro areas with over a half million people. In this study several metro areas in the New York-New Jersey-Connecticut megalopolis scored higher than Seattle, despite having questionable weather, and Honolulu ranked fourth, behind San Jose, San Francisco and Stamford.[26]

The good news about the ambiguity of quality of life measurements is that metro areas can market themselves based on whatever strengths they happen to have, confident that at least some portion of the high value, footloose workforce will find those particular attributes attractive.

The minuses

So far things look pretty good, and you have been waiting for the other shoes to drop: the price that spatial equilibrium demands be paid in exchange for high wages and attractive amenities.

Housing costs

Most of the physical products we buy—food, clothing, gasoline, cars, toasters—get traded widely around the world and tend to have similar prices everywhere. At the same time, we know it is a lot more expensive to live in some places than others. The big differences in the cost of living among metro areas come from the non-traded sector, with real estate as the most visible component. Entrepreneurs cannot move buildings from an area of low demand to an area of high demand. Thus, imbalances between supply and demand that would naturally even out in the traded sector, lead to price differences in housing. The same modest house that sells for $50,000 in a small Midwestern town will sell for over $1 million in Los Angeles.

In Chapter 1 we first saw the phenomenon of the superstar city, the place where very high incomes can keep up with prices driven high by a shortage of housing supply. Seattle has veered into superstar territory, with the area facing affordability problems well before the bubble began to distort the market around 2005.

The National Association of Homebuilders has maintained its Housing Opportunity Index (HOI) for the Seattle metro area going back to 1991.[27] The index number indicates the percentage of homes sold in the metro area that would have been affordable to a buyer with that area's median income. Except for the bubble years, the HOI for the Seattle market hovered between 45 and 55. At first glance this might seem reasonable, but bad things happen when we drop below the median: incomes fall faster than house prices, and once a potential buyer falls 10 or 15 percent below the median income there is simply nothing for them to buy.

A clear pattern emerged in the Seattle area during the 1990s and 2000s, seen very clearly in the IRS migration data. In-migrants from other states and countries moved overwhelmingly into King County, and, at the same time, King County experienced a net loss of households to the adjacent counties. In-migrants tend to have higher earning power, so they could afford the expensive homes near Seattle, Bellevue and Redmond, while people who had grown up in King County but did not have the high paying jobs in the tech sector, were forced to look in Snohomish and Pierce counties for home they could afford. This, in turn, drove prices in those counties well beyond what local wage scales could support, sending even more buyers up and down the Interstate-5 corridor. Prices as far away as Skagit and Lewis counties reflected this pattern.

Fortunately, Seattle does not have the extreme affordability problems of a major superstar like San Francisco, where the HOI never gets above 30 and has dipped into the single digits. But price trends have excluded moderate income households from home ownership if they have wanted to live anywhere near the major job centers in the Seattle-Redmond axis.

That need to "drive to qualify" for a home loan brings us to the next challenge for the Seattle area.

Traffic

Transportation problems are embedded in the spatial equilibrium equation in two ways. First, transportation affects the cost of living. Recall from Chapter 1 that within a metro area, housing costs and commute costs will tend to mirror each other inversely, with low housing and high commute costs in outlying areas and high housing and low commute costs close to employment centers. This plays out in the superstar regions where low wage service employees must commute very long distances to work in employment centers. Second, congestion is a major quality of life issue: the most pleasant and amenity-laden region still cannot look good from a traffic jam.

The annual Urban Mobility Report of the Texas Transportation Institute (TTI) provides frequently cited measures of traffic congestion.[28] In 2010, among metro areas with more than a half million people, Seattle ranked seventh worst in TTI's Travel Time Index, tied with Houston and finishing behind the usual suspects of Los Angeles, Washington D.C., New York, San Francisco and, curiously, Austin. In the early 1990s Seattle ranked as high as second in the Travel Time Index, and it is not clear whether in the intervening decades Seattle's traffic got better, others' got worse or the methodology changed. In any case, Seattle's traffic has gone from not too bad in the 1980s to really horrible in the 1990s to just sort of horrible today.

Given that the state has added very few general purpose freeway lane miles in the area since the new Interstate 90 corridor was completed in 1992, we would have expected congestion to worsen, especially since housing prices near the Seattle-Redmond job axis have gotten so high that many mid-level employees must commute from 10 or 20 miles away. But things have not worsened and may have gotten better. According to the Census Bureau, in 2000 59 percent of commuters in the Seattle area could make their morning trip to work in less than a half hour, and by 2010, 63 percent reported commuting within that time. With a nine percent increase in commuters and little new infrastructure built during that decade, that is a notable accomplishment. [29]

We can attribute some of the leveling off in the deterioration in commuting to the dispersal of employment. In 1995 Seattle had 46 percent of the jobs in King County, with 19 percent in the large Eastside cities of Bellevue, Redmond, Kirkland and Issaquah. By 2010 Seattle's share had fallen to 42 percent of King County jobs, and the share of the four Eastside cities had risen to 22 percent.[30] This meant a higher likelihood that people living on the Eastside were working on the Eastside, lowering the percentage of commuters ever getting on those congested interstate freeways that TTI fingered.

Is transit helping? Yes, a bit, but not as much as we might think, considering the investments the region has made in fixed rail and express bus service. In 1990 6.4 percent of commuters in the Seattle area reported commuting on public transit. By 2010 this had risen to 8.5 percent—an improvement, but hardly revolutionary.[31] During the time transit was gaining its two percent of commute market share, the region added 230,000 single occupancy commuters to the roads and highways.

Weather

The 1985 neo-noir film *Trouble in Mind* took place in Rain City, a slightly futuristic, slightly dystopian place full of losers, creeps and sad stories. Whether the filmmakers named their locale Rain City and then went looking for a place that fit the description, or whether they decided to film it in Seattle and then came up with the name, the association is clear. Everyone knows that Seattle means rain.

The Rappaport study on the impact of climate on migration patterns scores Seattle in the same category of meteorological misery as Erie, Rochester and Sault Ste Marie, but not because we freeze our collective tushes off in the winter.[32] Rather, the pervasive dimness drives people mad. We don't see the sun for long stretches, and the region's high northern latitude makes winter days short. In Seattle we drive with our headlights on most of the year. The Twilight Saga took place in Forks, on Washington's Olympic Peninsula because vampires need to live in places with very weak light.

And it does rain, but not as much as one might think. We never tire of saying that New York City gets more rainfall in a year than Seattle. But the big difference is that New York gets its rain in huge, fast dumps during summer thunderstorms and we get a relentless light dripping for days at a time. We love interval windshield wipers. Seattle natives tend not to carry umbrellas. A hat—the dorkier the better—works fine and umbrellas just poke people and get blown inside out. Seattle is known as the worst-dressed place in the country and I would chalk that up to the weather. In addition to ghastly hats, we wear clunky shoes since the puddles never dry out, and instead of stylish overcoats we wear elaborate Gore-Tex parkas to fend off the horizontal rain and the bone-chilling damp wind that blows off Puget Sound.

People do get used to it. My father grew up in Honolulu and although he always wore a hat when the temperature dipped below sixty degrees and could never understand fogging car windows, he lived most of his life happily in the Seattle area. Friends and neighbors from Northern California, which has perhaps the loveliest climate on the planet, have no plans to go back. So when it comes to weather as an amenity value, my sense is that it works as a negative in the recruiting process—why would anyone go to a place known as Rain City—but becomes a neutral factor in the all-important retention calculation.

A friend who works at Microsoft says that he considers the weather a plus for the software industry. When the atmosphere outside is dark and gloomy, programmers would just as soon stay inside and write code. He is baffled by the productivity of Silicon Valley, with its terrific weather.

I must say that we do get a reward, most years, for enduring a Seattle winter and spring (the two are often indistinguishable). Summer in the Puget Sound region, which starts after July 4, can provide the most pleasant weather anywhere. It stays surprisingly dry, with low humidity and no rain for weeks at a time, and once the morning clouds lift the temperature stays in the upper 70s day after day. And the other side of the short winter days are the long summer evenings when the sun sets at nine o'clock and even the warmest days cool down. Many Seattleites leave town in the winter when preservation of sanity suggests an escape to California, Mexico or Hawaii. In summer we stay in the area, camping, boating, fishing, hiking or just sitting on a beach. Like many people, I keep photos of these days on the start-up screen of my phone to get me through February.

Adding it all up

The portrait that emerges from these assets and liabilities suggests a successful but perhaps vulnerable region. It has grown more than all but one of its cold weather counterparts, Denver, and has higher productivity and incomes than most fast-growing large metro areas. The region has continually attracted well educated people, even during the economic downturn of the 2000s and has become among the best-educated places in the country. It hosts a number of large, world-leading businesses that have excellent prospects for the future and its connections around the globe continue to expand.

The primary vulnerability comes from the region's need to import talent. World-leading firms can and must hire the best people available, no matter where they come from, so national and international recruiting will always be a feature of business practices in the region. But while we know what brings people here—an attractive job with a great employer—we do not know two important things. First, how many top people decided NOT to move to Seattle and why did they choose other places? Second, why do people leave after growing up in the area or after being recruited here?

This loops back to my concern about the ability of second-tier regions to recruit and retain talent. Sure Seattle has first-tier companies and institutions that any young and talented person would be happy to work for, but those people are shopping not just for a company but for a region that will offer multiple opportunities over a lifetime. Given the head start of Silicon Valley in IT and Boston and San Francisco in life sciences, Seattle will always be a second tier aggregator of talent—maybe a very strong second, but never number one.

Cornell University economist Robert Frank has written about what he sees as an increasing tendency toward winner-take-all patterns in markets for talent at the corporate and entertainment level. That phenomenon could take hold in regional talent markets more generally, where second place is a very long way from first place.[33] Recall the scene in *Glengarry Glen Ross*, where the sales chief says that first prize in the monthly sales contest is a Cadillac Eldorado and second prize is a set of steak knives. The big talent destinations will always offer a better menu of opportunities. The scary part is that as more talent moves to a metro area, more opportunities arise in that place as new firms set up shop where they know the talent congregates: a virtuous cycle that we will come back to later in the book. As noted above, there is no obvious labor market dynamic through which San Francisco, New York, Los Angeles, Boston or Silicon Valley get overloaded with talent. The superstar city theory says that these places can go on indefinitely soaking up smart people, making them rich and selling them expensive houses.

I don't mean to say that Seattle cannot win its share of talent. It clearly does and will continue to be an attractive place. But we need to be like Avis in the old ads and try harder. Right now I cannot identify any concerted effort to keep the pipeline flowing, except to assume that the big national recruiters will continue to bring people to Seattle and keep them long enough that they put down roots.

On the rough continuum of development patterns from the Sunbelt cities (high growth, low cost) to the superstar cities (low growth, high cost) Seattle sits near the center, leaning toward the superstar side. A combination of weather and growth politics might suggest that Seattle will never be a high growth region, but Portland, Oregon, which shares both weather and political attitudes with Seattle, grew faster than Jacksonville, Tampa and Miami over the past 20 years. With a post-bubble moderation in housing prices and a strong base of business activity, Seattle could be in for a major growth spurt in the teens.

The Seattle economy still feels young and not quite fixed. The main drivers of growth are no more than a generation old, and we have seen the instability that plagues technology-based industries. The wireless communications business, pioneered in the Seattle area by Craig McCaw, was born, grew up, and receded in less than twenty years. What assurance can we have that the big new economic forces driving the region today will still be around in another generation? As I write, the business press is questioning the future of two firms that have seen extraordinary success in recent decades: mobile phone maker Nokia and Blackberry maker Research in Motion. Their struggles should serve as a wake-up call to any leader presiding over an economy based on fast-moving industries.

To protect ourselves we need to generate a constant flow of new businesses, understanding that many, if not most, will fail, but that some will provide that next wave of growth. So while I remain optimistic about the region's long-term future, sometimes it feels like we are the guy on the Ed Sullivan show who spun plates on sticks. He has to keep the first plates spinning while always trying to start new ones.

Now, having taken a look at a snapshot of the Seattle region in 2012, let's go back to Arthur Denny in 1851 and see where it all came from.

Chapter 3

Sawdust to Software, Fish to Flight

T he organizers of the Century 21 Exhibition exuded optimism, and looking back after fifty years we cannot fault them for it. We may not commute to work with a jet pack, but the technologies of today, had anyone predicted them in 1962, would have inspired equal wonder: all that computing power in your pocket, connected instantly to the entire world! Fair organizers got their wish: Seattle has become a major center of advanced technology.

The fair organizers got their other wish, too: Seattle has emerged from a dark corner of the country to become a recognized hub in the global web of economic regions. The international flavors on display in 1962 may have seemed exotic at the time, but today, Seattle residents experience the real thing in their neighborhoods or as they travel the world.

Technology and global connectivity, the two aspirations of the fair, happened.

Those organizers could not predict the journey we would take over the next fifty years, but if they had, they would have told us to fasten our seatbelts and get ready for a bumpy ride. From 1962 to 2012 the Seattle economy experienced spectacular growth and spectacular crashes and saw its once-dominant resource industries replaced by newly dominant technology industries. Many residents have grown fabu-lously wealthy, and we mostly dodged the crushing urban poverty that afflicted so many cities over that time period. The suburbs just taking shape in 1962 have grown both out and up, rivaling the central city in economic strength.

Let's take a closer look at the arc of this story. We'll begin with a brief run from the city's founding through the 1950s, pause for a snapshot of the region in 1962, and then move through the ups and downs that followed. The narrative will be brisk, focusing mostly on the economy, so long-time residents will find many things missing. But I do hope that you will get a general sense of how the regional economy evolved, and I hope the chapter gives you a sufficient historic framework on which to hang the discussions of economic factors and industries that follow.

Origins

The Denny party that landed on Alki Beach in 1851 consisted of a small group of Midwesterners who had headed toward Oregon simply because it was west of where they had been. After receiving some dubious advice along the trail, they decided to head north after they got to the Willamette Valley, their original destination. An advance party that came over land began building an encampment on Alki Point, and the main party, which included a newborn baby, arrived on the schooner *Exact* on November 13, 1851. No one had told them that mid-November has just about the worst weather of the year, and they settled in for a miserable winter. Within a few months they had moved to the sheltered waters of Elliott Bay, setting up their new town of Duwamps.[1]

The future of Seattle came into much better focus when two men, Henry Yesler and Dr. David S. "Doc" Maynard, arrived in 1852. The Dennys had been marginally successful farmers in Illinois, and probably thought they would take up that life again in the Northwest, with perhaps the same level of success. But Yesler saw the trees, and set up the town's first sawmill. The Yesler Mill provided an economic base for the new town, and brought cash from the gold rush boomtown of San Francisco that had greatly needed Seattle's lumber and pilings.

But as Roger Sale points out, Maynard helped keep Seattle from becoming just another timber camp. He pushed for growth beyond the mill, and expanded trade with San Francisco. Maynard, Arthur Denny and other pioneers figured out how to make the leap from mill town to "city." As lumber camps and company towns spread throughout Puget Sound, Seattle became the commercial center where business got done. It had stores, banks, schools, a hospital, and by 1861, the Territorial University. The waterways of Puget Sound were soon dotted with steamers delivering goods from Seattle merchants to settlements across the region.

These early burghers wanted to make Seattle a place where ambitious men would bring their families and carve a real civilization out of the wilderness—and make lots of money in the process. The Willamette Valley in Oregon had become a sort of extension of the Ohio Valley, where so many of its settlers had started, and Seattle too could become a thriving, upstanding community. Seattle's founders saw California, driven by the gold rush, as a rough place suitable only for men and for the merchants and low elements preying upon them.

Seattle did, indeed, become a mercantile, bourgeois city, and although it had more than its share of saloons and brothels, the town that spread to the north from Yesler's mill became a pleasant place to live. As merchants and local manufacturers figured out how to capture markets for goods and services throughout the Puget Sound basin and beyond, Seattle outpaced the original centers of Olympia and Tacoma. The founders knew all along, however, that to become a major city, Seattle would need a transcontinental railroad terminus. The story of how the railroad finally came to Seattle is a long and convoluted one, and the arrival of the Great Northern in 1893 set the stage for a brief era of spectacular growth.

The national economy suffered a deep depression for much of the 1890s—whoever came up with the phrase the "Gay '90s" clearly did not live then. The general economic malaise slowed the growth of Seattle at first, but, ironically, contributed to the most important event in the city's early history: the Klondike Gold Rush.

Miners and trappers had roamed around the Yukon for years, bringing back pelts and bits of gold, but not impressing anyone very much. Then, on August 16, 1896, George Carmack and his brother in law Skookum Jim Mason hit a major strike on the Klondike River, near Dawson. Other miners in the area converged on the site and spent the winter digging through the permafrost, extracting amazing amounts of gold. When the spring thaw came, the newly wealthy miners headed south, and on July 17, 1897, the steamer *Portland* arrived in Seattle with a "ton of gold." And the rush was on.

With a poor economy and idle factories around the country, unattached men had little to lose by heading to the gold fields. They came from all over the U.S., Canada and even abroad, most having no idea at all where they were headed and little idea what it meant to get to the arctic and mine for gold. But one group of people did know a thing or two: the merchants of Seattle. Seeing a major opportunity, the Seattle Chamber of Commerce hired a former newspaperman, Erastus Brainerd, to put the word out that Seattle was far and away the best place from which to depart for the Klondike. Through a series of sometimes ethically questionable publicity tricks, Brainerd succeeded in convincing about 80 percent of the 40,000 souls headed for the Yukon to come through Seattle.

Since the Royal Canadian Mounted Police would not let anyone into the Yukon without a year's worth of supplies—a kit worth about $10,000 today—those ready to provide those supplies stood to make a fortune. And the merchants of Seattle did just that. The fact that Seattle had become the commercial hub of Western Washington meant that it had not just the merchants, but also local manufacturing capacity—food processors, tent makers, stove works—for many of the needed goods. And the new transcontinental railroad could bring in other goods quickly.

The Klondike Gold Rush, and the Nome Gold Rush that followed the next year, had a totally transformative effect on Seattle. Supplying the miners brought a much-needed influx of cash into the city, relieving a suffering local economy. And, a few lucky miners and adventurers actually brought wealth back to Seattle: George Carmack himself settled in the city, and Johan Nordström founded his shoe store with money he made trading mining claims in the Klondike.

But most important, a large number of the returning miners, generally penniless, settled in the Seattle area. Now, being a descendent of some of those miners I might romanticize this part a bit. But I can't help thinking that the sorts of people who would head to the arctic in the first place, and survive the ordeal, make a pretty good root stock for an ambitious, risk-seeking, tough population.

Once the national economy got back on its feet, Seattle's position as a port on the Pacific, with direct rail connections to Chicago, led to a growing connectedness to Asia. Steamships had replaced sailing vessels and could now take the great circle routes in the North Pacific. This made Seattle the closest port to Japan and China, where Northwest wood products and fish would find a healthy market.

By 1909 Seattle felt very good about itself and celebrated its new stature with the Alaska-Yukon-Pacific Exposition, its first World's Fair. The Exposition brought visitors from around the country to the fair-grounds on what is now the University of Washington campus. But this big splash turned out to mark the end of Seattle's growth spurt, and a long period of uneven growth would follow. In 1912, perhaps symbolizing the new era of slow, cautious expansion, voters rejected the Bogue Plan that laid out an ambitious growth strategy for the entire region. The time for thinking big had ended.

The primary economic drivers of the previous decade—trans-continental railroads, ports, Alaska and Asian trade—had leveled off. The resource economy and shipyards hummed along, but with the excep-tion of the years around World War I, when shipbuilding boomed, little of major economic consequence happened for three decades. Seattle's remoteness caught up with it, as the heavy manufacturing industries of the nation continued to concentrate in the Northeast and Midwest. The western Washington timber harvest did grow, from 3.5 billion board feet in 1909 to a pre-depression high of 6.6 billion board feet in 1929. But any industry not tied to water, trees or agriculture had a difficult time estab-lishing a foothold.

Organized labor began a difficult, but ultimately successful drive to unionize much of the economy, culminating in Dave Beck's leadership of the Teamsters. The general strike of 1919—the only one in American history—made an impression on the nation, fostering a radical image that remained for many years. Although the strike did not achieve much by itself, the trend toward widespread union membership did stick, and the state remains a union stronghold.

During the 1930s, when the Depression sapped the life of the city, some important developments were underway that would color the post-war period. On the other side of the mountains, the federal government began its massive program of dam building on the Columbia River. The irrigation capacity of the new reservoirs allowed the tree fruit industry to expand, and abundant cheap hydropower would finally give industry in the Northwest some way to mitigate its disadvantageous location.

Around the same time, the Boeing Company started making some major advances in commercial aircraft. The trimotors that had dominated civil aviation in the 1920s were slow, noisy and uncomfortable, and, still having wood and cloth components, a maintenance nightmare. Boeing was the first American manufacturer to attempt an all metal, streamlined passenger plane similar to what we see today. The 247, launched in 1933, never saw a great deal of commercial success and Douglas planes, including the legendary DC-3, soon eclipsed it. But this plane, and its military and commercial successors in the 1930s, proved that Boeing had enough engineering talent to become a major player once the Army started gearing up for World War II.

If the Seattle economy slept through the 1930s, the city found its footing culturally during that time. The unsophisticated town that Sir Thomas Beecham famously referred to as an "aesthetic dustbin" in 1941 actually had quite a lot going on.[2] Mark Tobey and the Northwest School of painters gained national prominence, and the Cornish School (later Cornish College of the Arts) had attracted avant-garde artists like Merce Cunningham and John Cage. Seattle's proletarian past may have put a damper on the "serious" arts, but it appears to have provided fertile soil for artists trying to break from those conventions.

World War II changed Seattle as it changed the entire country. The region found itself no longer on the outskirts of the country, but strategically positioned on the edge of the Pacific Theater, and with capacity in key munitions industries. All of this war activity required skilled workers, and people flocked from across the country to work at the newly resurgent factories of Seattle, Tacoma and environs. Between 1940 and 1950, the population of Seattle increased from 368,000 to 467,000, and the population of King County increased from 504,000 to 733,000. During this same time, Tacoma grew from 109,000 to 143,000.[3]

But after the war effort ended, and the military stopped ordering ships, tanks and planes, Seattle again faced economic trouble. In spite of the post-war housing boom, timber harvests remained modest, and the boom in consumer products to satisfy the pent up demand of the country would largely pass Seattle by.

Once again, however, the federal government stepped into the breach, looking to take advantage of the jet engine and swept wing technologies that U.S., British and German scientists and engineers had worked on during the war. The Boeing B-47, with six jet engines, first flew in December, 1947, and solidified Boeing's position in jet technology. The B-52 followed, entering service with the Air Force in 1955.

Since the 1930s Boeing had gotten the majority of its business from the military and post office, while Douglas and Lockheed ruled the commercial market. In the early 1950s Boeing decided to challenge these two builders, while keeping a foot firmly on the military side. It designed the B-367-80 prototype to appeal first to the Air Force, which needed a jet tanker that could keep up with its jet bombers during aerial refueling. But Boeing could convert the "Dash-80" airframe to a passenger model that would provide a major size and speed advantage over the prevailing propeller planes. This new plane, the Boeing 707, would transform air travel and the Seattle economy.

Douglas also came to see the future in commercial jets, recognizing that although it dominated the commercial market with its large, comfortable propeller planes, those slower planes would never compete with jetliners. The Douglas DC-8 and the Boeing 707 had their maiden flights within a few months of each other and competed fiercely for customers. Boeing ultimately won that battle, building twice as many 707s as Douglas built DC-8s. "Boeing" became synonymous with passenger jets and the company began its dominance of the global commercial jet market.

Now, finally, after decades of little economic progress and a heavy dependence on military purchasing, the Seattle region had a new industry that could drive growth and lessen dependence on natural resources. Boeing had attracted commercial aircraft customers all over the world, so Seattle's isolated position in the country did not present any significant disadvantages. Military programs had drawn an impressive talent base to Boeing, both in the engineering departments and on the factory floor, paving the way for further expansion.

But by today's standards, the economy of the region was still pretty backward. Roger Sale asserts that the Seattle economy changed little from 1907 to 1967, and with the exception of Boeing's initial rise, he is largely correct. In the 1950s the state and the Puget Sound region still relied on the traditional resource-based industries and a strategic position on the Pacific Rim. The North Pacific fishing fleet had taken root in the Seattle area, with its mild winters and excellent repair yards, and the Navy kept the larger yards busy. Kenworth trucks rolled off the line, and the city had a steel industry to meet local needs. But otherwise, Seattle had simply not evolved very much.

The stagnation of the Seattle economy did not escape the notice of regional leaders. In a 1957 speech to the Seattle Rotary Club, Fred Haley, Tacoma civic figure and CEO of the Brown and Haley Candy Company, described the regional economy in stark terms:

> The Pacific Northwest is not yet an industrialized area. Neither, contrary to popular opinion, is it rapidly becoming one. . . Ours is essentially a colonial economy. . . Like other colonial economies, we export our natural resource products in raw or semi-fabricated form and import the finished consumer and capital goods.[4]

Haley had drawn upon a 1954, book *Industry in the Pacific Northwest and the Location Theory*, in which economist Edwin Cohn describes the pattern that Haley had noticed.[5] Because of its relatively small size and remote location, Washington would never be a suitable location for conventional industry. The only industries that would make sense for the region would be those related to maritime trade and those that process local raw materials in order to lower the cost of shipping. Or, he noted, we might get some of those accidental "footloose" industries that started here just because the founder happened to live here. Observing the pattern of the next fifty years, Cohn was on the mark. The industries that would develop would have negligible transportation costs (software, airplanes) or idiosyncratic origins (Starbucks, Amazon). We'll revisit this theme later in the book.

Seattle in 1962

By the time President Kennedy opened the Century 21 Exhibition, the region had already begun to move away from the world Fred Haley had described. The labor force had grown only about 20 percent since World War II, but that was impressive enough, given the need to absorb all those wartime workers into the peacetime economy, as the region had done in the 1920s. Forest products and food processing had fallen to about 20 percent of manufacturing employment. Aerospace already constituted half of the region's manufacturing workforce, a position it would hold through the decade. But even with a growing high-tech manufacturing base, the region maintained its blue collar feel. Non-traded services, including healthcare, legal and financial services, made up only about 20 percent of the economy.[6]

Imagine what the city looked like from Elliott Bay in 1962. The waterfront still had steamers loading and unloading at the original piers, with some massive fish canneries to the north of downtown. The Smith Tower, built in 1914, and the Northern Life Tower, built in 1928, dominated the skyline, with just a few newer "modern" structures like the Norton Building, showing any signs of recent construction. Mostly what one saw were the brick and terra cotta offices and stores of an earlier era. The action at Boeing Plant 2 in the Duwamish had not generated much in the way of demand for new service businesses in the downtown core, and it remained quiet.

As an indicator of the image the region had of itself, consider the cover of Seattle-First National Bank's Annual Review for 1962. It had six images: Grand Coulee Dam, a log truck, a family camping, a tractor, a Boeing 707 and the Space Needle. That set of illustrations pretty well sums up the economy of the time.

Like the rest of the country, King County experienced the beginnings of suburban growth in the 1950s, and by 1962 the landscape outside of Seattle had changed. Between the 1950 and 1960 censuses, Seattle added about 90,000 people but much of that growth came through annexations of neighborhoods to the north and south. During that same time, the areas of King County outside the Seattle City limits added 110,000 net residents, even after losing tens of thousands to Seattle annexations. Half a dozen new cities had incorporated in the 1950s in East King County, and older cities in the county like Kirkland, Kent and Auburn experienced major population growth. [7]

After decades of neglect, the region had begun to catch up on basic infrastructure. Since the area had not grown much, the old road and utility networks had provided adequate service. But with new suburban growth, the region would need to begin investing again. Metro started construction on its new sewage collection and treatment system in 1961, and smaller communities began to hook into the Seattle water system. The State Route 520 bridge across Lake Washington would open in 1963 and the Interstate freeway system would soon open up vast areas for easy commutes.

Residents and leaders may or may not have recognized that they had a soporific economy, but they did know they lived in a special place. The lead editorial in *The Seattle Times* World's Fair souvenir edition did not tout the fair itself, but rather the natural beauty of the Northwest, which it urged fairgoers to enjoy. The newspaper's Sunday magazine was even named "Charmed Land." And then, as now, we were told we could go boating and skiing in the same day.

So, perhaps befitting its place on the fringes of the map, the Seattle of 1962 found itself somewhat on the fringes of American life, earning the disdain of Holden Caulfield. The post-war industrial growth that fired the Midwest never got to the Puget Sound area, and the California life-styles celebrated in movies and songs never got beyond Siskiyou Pass.

But I think the copywriter who named the "Charmed Land" magazine was on to something. For an individual or family not looking for too much excitement or cultural sophistication, the region could be an exceptionally nice place to live. My own dim memories begin at about this period, and I recall few complaints about the lifestyle at the time, and those I know who also grew up here have fond memories. Seattle was a minor league, provincial town in most respects, but maybe those bothered by such things were the ones who left.

In any case, the charmed land was about to get on that bumpy ride that has not landed yet. Fifty years of slow growth and plodding indus-trial development would give way to fifty years of dramatic ups and downs, with the region emerging as one of America's most vibrant metropolitan areas, queasy but still smiling.

1962 to 1969. The Boeing ramp up years

Fred Haley's observation in 1957 that the Puget Sound region lacked a strong industrial base would have sounded odd by the late 1960s: the region had, indeed, become an industrial area. In 1966, ten years after his speech, Boeing employed about 85,000 people in King and Snohomish Counties. At their peak, Boeing's operations supported upwards of 40 percent of the economy in the two counties. If the region had resembled a colony in the 1950s, ten years later, it looked like one big company town.

We'll cover more details of the aerospace industry later, but for the story of Seattle in the 1960s to make any sense we need to understand the product strategy of Boeing's commercial arm. The company rolled out three airplane families during the 1960s—and worked hard on a fourth—in an effort to dominate the market and outmaneuver its rivals, Douglas, Lockheed and the new kid, Airbus.

In the 1950s the airline industry needed a large fast plane that could fly across oceans without refueling. The 707, modified with larger fuel tanks, met this need, carrying 150 passengers over 4,000 miles. But the industry did not need that much capacity for most domestic routes, looking instead for a smaller jet that would provide speed and non-stop range on transcontinental routes and land on the short runways that most airports still had. In 1964 Boeing introduced the 727, a tri-jet that would go on to become the best-selling jet to-date. But even with the smaller 727 the airlines needed a jet that would have the better economics of twin engines and be small enough to serve minor markets. In 1965 Boeing introduced the 737 to meet this need.

By the mid-1960s Boeing produced three families of aircraft, mostly from its massive new plant in Renton. In addition to that plant, Boeing had built fabrication facilities and military and space operations throughout the Kent-Auburn Valley, and was still conducting operations at the original Plant 2 just south of Seattle. These programs had required a large ramp up in employment on both the engineering and production side.

But more was to come. In the early 1960s, as the Jet Set popularized the idea of hopping around the globe, and resurgent economies of Europe and Japan produced newly affluent travelers, aircraft manufacturers could see a market for larger intercontinental airplanes. In March, 1966, less than a decade after putting its first commercial jet into service, Boeing launched the program for the 747. Everything about this program was outsized, including the new assembly plant in Everett, which remains the world's largest building.

And Boeing still had more on its plate in the mid-1960s. The aerospace industry had long known about the questionable economics of supersonic flight, and a 1961 Kennedy Administration suggestion for a program to develop a supersonic commercial plane drew sharp opposition. But by 1962, a British-French consortium had launched the Concorde. Not wanting to lose out on a market estimated at upwards of 500 planes, the federal government held a design competition for a supersonic transport, or SST. Boeing, Lockheed and North American submitted proposals, with Boeing declared the winner in December, 1966.

As huge engineering teams worked on the 747 and SST programs, the rest of the company did not stand still. The older jets received continual upgrades and modifications as new technologies and new market requirements dictated. And while Boeing located much of its space and defense operations in Wichita, Kansas, Huntsville, Alabama and Philadelphia, Pennsylvania, some Pentagon and NASA programs wound up in the Seattle area.

By 1969, Boeing and its suppliers employed 104,500 people in King and Snohomish Counties. The perception I had growing up that every other adult worked at "Boeing's" was not far off the mark.

This surge in employment at Boeing led to a major upswing in overall population in the region. After moderate growth in the 1950s and early 1960s—most of which consisted of children being born during the Baby Boom—the Puget Sound region saw a dramatic population increase from 1963 to 1968. Over that time period, King County added 165,000 people, Pierce County added 55,000 and Snohomish County added 54,000. In all, the region added about 275,000 people in five years, an 18 percent increase in population. The region grew nearly as much in this five year period as it had during the entire decade of the 1950s, when the Baby Boom was in full swing. Moreover, the birth rate had plummeted after 1964, so most of the population growth in the mid-1960s came from net in-migration. In 1968, the peak year for in-migration, 65,000 more people moved to the region than moved out.

Whereas growth in the region in the 1950s had consisted mostly of babies, and therefore *larger* households, growth in the mid-1960s consisted mostly of in-migrants, and therefore *more* households. Suburbs that had begun to spread out from Seattle in the 1950s really began to move in the 1960s. Completion of the SR-520 bridge and the Interstate system meant easier commutes to Boeing's facilities in Renton, Seattle, Kent and Auburn, and also to the new plant in Everett.

And with all these new Boeing operations and employees, the multiplier effect began to kick in. Boeing attracted suppliers to the area, from companies such as Heath Tecna, in Kent, that built plastic components for aircraft interiors, to providers of basic operational services. Then, all the new households in the region would need stores, schools, healthcare and other day-to-day goods and services. Later studies pegged the Boeing multiplier at about four, meaning that every job at Boeing itself generated three additional jobs throughout the economy.[8]

With Boeing adding about 60,000 employees during this time, another 180,000 jobs would appear in the economy through the multiplier effect, for a total added impact of 240,000 jobs. Employers in the region added a total of about 275,000 people during this time, so we can safely conclude that Boeing drove nearly all of the net job growth in the region during the mid-1960s. A company town, indeed, and one getting ready for a major fall.

These were also the years of social upheaval across the western world. Although this book does not focus on those forces of history, it is worth noting that while Seattle had its share of visible challenges to the status quo—UW students taking over Interstate 5, the Black Panther Party holding military style drills—the region was fortunate to escape with little permanent social or physical damage. Roger Sale, a close observer at the time, attributes this not to any local enlightenment, but rather to the relatively small scale of Seattle's inner city issues. Whatever the reason, Seattle was fortunate to have one less problem to dig itself out of as the very difficult early 1970s came along.[9]

1969 to 1972. The Boeing Bust.

If the Klondike Gold Rush served as the first defining event in Seattle's economic history, the Boeing Bust was the second. Ironically, Seattle benefitted from the gold rushes because it had avoided becoming a company town that served only the needs of the local mills. It had become a regional business center with manufacturing capacity, and therefore could supply the diverse needs of the miners. But seventy years later it had become a far less diversified place, depending heavily on one company. And when that company ran into trouble so did the region.

From an engineering perspective the 747 was a major success. No one had attempted to build a commercial airliner that large, and when it finally took off for the first time on February 9, 1969, it flew beautifully.

But problems with production delays and engines pushed the program farther and farther from its original delivery date, and, critically, farther from the cash generated by delivering finished planes. The 747 program had run far over budget and both the launch customer, Pan American, and Boeing's banks had run out of patience.

Meanwhile, sales and deliveries of the rest of Boeing's family of planes had leveled off. Orders peaked in 1965, with Boeing selling 135 707s, 187 727s and 83 737s, for a total of 405 planes. By 1969, orders had fallen to 134 planes, including thirty 747s.[10] This meant that in 1969 Boeing accepted just over one fourth as many orders as 1965 for its three narrow-body planes. Airlines had begun to sober up about the overly optimistic forecasts for passenger growth that had driven orders in the mid-1960s, and with a national recession taking hold in 1969, they needed to cut back.

With new orders falling steadily from 1965, and existing orders facing cancellation, Boeing had stretched out production, peaking at 376 deliveries in 1968 and dropping to 141 in 1971. And to make matters worse, deliveries of its most profitable planes, the older 707 and 727, which had long paid back their initial investment, had fallen quite a bit. 747s made up nearly half of all deliveries in 1970 and 1971, and that program was still struggling with production issues, making each plane far less profitable than the older models. Cash flow had become a huge problem, and the hemorrhaging of money had to stop before the company went bankrupt.

In mid-1969, William Allen, the man who had led Boeing into the jet age, retired as CEO, turning the fate of the company—and the entire regional economy—over to T. (Thornton) Wilson. Wilson knew that if he and longtime Boeing managers did not make the necessary and extremely painful cuts, the board and the firm's bankers would bring in an outsider who would likely do irreparable harm to the company's engineering heritage. So beginning in late 1969, Wilson and his line managers began cuts. With the cancellation of the SST program in early 1971, the cuts would eventually extend to 60,000 employees in King and Snohomish counties.

Then came the signature image of the Boeing Bust, when two local commercial real estate brokers, Bob McDonald and Jim Youngren, rented the famous billboard near SeaTac Airport that said "Will the Last

Person Leaving Seattle Please Turn Out the Lights." The billboard lasted only a couple of weeks, but it seemed to capture the mood that had hung over the city for a year and a half, by then. Images of the billboard traveled around the world, and in May, 1971, *The Economist* ran a story about Seattle headlined "City of Despair."

Less than a decade earlier, Seattle had bounded onto the world stage with the Century 21 Exhibition. In early 1969 the region had again made global headlines with the first flight of the 747, a stunning achievement for a remote, third-tier city. Now a "city of despair?" The rapid job losses, much of which hit the elite engineering staff, certainly shook the confidence of the region, which had long enjoyed relatively steady growth. Unemployment reached over 13 percent, twice the national average.

Looking back, though, just how bad was the bust? Did everyone leave town?

No. That was the remarkable thing. Out-migration, while significant, was not excessive, considering the magnitude of the economic shock. Each year from 1970 through 1974 the three county region experienced net out-migration, with a total loss of about 85,000 people over four years. But in the preceding five years, the region had experienced a net inflow of about 210,000 people, so looked at over ten year period, from 1965 through 1974, the region still gained a net of about 140,000 people.[11] It appears that a substantial portion of the skilled, ambitious people who moved to the region during the boom chose to stay in spite of the tough times. And although we cannot know for certain, I would imagine that a large number of the people leaving consisted of relatively recent Boeing recruits and individuals working in construction and other fields that tend to attract footloose workers.

Overall regional employment did not suffer nearly as much we might suspect. With Boeing cutting 60,000 people, and its suppliers in the region cutting perhaps another several thousand, we would expect the multiplier effect to result in total job losses in excess of 200,000. But from 1969 to 1971, the low point for regional employment, job losses totaled 59,000 in King County and 15,000 in Snohomish County. Pierce County saw a loss of 16,000 jobs, but 13,000 of these stemmed from reductions at Fort Lewis and McChord Air Force Base. So, over the three counties, the Boeing Bust consisted of a loss of 78,000 non-military jobs.[12]

These jobs losses fell overwhelmingly in two areas: manufacturing and construction. The rest of the private sector in the three counties lost only 16,000 jobs in the three years, and gained all of those back by 1972. It appears that the multiplier effect does not work very powerfully in reverse over the short run. Jobs from the multiplier effect come from two sources. "Indirect" jobs get created at suppliers, and we would expect them to fall at the same rate as Boeing production. But the second source, the "induced" employment, comes from consumer spending, and these jobs fell at a much lower rate. Unemployed people still need stores, schools, hospitals and other services. So lower than expected out-migration meant that much of the economy that had built up during the 1960s would remain intact—with slower business, undoubtedly, but still intact. While manufacturing employment fell 30 percent and construction employment fell 23 percent, retail employment fell only five percent, government fell three percent and the large catch-all of "other services" fell only one percent.

I certainly do not mean to minimize the real difficulties the region faced during the Bust, which my family felt directly. My father had worked as an industrial engineer at the Kenworth Truck Company and was laid off during this time. The truck industry had hit one of its cyclical downturns at the same time that Boeing was contracting. At any other time my father would have easily found work with another manufacturer, but not in 1970 when the region was awash in technical talent.

Recessions, however deep or prolonged, take a psychological toll on the workforce. No one feels safe. And it is difficult to overstate the impact of watching the industry that had created such rapid growth over the decade and become such a defining feature of the zeitgeist shed more than half its workforce. The region would bounce back soon enough, but the scars would remain.

1972 to 1980. Recovery and diversification

In 1972 the regional economy hit bottom and began to crawl back. Although manufacturing employment stayed persistently low early in the decade, services began to take up more of the employment pie. But just as the region could see a light at the end of the tunnel, the nation got rocked by the OPEC oil embargo, gas lines and the general turmoil of the mid-1970s. Hard to catch a break.

During this period of slow recovery we can see the beginnings of activities and trends that would blossom later. Not surprisingly, economic diversification took center stage. Conventional economic development—activities to recruit new businesses and retain existing ones—had fallen off the civic agenda long before. The old resource-based industries did fine and could not go anywhere, and for a decade Boeing had provided all the industrial growth the region could handle. The economic development agenda had consisted mostly of infrastructure catch-up through programs like the Metro sewer system, the Interstate Highway program and Forward Thrust.

No one wanted to go through another bust, and as the cyclical nature of the airplane business became obvious, local leaders knew that another aerospace downturn would inevitably hit the region. So the hunt began to find new industries to mitigate the inherent instability of aerospace. The first step was to get organized. The Seattle Area Industrial Council had withered during the Boeing boom of the 1960s (hard to make the case for industrial recruiting) and by 1969 did not have the horsepower to deal with the crisis. The chamber of commerce did not have the capacity to do business recruiting either, so the chamber, along with government and civic leaders formed the Economic Development Council of Seattle and King County, predecessor to today's Enterprise Seattle.

The new group faced formidable barriers to traditional industrial recruitment, however. The region had not gotten any closer to the major national markets, and with high oil prices coming into play, transportation costs became a larger factor. Moreover, at a time when industries flocked to Southern "right to work" states that had made compulsory union membership illegal, the region's heavily unionized workforce, skilled as it was, looked less attractive.

Making the competition even tougher, the nation's manufacturers had just begun to feel the pressure of foreign competition—high gas prices led to a surge in imported small cars—and regions around the country had responded by stepping up their own efforts to recruit and retain business. Economic development agencies in Washington, hobbled by the state's unique prohibitions on gifts of public funds and lending of the state's credit, could not compete with other states that offered attractive recruitment packages.

So it should not come as any surprise that, in spite of cheap energy and no income tax, the Seattle area had a very difficult time competing for most industries. The businesses already in the area stayed, but recruitment efforts did not have any major successes bringing new large operations to town. Quietly though, small manufacturing firms began to grow throughout the region. The medical device and measuring instrument industries, with firms like Physio Control and the John Fluke Manufacturing Co., began to grow into serious employers. In 1971, several former Boeing employees started Flow, which made innovative water jet cutting equipment. Advanced Technology Laboratories built a medical diagnostics business out of ultrasound technology developed at the University of Washington. The catch-all category of "diversified manufacturing" experienced significant growth as the decade wore on.

Trade and port activity also grew in the 1970s. The Port of Seattle had adopted containerization early on, and as trade increased in the 1970s, the Puget Sound ports saw growth in cargo shipments. Total trade through the Washington Customs District grew from $3.2 billion in 1970 to $21 billion in 1980, or a three-fold increase, adjusted for inflation.[13] And substantial activity on and near the waterfront resulted from construction of the Trans-Alaska Pipeline from 1974 to 1977. Contractors assembled huge barges on the Puget Sound waterfront, many with prefabricated building modules, and had them towed to the North Slope. Seattle, which had always served as the supply and service base for Alaska, saw that activity increase significantly around the Pipeline.

Seattle finally broke out of its "minor league" status in the mid-1970s. Literally. Although it had had an NBA team, the Supersonics, since 1967 (the SST program got cancelled, but the name lived on!) and the Pilots for one Major League Baseball season in 1969, Seattle sports fans had subsisted on the Rainiers and the inconsistent University of Washington Huskies. With the completion of the Kingdome in 1976, the Seahawks and Mariners would bring big league sports, however badly played, to Seattle.

And in keeping score of Seattle's increased visibility during the 1970s, we cannot ignore King Tut. The *Treasures of Tutankhamen* exhibit was a global phenomenon in the 1970s, touring the USSR, the U.S. and Europe, drawing millions of visitors at each stop. Originally, Seattle and Los Angeles were the only Western U.S. stops, but San Francisco later intervened and joined the tour. This was a very big deal. Exhibit organizers needed crowds, so Seattle's selection meant they had confidence that the city could pull them in. And it did. The exhibit ran from July 15 to November 15, 1978, drawing 1.3 million visitors. I had been away that summer, and when I returned in August I could not believe the teeming masses downtown and on the waterfront. It felt good. The "City of Despair" had come a long way in eight years, shaking off the Boeing Bust and taking what seemed like a more secure place on the national stage.

1980 to 1983. The housing recession.

Inflation had reached very high levels in the late 1970s, and at the same time, the economy stalled. Observers coined a new word to describe the misery: stagflation. With the encouragement of the newly inaugurated Reagan Administration, Federal Reserve Chairman Paul Volcker set out to break the back of inflation by driving interest rates to unprecedented levels. The plan worked, but the housing industry paid the price. With mortgage rates in the neighborhood of 18 percent, buying a home made no sense to many people, and homebuilding slowed dramatically. This had two devastating impacts on the economy of the Seattle area.

Construction itself slowed significantly. The region had experienced a major surge in in-migration during the late 1970s, and developers had responded with a big increase in construction of homes and the accompanying retail and service businesses. Construction employment in the three-county area jumped from about 38,000 in 1975 to 67,000 by 1979. But by 1982, construction employment had fallen back to about 54,000.[14]

Then, the national downturn in housing caused by high interest rates led to a big drop in demand for building materials, including wood products. In the early 1980s wood products still constituted the region's second largest segment of manufacturing, so the 32 percent drop in harvest and 25 percent cut in employment from that sector between 1979 and 1982 hit the region hard.

The double-dip recession that lasted from 1979 through 1982 nationally was particularly harsh. Unemployment in the state hit 9 percent in June 1981 and topped out at 12.2 percent in November 1982, staying over 10 percent until January 1984 and not getting below eight percent until January 1987.[15]

Like the Boeing Bust, we cannot understand this economic strife without understanding the underlying demographic shifts that played out during the late 1970s and early 1980s. Even with those very high unemployment rates, total employment in the region actually grew during most of this time—very slow growth, but still positive—and total personal income flattened but did not fall. Only one year, 1982, saw an actual drop in total jobs, and that was only about 7,000.

Even though jobs kept growing, the slow pace of that growth could not keep up with expansion in the workforce. Unlike the Boeing Bust, when net out-migration began as soon as Boeing started its layoffs, people kept moving to the region in the early 1980s, even though job growth had leveled off. In 1979 and 1980, as the national economic ship headed for the rocks, the three county region experienced a net gain of over 100,000 people. And even in 1981, with an economy clearly struggling badly, the region experienced a net gain of over 40,000 people. In only one year, 1983, did the region see a net outflow, but by then it was too late to stem the growth in the labor force that drove the unemployment rate up. Between 1980 and 1982, the region experienced a net gain of 114,000 people and a net gain of only 1,600 jobs.[16]

A second demographic feature of those years, the entry into the workforce of the biggest bulge in the Baby Boom, exacerbated the unemployment problem. Total births in the nation reached their peak between 1957 and 1961, so this cohort started hitting the workforce in 1975, and the college graduates began to arrive in 1979. The national economy had spent the previous decade absorbing the earlier Boomers and large numbers of women who had re-entered the workforce, and now the tail end of the Boomers were arriving on the job market at an even faster pace, just in time for a national recession. I am keenly aware of this particular demographic phenomenon, having graduated from college in 1982, facing intense competition for very meager prospects.

While the region bounced back from the Boeing Bust with an industrial structure not too different from the 1960s, some significant changes came out of the recession of the early 1980s. The wood products industry, the Puget Sound region's original economic mainstay, never recovered, and by the early 1990s had shrunk to about 20 percent of its pre-1980 size. Manufacturing overall, which had hit a post-Bust peak of 33 percent of the economy in 1981, began a long slide, dropping below 30 percent in 1990, on its way to 21 percent today. Meanwhile, business, legal and financial services and healthcare began to grow rapidly, with some major service sectors nearly doubling between 1979 and 1989.[17]

1983 to 1990. Discovering technology and the world

The economy of Seattle today is so strongly tied to information technologies, gaming, life sciences and other "high tech" businesses and research institutions we can easily forget how new this identity really is. In Seafirst Bank's 1984 Annual Review of Pacific Northwest Industries, an article about the Seattle economy starts with a long description of the evolution and diversification of manufacturing in the region, followed by a review of port and trade activity and acknowledgement of growing service businesses. It assesses the future by stating:

> "For the Seattle metropolitan complex, the past generally should be prologue to the future: a hub of Northwest business services, distribution and transportation services; a growing force in the nation's visitor industry; and an important and increasingly diversified manufacturing center."

Not a single mention of information technologies or any other technology-based business or research activity!

But by 1984 technology-based businesses had begun to grow rapidly in the region. Microsoft had moved from New Mexico to Bellevue in 1978, and by 1984 had 600 employees and $100 million in revenue. Aldus, formed in 1984 by Paul Brainerd and five other refugees from Atex, developed the first desktop publishing software, PageMaker, for the new Apple Macintosh. Attachmate and Walker Richer & Quinn were figuring out ways to hook the new world of microcomputers into traditional corporate mainframe systems. And in the old Butter and Egg District of Western Avenue in Seattle, Immunex was developing intellectual property that would pay off handsomely in the future.

Even with Bill Gates' appearance on the cover of *Time* magazine in April, 1984, with huge glasses and a six-inch floppy disk, the region's business establishment had not begun to appreciate the growing presence of industries driven by new technologies. To be fair, though, the battle for the heart of the computer industry had not yet ended. In hindsight we can see that the desktop personal computer would win out over the mainframe and the mini-computer, and that open software platforms would win over proprietary ones, but at the time it was not clear that Redmond could compete with Silicon Valley and Route 128. Thankfully, however, the lack of recognition of this new industry did not matter at the time: Microsoft went public in 1986, creating a generation of young millionaires who could not care less what the establishment thought.

The 1980s saw the birth of another technology industry that would, for a time, give a boost to the region: wireless communication. Craig McCaw used the family cable TV company as a vehicle to buy up licenses for the new cellular phone technology and began building a network. While working at Captains Nautical Supplies in the early 1980s, I remember selling topographic maps to some outfit called McCaw Cellular, having no idea at all what the business did. The early phones were clunky and expensive, but McCaw could clearly see the potential for the phones and the service behind them to follow the pattern of other technologies and become far smaller and cheaper. Clever maneuvering in the cellular license market allowed McCaw to become big enough to get the interest of AT&T, which eventually bought the company.

A second major development of the 1980s did receive recognition at the time, though: the region's growing global position.

Sometime in the early 1980s Americans began to wake up and discover that they no longer ruled the planet. World War II had left industry in North America fully intact, while bombs had destroyed industry across Europe and Japan. This meant that American businesses could have their home markets to themselves and could enter foreign markets to the extent that trade barriers allowed. This began to change by the 1960s as European and Japanese industries finished rebuilding, and by the 1980s those newer industries presented a serious challenge to their now-aging American counterparts. The Tokyo Round of the General Agreement on Tariffs and Trade (the GATT, predecessor to the World Trade Organization) had opened markets around the world, and for the first time in a couple of generations, U.S. industry had to struggle to maintain sales at home and abroad.

The buzz in the mid-1980s was all about the "new global economy" the nation had just discovered. In most places in the country this new economic order presented a major threat: one industry after another felt the pressure of imports and new competition in once-exclusive foreign markets. The U.S. trade deficit began to balloon in 1983, and pressure mounted on Congress to go after "unfair trading practices" and to institute outright protectionist measures. Globalization mostly meant threat, rather than opportunity.

But not in the Northwest. We benefitted from all this globalization in ways that few other parts of the country did. Even then, Boeing exported more than any other U.S. firm, a large share of the state's agricultural output went overseas, and the Seattle area had thriving businesses such as clothing that depended on imports. In addition, many of the imports that had begun to displace U.S. products were passing through the ports of Seattle and Tacoma, employing Longshoremen, truckers, railway workers and a long list of service businesses. So while the rest of the country wrung its hands and gave furious speeches about the machinations of Japan's Ministry of International Trade and Industry, Washington State and the Seattle region generally cheered these developments.

The economic vision that had emerged by the end of the decade appeared far more forward looking than that of the 1984 Seafirst report. *Washington Works Worldwide*, the final report of the State Economic Development Board, issued in November 1988, envisioned:

> *A Washington that has become an international crossroads of world trade and world cultures; a Washington where globally-competitive businesses produce high value added, high quality, highly innovative and constantly-improved goods and services for the global market-place; a Washington where well-paid workers are highly educated, multi-skilled and adaptable to the new challenges of an information-intensive, ever-changing international economy; and a Washington where quality of life, communities, natural environment, and standard of living are known and admired throughout the world.[18]*

As with most economic development strategies, this one missed the mark in some crucial areas (like the Seafirst report noted earlier, it does not mention software), and ended up gathering the proverbial dust on shelves, but the vision that is posits looks remarkably like what we have aspired to in the years since. It also looks very much like the underlying ideology of the regional leadership coalition, discussed in Chapter 7. The 1980s saw the solidification of an ethos that embraced globalization, education, technology and, most important, change. As we will discuss in Chapter 8, the region did not have an aging industrial structure to pro-tect and could afford to indulge in an ambitious agenda of innovation and globalization.

Underlying that confidence, however, was the old standby: Boeing. The firm had recovered from the Bust, introduced two new models in the early 1980s—the 757 and 767—and by the mid-1980s had almost reached the employment levels of the late 1960s. Orders and deliveries picked up in 1985, and by the end of the decade the company was again flying high. It launched a major redesign of the 747, the 400, in 1985 and began deliveries of that monster in 1989. Then, in 1990, to make sure its engineering teams did not get a moment's rest, Boeing launched the 777, which would revolutionize long-range air travel as the 747 had done a generation earlier.

The prosperity that began to settle over the region in the late 1980s, welcome as it was to many in the region, was accompanied by a building boom that ended up generating a significant backlash. In Downtown Seattle, four major skyscrapers went up almost simultaneously, begin-ning with 1201 Third Avenue, which broke ground in 1986, the same year the long-delayed Westlake Center project got underway. Then, the downtown transit tunnel began construction in March 1987, creating massive holes in the ground on Third Avenue and on Pine Street, in the heart of the retail district. The convention center was under construction from 1985 to 1988. I recall moving back to Seattle in September 1987 and thinking the place was a real mess.

Compounding the construction disruption was the unanticipated out-come of a new Seattle downtown zoning code that provided a number of density bonuses in exchange for public amenities. Well, no one figured that developers might take advantage of *all* the bonuses, but they did, resulting in some very large buildings like 1201 Third and Two Union Square. A group of citizen activists had had enough, and successfully launched an initiative—the Citizens Alternative Plan (CAP)—that over-turned the existing code and placed severe restrictions on building heights in the downtown.

Regionally, the picture did not look much better. Major population and housing growth in the decade eliminated what little extra capacity the freeway system had, and the region received its "second worst" traffic award from the Texas Transportation Institute. The newly-expanded Interstate 90 led to a housing boom on the previously sparse Sammamish Plateau. Reaction throughout the region to rapid growth ultimately led to the state Growth Management Act, which the legislature adopted in 1990.

The building boom ended up having its own self-correcting mechanism, however. Three of the four big new buildings had trouble finding tenants and ended up in foreclosure, bringing downtown construction to a halt. The transit tunnel took buses off the street and the convention center provided a welcome new supply of parking. Overbuilding in the suburbs led to flat housing prices for most of the 1990s. The late 1980s had an undeniably ugly side, but all that construction provided the infrastructure for the big growth spurt of the 1990s.

All in all, by the end of the 1980s Seattle appeared finally to have overcome the geographic problem that Edwin Cohn and Fred Haley had identified as the reason for the "colonial" economy of the Northwest. Distance from markets did not matter for the aerospace industry or the newly emerging technology industries, and the prominence of these sectors allowed the region to embrace globalization in ways that most other parts of the country could not. The region was poised for the 1990s.

1990-1991. Dodging a recession for the first time.

But before we could begin the era of Seattle's ascendance, a shallow national recession got in the way. In the 1980s the nation experienced the longest peacetime economic expansion on record, but a confluence of events late in the decade brought the long recovery to an end. The "Black Monday" stock market crash of October 1987, although temporary, unnerved many people, and the savings and loan crisis of the late 1980s shook confidence in real estate and banking. Finally, the first Gulf War, launched in August 1990 led to a spike in oil prices that further shook the economy.

The National Bureau of Economic Research defines a recession according to several measures, and this downturn barely met those criteria, with the economy moving in the wrong direction from the third quarter of 1990 through the first quarter of 1991. Anemic growth through the rest of 1991 did add to the pain, although demographics— the much smaller Baby Bust generation had begun to enter the work- force—helped.[19]

In the past, national recessions had hit the Northwest harder than in most areas since the region depends so much on sales of capital goods, like airplanes and trucks, which profit-starved businesses delay pur- chasing. But for the first time, the Seattle area dodged the national recession. Employment actually grew a modest half percent from 1990 to 1991, and over one percent from 1991 to 1992. Two factors contributed to the region's ability to weather this national downturn.

Mercifully, aerospace performed well during those years. The travel industry usually falls victim to a recession early on and recovers last. Leisure travelers take fewer long distance trips, but the real trouble comes as businesses tighten their travel budgets and buy fewer of the expensive seats at the front of the airplane. And when cash flow slows, airlines delay delivery of new airplanes. This pattern did not repeat itself in 1990-91, however. Orders did fall from 563 planes in 1989 down to 112 in 1994. But deliveries, which drive jobs in the regional aerospace industry, actually went up. Boeing delivered 284 airplanes in 1989, 385 in 1990, 435 in 1991 and 446 in 1992. And even better, these delivery figures included a lot of very expensive 747-400s, meaning strong cash flow.[20] Aerospace employment in the region experienced its post-Bust peak in 1991 at 112,600, falling to 99,600 in 1993 which would be the average for the decade.[21] These jobs losses were far lower than in previ- ous recessions and were attributed mostly to the ramping down of the aggressive development programs of the 1980s and early 1990s.

The other factor in the region's ability to dodge the national recession was the growth in diversification of the economy toward service and technology-based industries. While the goods producing sector lost 9,000 jobs in the King-Snohomish region between 1990 and 1992, the service producing sector gained 28,000 jobs, including 4,000 in the software industry. This pattern of flat manufacturing employment and growing service employment would continue through the decade.[22]

1991 to 1999. In the spotlight.

The mid to late 1990s proved a good time for the country as a whole, and especially for the Seattle area. Several businesses headquartered in the region assumed national and international prominence and Seattle gained a new cultural cache. Recall James Lyons' suggestion that after all the things that had gone wrong in urban America during the 1980s and early 1990s—deindustrialization, drug and murder epidemics, riots—Seattle seemed a place where things went right, a place of new industries and attractive lifestyles and little baggage.[23] Seattle's rise to prominence floated in on four distinct but interrelated streams.

First, Microsoft's growing dominance of the software industry brought global attention to the region's technology industries. Unlike Silicon Valley, which boasts multiple large technology companies, Seattle had Microsoft and a handful of smaller firms. But no firm in Silicon Valley totally dominated a sector the way Microsoft did and, to that point, no Silicon Valley firm had created the same kind of conspicuous wealth.

Second, Starbucks led the way in defining a particular Seattle cultural image. The Seattle brand began to mean something beyond Boeing and a vague sense of environmentalism. Seattle's brand image fit perfectly with the newly dominant value system embraced by what David Brooks defined as the "Bourgeois Bohemians," or Bobos: a leftish social and environmental consciousness wrapped around an upper-middle-class capacity for consumption.[24] Seattle offered the perfect lifestyle for middle-age baby boomers clinging to their old sense of adventure and exceptionalism but not straying too far from safety and comfort.

Third, a homegrown music movement, Grunge, provided a much-needed shot in the arm to an industry in desperate need of something new. Although much of the action gravitated to Los Angeles eventually, grunge was unmistakably associated with Seattle and exported to the world. It retained enough of a sense of authenticity for long enough to make a permanent mark on national and international culture and became embedded in the Seattle brand.

Fourth, Seattle became increasingly identified with the Pacific Rim and a positive view of globalization. As noted, few areas of the country could find as many advantages and as few disadvantages as Seattle in the new world economic order. The region's newly emergent global leadership and growing cultural sophistication led to the notion that Seattle could become the "Geneva of the Pacific Rim." The Asia-Pacific Economic Cooperation (APEC) summit in 1993 was a major success, and although the World Trade Organization (WTO) meetings of 1999 did not work out quite as envisioned, the choice of Seattle as the venue for that event really did make sense.

Consider how the overall landscape changed from 1992 to the eve of the dot-com crash of 2000.

Did everyone move to Seattle, as the Newsweek cover suggested? Well, yes and no. The three county region gained about a half million people during the 1990s, or the equivalent of the population of Seattle itself spread almost entirely through the suburbs of three counties. While the region had never seen census-to-census growth this large before, in percentage terms it did not match the growth surge of the 1960s.[25] Remember, though, that in the 1960s the region had just opened a spacious freeway network, whereas the population arriving in the 1990s faced a transportation system already operating at capacity.

Over the decade, 57 percent of the population growth came from net in-migration, with the balance from natural growth. The net in-migration rate for the 1990s only slightly exceeded the average over fifty years, so although it may have seemed like the region was getting flooded with newcomers, the migration pattern followed past decades fairly closely.[26]

The region did get notably wealthier during the decade. In 1990, the Seattle metro area had the 13th highest per capita personal income (PCPI) among regions with more than a half million people. By 2000, Seattle had moved up to seventh place, passing regions such as Chicago and Minneapolis. During the decade, PCPI increased 57 percent nationally (not inflation adjusted) and 72 percent in the Seattle area. The average wage per job provides an indicator of the wellbeing of the workforce, and on this measure, the Seattle area performed equally well. In 1990, among regions with more than a half million people, Seattle ranked 16th highest for average wages, and by 2000 it ranked seventh. Average wages grew at the same rate, 72 percent, as PCPI.[27]

By both measures, the Seattle area moved into heady company within the national rankings of successful regions. The only large metro areas that had higher wages and incomes in 2000 were the San Francisco/San Jose, New York/Connecticut, Boston and Washington metro areas. And like the San Francisco area and Boston, the majority of income growth could be attributed to information technology industries, especially the stock options granted by fast growing companies. Clearly, the high incomes and wealth created by the software industry were not available to the average worker in the region, whose income performed about the same as his or her counterpart elsewhere in the country. But as we will see in Chapter 6, software did provide the main engine of growth for the decade.

The prospect of getting rich at a young age through an ownership stake in a valuable new company was something very new for the region. Employment at Boeing and other manufacturers and at the ports had always paid well, but not enough to afford a nanny for the kids, his-and-hers BMWs, a vacation home in Montana and other goodies that seemed standard for the new tech generation. By the latter part of the decade, a large cohort of wealthy Microsoft alumni helped launch the next big technology wave: internet commerce. Although dot-com mania spread all over the country, the Seattle area had its share of start-ups and, fortunately, the biggest success, Amazon.

As we will see next, the region came back to Earth with a thud by the end of the decade. But we had fun while it lasted. Few regions of Seattle's size get the chance for that much exposure and wealth creation and we have a lot to be thankful for. The question is, what did the decade leave us, besides miles of unlit fiber optic lines and a surplus of ping pong tables and Herman Miller Aeron chairs?

To begin with, the 1990s marked a continuation of the shift in the regional economy away from goods producing and toward service producing activities. Manufacturing employment fell from over 19 percent of employment to below 15 percent, and within that, aerospace fell from over 10 percent of employment to below seven percent, the lowest employment share for that industry since the 1930s. Construction and government retained about the same employment share over the decade, so services picked up all the share that manufacturing lost.[28]

The growth in employment share encompassed quite a number of services industry categories, but software had an impact far beyond its numbers. In 1990 about 7,000 people worked in the "software publishing" business. This grew to over 31,000 by 2000, constituting about 2.2 percent of employment in the three counties. But the impact of those jobs was much larger. A 1996 economic impact study found that the software industry had an employment multiplier of 4.4, and a 2009 study found that the multiplier had increased to 6.8.[29] So, in the 1990s each job in software added another 3.4 to 5.8 additional jobs. Those jobs come from purchases by the industry itself (mostly legal and financial services, but also those ping pong tables and the catering at elaborate company parties) and household purchases by employees (big houses, personal services, dinners in nice restaurants, private schools). So, the 24,000 jobs created in the Seattle area software industry in the 1990s created between 84,000 and 140,000 additional jobs in the region. At the high end that would constitute just under half of all employment growth in the decade. In short, we can attribute a substantial portion of the growth in the service, construction and government sectors to purchases by the software industry and its employees.

By the end of the 1990s we could see, for the first time, an industry with an economic impact approaching that of aerospace. We finally had a second tent pole to hold up the regional economy, which had continued its dependence on aerospace since the shrinkage of the wood products and fishing industries. And unlike aerospace, which fluctuates with business cycles, software (excluding e-commerce) just kept growing, providing a stability that would keep the region moving forward during the turbulent 2000s.

Another legacy of the decade, related to the first, came in the form of a large cohort of talented people who moved to the region and stuck around, even when the going got tough. Like the recession of the early 1980s, the downturn of 2000 did not result in a mass out-migration. Net in-migration continued at a strong pace through 2002, and dipped to a relatively low level in 2003, but never turned negative. Migration from the San Francisco Bay area to Seattle remained positive even after the dot-com crash. As the region clawed its way back from the post 9/11 recession, it would have the talent in place to make new things happen.

Finally, the 1990s saw the solidification of Seattle's new image as an attractive, culturally sophisticated region. Throughout the decade Seattle became the setting for movies and TV series that portrayed the area in a very positive light. Real images of Seattle (the movies and TV series rarely filmed in Seattle itself) during the WTO riots scuffed up that new image a little, but a decade later the city has still proved a winner as a setting.

1999-2002. Confidence takes a hit

As the party of the 1990s began to wind down, a series of shocks, both large and small, rattled the fragile confidence the region had built up since the deep and long recession of the early 1980s. Although the national recession of this period remained fairly shallow and short, the Seattle area returned to the old pattern of feeling the impacts more strongly.

The trouble started with the event that civic leaders thought would celebrate Seattle's arrival on the global stage. The riots at the World Trade Organization (WTO) summit in 1999—the "Battle in Seattle"—not only broadcast an unflattering image of Seattle, they caused new rifts locally. Organized labor in the region had generally stayed away from national fights against trade expansion, but local labor leaders got pulled into the WTO protests in ways that unnerved their business and civic counterparts. Similarly, local environmental groups that had worked comfortably within the community now seemed radicalized. Law enforcement became a villain in many people's eyes, and city government appeared confused and inept. We discovered that 15 years after the region had embraced a globalized future, public support for international trade and investment had thinned. The world media began calling violent anti-globalization protesters, wherever they appeared, "Seattle people." The brand image we had carefully built up suddenly had a new and sinister component.

Next came the bursting of the dot-com bubble. Internet commerce began to show up as a measurable portion of the economy in the late 1990s, and by 2000, 30 percent of households had internet access and could potentially shift their purchasing to on-line merchants. The potential for this new economic activity seemed almost limitless, as did the array of products and services that might be captured from brick-and-mortar stores. Thus began the dot-com craze and the irrational exuberance that led investors to turn billions of dollars over to entrepreneurs who had little or no experience as merchants.

As these entrepreneurs saw the enthusiasm of investors for technology stocks, they moved their new firms toward public offerings far earlier than start-ups had in the past. So when it turned out that the business models of most of these companies had little merit, serious financial risk had spread beyond traditional venture capitalists and toward millions of other investors who had jumped onto the bandwagon. When the NASDAQ peaked in March 2000, and the e-commerce industry started to implode, the collapse happened fast. The Seattle area, with a large number of start-ups and investors, felt the pain more acutely. Thousands of people who had flocked to work in these firms, many with few technical skills, found themselves on the street with poor prospects.

Then, in what the Seattle Times called "a stunning blow to Seattle's prestige," Boeing announced that it would move its corporate headquarters away from the Puget Sound region. The company announced the decision to move in March 2001, and by May had settled on Chicago for its new "head shed." While the move had minimal impact on employment in the region, the loss of the marquee name from Seattle's list of headquarters hurt deeply. The region had spent fifty years overcoming the disadvantages of location, only to discover that Boeing's top leaders found Seattle the wrong place for their newly expanded company.

But perhaps the headquarters move just confirmed of what many believed: Boeing had ceased to be a Seattle company. In the 1990s, Boeing had acquired major assets from Hughes Aerospace and Rockwell International in Southern California, and then with its 1997 merger with McDonnell Douglas, Boeing had taken on huge operations in St. Louis. Much of the leadership of the newly merged company—including Harry Stonecipher, who would become chairman in 2003—came from Douglas. The grim joke making the rounds at the time said that Boeing did not buy McDonnell Douglas, but rather, Douglas bought Boeing using Boeing's money. Everyone knew the painful truth: the Boeing of old, with a board made up of Northwest business and civic leaders and with daily executive lunches at the Rainier Club, would not return.[30]

But if the headquarters departure had minimal jobs impact, the other shoe would fall in a few months. The terrorist attacks of 9/11, all of which involved Boeing aircraft, put an immediate crimp in air travel. Fear of further attacks combined with the new hassles of security and the general economic downturn of the time to reduce air travel by 15 to

30 percent between 2001 and 2002.[31] This, in turn, cut back the immediate need for new planes and the cash that airlines would have to pay for them. Boeing anticipated this dynamic and, within weeks of the attacks, began drastic cutbacks in production schedules and employment. In all, Boeing would cut 25,000 jobs by 2004.[32]

A further disturbance in The Force came courtesy of the Antitrust Division of the United States Department of Justice which, in May 1998, sued Microsoft for anticompetitive practices. The case went to trial in October 1998 and proceedings dragged on for nearly two years, with national media regularly painting Microsoft in an unflattering light. The case finally got settled in November 2002, with little long-term damage done to Microsoft. But although Microsoft had always had a reputation for aggressive business practices, the judgment clearly asserted that the company had monopolist tendencies. Bill Gates was now less a Thomas Edison or Henry Ford and more of a John D. Rockefeller. The case had no impact on the local economy, but like the departure of Boeing's headquarters, it bruised the region's collective ego.

On the cultural front the prominence of the previous decade eroded in the natural course of events. No second-tier city can remain in the spotlight forever, and with the aging of grunge, the bursting of the technology bubble and a general lack of novelty, Seattle's time came to an end. Frasier would continue to the 2004 season, but the series and its stars showed their age. Pop culture's short attention span had moved on.

Make no mistake, though. The recession of 2001 had far more than just a psychological impact. Between the peak employment year of 2000 and the low point of 2003, the region shed 80,000 jobs, or more than a quarter of all the jobs created in the previous decade. Employment levels would not recover until 2006, and aerospace employment in the region would not recover for a full decade.[33]

Many of us had believed that the relatively shallow recession of 1991, and the region's ability to evade its worst effects, demonstrated that business cycles in general had eased, that the region's diversification efforts had paid off, and that we would not see another Bust. We were wrong. The hammering the region took beginning in 2000 came as a result of the continued prominence of the highly unpredictable aerospace industry—still the biggest employer in the region—and the instability of technology-based industries. We had not made geography irrelevant and had not invented a magical new form of metropolitan economy that would have only an upward trajectory. In the 1990s we created a great deal of wealth but remained vulnerable: after 150 years the region still had a stress-inducing risk-reward profile.

2002-2008. The suburban boom.

As in the past, the Seattle area lagged the rest of the country recovering from the recession. Regional employment bottomed out in 2003 and turned only slightly positive in 2004. Construction came out of the chute fastest, presaging the building boom that would define the recovery, and ultimately end it. Software continued its uninterrupted growth trend, and aerospace gradually clawed its way back from a low of 59,000 employees in 2004 to 79,000 by 2008. Other than the outsized role of construction, the recovery was fairly balanced, adding a total of 155,000 jobs from 2003 to 2008, more than making up for the job losses of the recession.[34]

From a 2012 perspective—slightly up from the bottom of the pit we dug ourselves into—it can be difficult to remember just how positive things looked in the mid-aughts. Yes, construction seemed aggressive, but the regional population had continued to grow, with in-migration nearly at levels of the 1990s. And those in-migrants came here to take jobs that paid very well, so all those expensive condominiums in Bellevue, Kirkland and South Lake Union appeared to be marketable. And whereas the construction industry in the Sunbelt seemed supply-driven—build it and they will come—construction in the Northwest always seemed demand-driven. We expected housing prices to rise given the building restrictions of growth management, so we failed to see the price bubble embedded within natural market dynamics.

Geography became the story of the decade. While the economy grew in a relatively balanced way across sectors, it did not grow in such a balanced way across the region. In the 2003 to 2008 period the suburban tail began to wag the central city dog.

The dot-com crash hit the city of Seattle particularly hard, since many of the start-up firms had preferred the funky old buildings of the city to the shiny, but rather sterile suburban office parks that the geeks had always felt at home in. In Seattle, Fremont, Pioneer Square and

Sodo had cheap, cool space, like the South of Market district of San Francisco that had attracted "dot-commies" from Silicon Valley. So when the crash came, Seattle took a disproportionate hit. The dot-com startups had been spending all that investor cash in the local economy, so when the cash dried up, local service businesses felt it.

Within the city limits of Seattle between 2000 and 2003, over 40,000 jobs disappeared. Seattle had about 42 percent of the jobs in the county, but sustained 57 percent of the county job loss. In contrast, the suburban agglomeration of Bellevue-Redmond-Issaquah, with about 20 percent of the county's jobs, sustained no net job loss from 2000 to 2003. Once the recovery started, Seattle gained relatively few jobs, while the Eastside suburbs gained substantially. Software, still overwhelmingly a suburban industry, continued to grow, and most construction-related businesses have suburban headquarters and a suburban employee base. By 2008, the peak year for regional employment, Seattle had still not gotten back to employment levels of 2000, while the three Eastside cities had gained a total of 32,000 jobs beyond their 2000 level. And other suburbs experienced positive job gains as well, with Kent, Auburn, Bothell and Federal Way all posting strong employment growth through the recovery.[35]

A second noteworthy feature of the 2000s was the emergence of the life sciences as a major economic force in the region. The University of Washington had always had a large and busy health sciences research operation, but by the turn of the century, other institutions were growing and creating a large cluster of research enterprises that, cumulatively, have an important economic impact. The Fred Hutchinson Cancer Research Center, with its move to South Lake Union in the mid-1990s started the trend. The nexus of the UW and the Hutch created an environment where other health research institutions could flourish. Then, when the Bill and Melinda Gates Foundation began to focus more intently on global health issues, the cluster began to move in that direction.

In the turbulent decade of the 00s, the life sciences brought a welcome stability, having the great advantage of steady growth, although with lower jobs multipliers. It appears that the region has added yet another pole to hold up the economic tent.

2008-2012. Crash and weak recovery.

Once again, we really thought we could dodge this one. After all, Boeing had stabilized and was increasing deliveries while trying desperately to get the first Dreamliner out the door. Software had slowed but not stopped, and the newly-recognized life sciences industries were growing. Yes, construction had slowed, but we were not like those profligate builders in the Sunbelt throwing up zillions of homes for the flippers to flip. Seattle had the NEW economy based on solid fundamentals and growing, globally-competitive sectors.

It almost worked. We did hold off longer than most other areas of the country, but the creeping national fungus of financial sector rot eventually caught up. And when it arrived, it did not have the stench of some venal New York bank, but of our own, homegrown entry in the national banking world, Washington Mutual. Yes, that nice little thrift with the cute commercials. Remember the "Friend of the Family?" With the implosion of WAMU we could no longer sit in our isolated, high-tech, Pacific Rim world and scoff at the irresponsibility of the Mid-Atlantic elite. The newly hollow building on Second Avenue reminded us of our connectedness to the traditional national economy.

We also learned just how optional homeownership can be. The home-building industry got hammered even as people continued to move to the area, get jobs, send their kids to school and do all those things that folks used to do in homes with mortgages. Now they seemed to do them from rentals. I don't think that the trend toward renting is at all permanent, and the kinds of households that have traditionally bought homes will do so in the future. So I don't think homeownership is any more of an "if" question than it ever was. But it has certainly become a "when" question, and the "when" keeps getting pushed further into the future. Quite logically, no one wants to buy a home as prices continue to fall. So as the recession wore on we found ourselves, along with much of the country, in a classic deflationary spiral: no one buys because prices keep falling and prices keep falling because no one buys.

And construction got hit hard, losing 31,000 jobs from a peak of 99,000 in 2007. Thanks to ongoing infrastructure programs like those funded by Sound Transit and the state DOT, as well as hastily-funded "stimulus" projects, civil construction lost only a small number of jobs. The bulk—over 20,000—of the job loss came in the "specialty trades," which includes the subcontractors that provide the vast majority of the workforce in residential construction.[36]

Home building led us into the recession, and, unlike past downturns, it did not lead us out. I think we are seeing a fundamental weakness in the idea of the multiplier effect in the short term. Growth in industries within the economic base should result in growth in the rest of the economy. But we now see that that much of the spending by businesses and households is highly discretionary. A household may have a good job, or even two of them, but still feel insecure enough to put off buying a home, buying furnishings, landscaping the yard, buying a swing set and doing all the other things that keep retail, construction and service industries humming. This suggests a growing reservoir of pent up demand, and no one has any idea when that dam will burst.

So here we sit in 2012, with Boeing again on a hiring spree, Amazon on a roll, Nordstrom reporting higher sales, non-Boeing manufacturing up sharply and lots of good signs within the core of the economy, and yet sluggish growth in many other sectors. Maybe we have entered a new economic era of highly contingent consumption. Because the fundamentals of life are now so cheap, we spend an increasing part of our incomes on services that we can easily live without if we choose to. I never buy into any of those "new era of austerity" arguments that assert some permanent march to simplicity, but it does seem that an increasing part of the consumption package is subject to the confidence of consumers. Lack of confidence, it appears, can drag on for a very long time.

THAT was a wild ride

The Seattle economy is not for the faint of heart. After a quiet fifty years prior to the World's Fair, the region jumped on an economic roller coaster that has kept climbing but with some stomach-churning dips along the way.

Industrial diversification has helped, but we still have not shaken off the instability that makes living here so challenging. Geography keeps getting in the way. The stable sorts of industries—consumer products, business services, retirement communities, distribution—that have kept the Midwest and the South humming along just don't locate here in the upper corner. Businesses that are indifferent to geography, either because they have low transportation costs or because their founders don't care about being in a remote place, seem to provide less stability.

But for those who don't mind a bumpy ride, Seattle has proven to be a good place to live and establish a career. With respect to incomes it has moved from a middling position to the upper tier, and with housing costs high but not ridiculous, real wages are quite good. In Chapter 9 we'll poke our nose out into the future to see where the roller coaster might be headed.

Chapter 4

What Changed, and Didn't, Over Fifty Years?

Fred Haley, the business and civic leader who provided such a brutally honest assessment of the state's economy in 1957, lived to 2005, and saw the state and region emerge from "colonial" status. Having a front row seat on the roller coaster of the regional economy for most of the past fifty years, what did he see change? What did not change very much?

Some themes run through the story arc of the previous chapter, and now we'll explore some of those in more detail. But don't worry, Patches Pals, we're not going to wax nostalgic about Bobo the Gorilla, the Bubbleator, the Last Exit on Brooklyn or other long-lost artifacts of Seattle's past. The food at the Dog House really was terrible (the tenderness of the steak was not guaranteed!) and we still do have Dick's.

As you read through these changes and non-changes, do a thought exercise: what if the reverse had happened? What if the things that are gone had stayed, and the new things that arrived on the scene had not? What if the things that never went anywhere had gone? Think through the implications. Do a George Bailey and imagine the absence of individuals and institutions that have colored the region over the past fifty years. Given the changes in the world around us, what would the Seattle area be like?

What has changed?

Shift from resource-based industries to high technology and service industries

For the first hundred years of its history, Seattle's economy depended on natural resources—much to Fred Haley's dismay. What manufacturing existed mostly dealt with those raw products: wood, wheat, fish. In 1962 Seattle still had at least a dozen sawmills within its city limits, cutting millions of board feet of lumber products per year. Mills in Tacoma and Everett produced far more lumber, as well as rolls of paper from the lumber left-overs. The fishing fleet brought in tons of fish, feeding them into canneries on the Seattle waterfront. The farms of the state sent fruits and vegetables to the region for canning and freezing and wheat for milling.

These processing industries made sense. Processing of raw products removes unnecessary weight and bulk, making it less expensive to ship them to distant markets. In making lumber and paper from logs, the processers left the bark behind, and could stack the product neatly onto rail cars or into the holds of steamers. It is just a whole lot more efficient to ship lumber and paper than to ship logs. Similarly, fish and food products are perishable and have large amounts of waste, and should be processed near the source.

The natural resource and processing industries also generated manufacturing specific to those industries. Northwest companies built timber handling equipment, fishing boats and fishing gear: Marco's Powerblock, invented in Seattle in 1955, revolutionized purse seine fishing around the world. Seattle had two massive plants that made cans for fish and vegetables. (One of those can factories now houses the headquarters of RealNetworks.)

But these industry clusters, valuable as they were, had limits to growth. They faced finite demand for products and had competitors with lower shipping costs. As long as these industries made up the majority of the region's economic base, the population of the region could not grow very fast. And it didn't. Without expanding industries, people elsewhere in the country looking for a new home would not choose the Northwest, and many ambitious young people who had grown up here would leave.

Today, forest products and fisheries together make up only about one half of one percent of the region's employment. Their declining economic presence over the past fifty years can be chalked up to several factors.

Most notably, there are fewer resources to exploit. Commercial fin fisheries ended on Puget Sound in the 1970s, and although tribal fisheries continue to operate in local waters, the catch is not large. The region has remained the base for the Alaska fleet, but there too, some fish stocks have diminished. And much of the catch of Seattle-based bottom fishing boats gets processed on board factory trawlers and transferred at sea to foreign buyers, never making it to shore. (The north and south parts of Puget Sound have active shellfish farming operations, but these do not require the infrastructure that the fin fisheries use.)

Timber faces similar constraints. With federal court mandated protections for the endangered spotted owl, logging on National Forest Service lands has dropped from over one billion board feet in 1988 to just 50,000 board feet in 2010. Private timberlands have moved to sustainable yield practices designed for efficient growth of structural timber and not much else. Loggers harvested 6.6 billion board feet of timber in Western Washington in the peak year of 1973, 18 percent of which came from federal lands. By 2010 the total annual harvest in Western Washington had fallen to 2.7 billion board feet, with only four percent coming from federal lands.[1]

Then, what processing remained moved out of the metropolitan core. Sawmills, paper mills and fish processors are not the toniest of neighbors, and these kinds of manufacturing activities have gradually moved to outlying areas. Or, perhaps more accurately, as the industries have gradually reduced capacity, the mills and canneries in the outlying areas have kept operating and have received upgrades while those in the urban areas have shut down. Today only a handful of sawmills operate in the three-county Seattle metro area.

And, like all competitive manufacturing operations, these industries have become far more efficient. Operators of the remaining mills in rural areas can process as many logs as the forests can produce and the market can absorb.

Finally, tastes change. Canned salmon used to be a popular item, since most households could not buy fresh fish. With the advent of frozen fish, and then fresh farmed fish, the canned product fell out of favor. The year-round availability of fresh fruits and vegetables has led to a fall-off in canned produce.

In many areas of the country that have depended on farming, re-source extraction and processing, these kinds of changes have resulted in dramatic drops in populations. Fortunately for the Seattle area, as resource-based industries became smaller, new industries took their place. But any industry that would take hold in the area needed to be indifferent to the distance of the region from supplies and markets. The region needed to get out of Fred Haley's transportation trap.

The most obvious way to get out of that trap would be to specialize in goods-producing sectors that have a high ratio of price to weight, so that transportation costs become a less significant factor. And that means that the value in the product must come not from materials but from design and process, i.e. technology. Consider that a refrigerator is worth about $2.50 per pound and a Chevrolet Suburban is worth about $7.50 per pound, whereas a Boeing 777 is worth over $900 per pound.[2]

Aerospace occupies the center of the region's high technology manu-facturing capability. Compared to the price of the product—tens and hundreds of millions of dollars—the cost of transporting materials, sub-assemblies, engines and components to Boeing's plants is small. And with deliveries going all over the world, Seattle and Everett are quite convenient places to turn the plane over to the customer and to supply spare parts. While Boeing's commercial arm has had issues with the Puget Sound area, remoteness of location has not been among them. Other high tech hardware manufacturers have grown up in the region, particularly in the medical and measurement device sectors. These instruments tend to carry a hefty price tag, so shipping costs do not make much of a difference to the firm or the customer.

Another way out of the transportation trap has been to build up ser-vice industries that have national and international markets. These include the obvious ones of software, e-commerce and tourism. And un-beknownst to many, the region has large and globally competitive architecture practices that design major buildings for clients around the world and is home to two of the nation's top ten firms, Callison and NBBJ. Retail industry headquarters, such as Nordstrom, Starbucks, REI, Zumiez, and Eddie Bauer also constitute a large service industry.

By shifting directly from a resource-based economy to a technology and services-based one, Seattle has made an unusual transition. Major resource industry capitals like Vancouver, Houston and Denver still serve as service centers for those industries. Boston and San Francisco made their transition out of resources long before technology-based industries arose. So Seattle has accomplished something quite remarkable in extricating itself from a "colonial" past in just a few decades. Resource industries remain an important part of the economy of Western Washington, but have mostly departed the urban areas and have been replaced by new industries that can operate comfortably up here in the corner.

From local to global

In 1962, Americans did not have much reason to engage with the planet. The Cold War had made the world a scary place, and most businesses did not operate in global markets or feel competition from imports. Like Candide, we tended our gardens.

Residents of Seattle had more reasons to engage the world, with Asian markets still buying timber and fish, and Boeing selling its new jet airliners around the world. But on the eve of the World's Fair, with its exotic international displays, shows and food, most people in Seattle kept a local focus. That would change over fifty years. Today the Seattle area has the capability to establish itself as an important node in the emerging global network of cities.

In commenting about the remarkable industrial accomplishments that have come out of Minnesota, a wag once said that in Minneapolis "you innovate or you freeze to death." That wag might have said a similar thing about Seattle: engage with the world or die of loneliness. That growing engagement has come from a number of places.

The region's major businesses have always had international customers. The state's forest and agricultural products have always found easy markets in land- and resource-scarce Asian countries: Washington wheat farmers have exported 85 to 90 percent of their crop in recent years. Ninety percent of the nation's exports of apples and other tree fruit come from Washington, shipped through the ports of Seattle and Tacoma. In all, the state's agricultural producers export about $6 billion worth of commodities.[3]

In 1975 Boeing delivered about 60 percent of its commercial planes outside North America. In 2011, of the 477 aircraft the company delivered, only 66, or 14 percent, went to North American customers (including the U.S. military). The company projects that, between 2011 and 2031, 79 percent of global airplane sales will go to customers outside North America.[4]

As noted in Chapter 2, technology firms emerging today are "born global." All software products come with a full array of language, currency and measurement capabilities. With foreign customers since the 1930s, Boeing has configured its products for global markets. The requirement to consider the needs of foreign purchasers creates a level of global awareness less common in industries that operate strictly in domestic markets.

The region's talent pools have become increasingly internationalized. As Boeing built up its engineering staff in the 1950s and 1960s it turned to Europe for engineers. This pattern of recruiting technical personnel from outside the U.S. accelerated in the 1990s as software firms began to hire programmers from India and elsewhere. Microsoft became a huge user of the H1-B visa program that allows firms to bring in people with specialized skills if they cannot find a sufficient number of people with those skills within the country. As a result, the foreign-born population of the region has shot up, exposing residents to neighbors, co-workers, classmates and teammates from all over the world.

And the foreign-born population has spread throughout the region. We used to think of an international population as a feature of central cities. But now, newly-arrived immigrants settle more often in suburbs than in the central city. According to the Census Bureau, by the late 2000s, foreign born residents made up 31 percent of the population in Bellevue and 29 percent in Redmond, with the two communities dominated by Microsoft employees. But we'll find an equally dramatic story in the south part of King County, where the foreign born population is 36 percent in Tukwila, 30 percent in White Center and 28 percent in Renton. Moving further south, foreign born residents make up 26 percent of the population of Kent, 24 percent of Federal Way, and 19 percent of Auburn. In contrast, only 17 percent of the population within the Seattle city limits was born outside the U.S.[5]

As leaders in the region embraced globalization more intentionally, they began to expand contacts overseas. The programs of the Trade Development Alliance have taken business, political and civic leaders to meet their counterparts in Europe, Asia, Australia and Latin America. This has helped create a strong layer of globally-aware regional leadership.

But even with all this global connectivity blossoming over the past fifty years, two areas of engagement have underperformed. Oddly, considering the extent of its global ties, the region has one of the lowest rates of foreign direct investment in the country.[6] Foreign interests own few major employers in the region, reducing the opportunity for businesspeople to get exposure to counterparts at foreign headquarters and reducing the number of foreign executives who cycle through the area. And international tourism has never really taken off in the region. Although it has many attractive features, the Seattle area still does not enjoy the recognition that draws large numbers of overseas visitors.

An emerging school of thought in urban economics suggests that the key to being a "global city" lies in the presence of specialized business services that facilitate international transactions.[7] Under this theory, a city can have a very global posture even if it has no port—London and Frankfurt being examples. Over the past fifty years Seattle has not developed this sector as much as might be expected, given the number of globalized businesses in the area and the prominence of the ports on Puget Sound.

The growing global outlook that the region has adopted over the past fifty years stems, in many respects, from the very isolation that worried Fred Haley. Because Seattle was such a problematic place from which to serve US markets, it had no large industrial complex rooted in feeding domestic consumption. Few Seattle area businesses had to be dragged kicking and screaming into the globalized economy that has become an inevitability. Few business or civic leaders spent their time decrying the impact of imports and railing against unfair trading practices, and local labor leaders expressed these concerns far less than their counterparts elsewhere in the country. Seattle area businesses have tended to look at other countries as potential markets and partners or as sources of imports rather than as threats. Few places in the country had an easier or more profitable time adapting to globalization over the past fifty years.

Redefining periphery

Seattle has not moved in fifty years, but the world has moved around it. Although still not in the center of the universe (notwithstanding the claims of Seattle's Fremont neighborhood) the region is not quite such a lonely outpost as fifty years ago. Seattle has been able to overcome its isolation in some important respects.

In general, the nation has moved toward the coasts and away from the middle. California long ago became the largest state, and its gravity draws people and investment from all over the world. Instead of worrying about the distance between Seattle and Chicago or New York, we more often think in terms of the distance to San Francisco or Los Angeles. Rather than feeling stuck in the far corner of the country, Seattle now can think of itself as part of a string of attractive, economically and culturally vibrant metro areas stretching from Vancouver to San Diego.

With the fastest growing trade corridors shifting from the Atlantic to the Pacific, Seattle has found itself in a key position. Via the great circle routes, Seattle is equidistant by air from London, Tokyo and Santiago, enhancing Seattle's potential as a global meeting place. Shipping routes from Asia to Seattle and Tacoma are one day shorter than routes to California ports.

Positioning on the Pacific Rim also has major implications for the region's military installations. Puget Sound already has the largest concentration of military assets on the West Coast, and with the Pentagon's recent strategic pivot toward East Asia and the western Pacific, these bases will likely play an even larger role in national security.

As noted, the Puget Sound area has relatively little foreign direct investment (FDI). During the 2000s I did a short study of FDI in the U.S., looking for patterns that would tell us why so few non-U.S. multinational firms have built or purchased manufacturing facilities in the Seattle area. I found that the most reliable predictor of the location of FDI within the U.S. was the distance of the site from New York City. The Mid-Atlantic area has the highest concentration of FDI, and investment density diminishes from there. I concluded that since most FDI has historically come from UK and Northern-European-based firms, they simply set up shop close to where they had landed. And since chemicals and materials make up a large part of that investment, proximity to the manufacturing centers of the country makes sense.[8]

If my assessment has merit, we should expect firms investing from Asia to establish their North American operations on the West Coast, as Nintendo did in Redmond. But other than Japanese auto firms, not many Asian multinationals have established major operations in the U.S. If this changes, Seattle could find itself in a very good position, no longer on the periphery of American industry, but as the landing point for Asian industry.

From Seattle-centered to multi-centered

Fifty years ago a large part of the population and the great majority of the economic activity in King County resided within the city limits of Seattle. The region had many other towns, but they served only as market centers for agricultural areas, mill towns or railroad depots. These towns could provide only the most basic goods and services, with more elaborate retail, medical care, entertainment, business or personal services requiring a trip into the big city.

The post-War suburban boom mostly took place in unincorporated areas of the county, with new neighborhoods incorporating or annexing to cities later. In 1960, 60 percent of King County's population lived in Seattle, and only two other cities in the county, Renton and Auburn, had populations over 10,000. By 2012, Seattle's share of county population had fallen to 31 percent, and King County had eight suburban cities with populations over 50,000.[9]

Pierce County followed a similar pattern to King County, with 46 percent of the county's population living in Tacoma in 1960, and only one larger town, Puyallup. Pierce County had a larger rural population in 1960, and today has an even larger share of suburban population than King County. Snohomish County has always had a more dispersed settlement pattern. Everett, with a population of about 40,000 in 1960, had just 23 percent of the county's population that year. This would fall to 15 percent by 2010.[10]

In the decades before 1960, Seattle had grown by annexing lands to the north and south as they filled in, and in doing so, it swallowed up previously independent cities such as Ballard and Georgetown. Seattle made its last significant annexation, Arbor Heights in Southwest Seattle, in 1956. So with the exception of three small slivers annexed subse-quently, Seattle had established its permanent boundaries by the early 1960s.[11] Since the area within the city limits was mostly built out by this time, most new residential development had to take place outside Seat-tle. Many of the new suburban subdivisions built in unincorporated areas annexed themselves to existing cities, causing those cities to grow rapidly. Bellevue, which had only about 6,000 people when it incorpo-rated in 1953, had over 60,000 residents by 1970 and passed the 100,000 mark in the 1990s. Kent had only 9,000 people in 1960, and was up to 40,000 by 1990. Redmond, a remote farming town of 1,400 people in 1960 grew to 36,000 by 1990.[12]

Annexation was not the only way to grow suburban cities, however. Residents of unincorporated areas kept creating new ones. The original towns of King County, like Kent, Auburn, Issaquah, Renton and Kirkland were established early in the twentieth century as market centers and railroad depots. Then city-building went quiet, with no new cities incorporated in King County between 1913 and 1953. Then came post-war suburban growth, and newly developed areas felt they needed their own city governments to wrest control of land use from the county and to provide better services. Eleven cities incorporated in King County between 1953 and 1960, including Bellevue, and my little city of Medina. Then, after a long lull, a flurry of incorporations in the 1990s provided ten new cities to King County and three to Pierce County, largely in response to the planning requirements of the new state Growth Management Act.

If suburban cities had remained just bedroom communities with local services, Seattle would have retained its position as the unquestioned center of a hub-and-spoke regional economy. But that did not happen. Starting in the 1960s, jobs began to move outward. Boeing had started this trend in a big way, setting up commercial aircraft production in 1957 in an old military plant in Renton, followed by facilities in the Kent-Auburn Valley and then the gigantic facility at Paine Field in Everett. Around the same time, medical device maker Physio Control moved to the boondocks out on Willows Road in Redmond. Fluke followed Boeing to Everett, and a string of medical and aerospace technology firms set up shop in the Overlake area of Bellevue and Redmond and the North Creek and Canyon Park areas of south

Snohomish County. Factories and warehouses began to fill in the Kent-Auburn and Puyallup valleys, and office and industrial parks sprouted along all the major highway corridors in the region.

Industries established themselves outside of Seattle for easily understood reasons: the old industrial areas of the city were simply full. Boeing and other large industrial and warehousing operations could never find land to build large facilities near the city. Moreover, the traditional urban industrial districts still had saw mills, pulp mills, steel mills, canneries and other old, dirty businesses that a technology firm might find incompatible with its clean processes.

But even the spread of industry out of the central cities might not have changed Seattle's position. After all, civic leadership usually emanates from the tall downtown buildings with their financial and professional service firms. In the 1980s, however, a string of tall buildings went up in Bellevue, and in the 1990s and 2000s the Eastside building boom continued. Now, one could feel the center of energy in the region begin to shift a bit to the east. By 2012 Eastside promoters had even begun to think that Bellevue would become a "twin city" to Seattle.[13] After all, Minneapolis started out smaller than its older and more established twin, St. Paul, and then surpassed it in size. Since the Eastside will likely never become politically unified, Seattle will remain the largest city by far. But with the core of Bellevue, Redmond, Kirkland and Issaquah approaching a population of 300,000, and with the bulk of job creation in the past decade taking place in these areas, there is no question that the old hub-and-spoke has changed forever.

Gentrification and urban living

Ever since the creation of industrial cities in the nineteenth century, people who could afford to move from the heart of the city did so. Cities were just not very nice places to be: they smelled bad. Whether the coal-fired blast furnaces or slaughterhouses of the Midwest or the pulp mills and sawdust burners of the Northwest, old-time industries did not make good neighbors. We tend to think of the suburbs as a post-War phenomenon, but, as noted in Chapter 1, they really started not long after large cities themselves developed. In Seattle, Washington Park and Madison Park were the original "streetcar suburbs" of the early twentieth century, and areas such as the Highlands, Laurelhurst and Magnolia allowed the wealthy to get away from the fetid city.

As suburban development accelerated in the 1950s and 1960s, most of the older neighborhoods within Seattle had become resolutely blue collar. Ballard, Wallingford, Beacon Hill, West Seattle, Upper Queen Anne, Crown Hill and similar areas, with their small homes and city schools, appealed mostly to the people who worked in the factories and mills of the city, at the shipping terminals or with the fishing fleet based along the ship canal. At the same time, some of the traditionally wealthy neighborhoods, such as Capitol Hill, lost favor and their giant houses became group homes or apartments.

Although some wealthy city-dwellers lived in fancy flats on Capitol Hill and First Hill, people of far more modest means occupied most of the multi-family housing in Seattle. And outside the city, apartments were rare: why live on top of your neighbors when you could have all that space to spread out in?

Racial segregation, both active and passive, mostly confined African American and some Asian American populations to the Central District and the Southeast part of the city. While these neighborhoods did not deteriorate anywhere near the degree to which similar neighborhoods did elsewhere in the country, (fortunately, Seattle never built high-rise low-income public housing) persistent poverty took its toll on the homes and their surroundings.

This pattern of stagnant or deteriorating city neighborhoods and burgeoning suburbs continued through the 1970s. Then things began to shift. Baby Boomers, who had spent the 1960s rejecting their parents comfortable suburban lifestyles, rediscovered city neighborhoods and began to move into them as the older, often original, residents of these areas moved on. But these new residents were different. They worked in government, at universities or in downtown office buildings, not at mills, factories or shipyards, and the character of these old neighborhoods gradually changed. The new residents had money to restore the homes, but often sent their children to private schools, shopped at the Puget Consumers Coop, drove Volvos, and otherwise exhibited sure signs of Bobo-ism.

The gentrification of Seattle started in the Wallingford and Fremont areas in the 1970s, and soon spread to Queen Anne Hill. Those gentrifiers still seeking "authenticity" began to move into Ballard and West Seattle which, in time, started to look more and more like Wallingford. Next stop would be the former ethnic enclaves of the Central District and Rainier Valley, where older African Americans and Asians eagerly accepted generous offers for homes they had bought for a pittance back when white people and lenders stayed far away. According to the 2010 Census, in the census tracts that make up the Central District, Seattle's historic African American neighborhood, less than 20 percent of the population is black, and two thirds is white. Rainier Valley remains a diverse area, but the charming Columbia City business district on Rainier Avenue now looks increasingly like Madison Park.

As the Boomers and their children moved into the cozy bungalows of Seattle, the next generation began to discover the joys of a more intense form of urban living. Like any big city, multi-family housing had always made up a large share of Seattle's housing stock. But few would describe living in these buildings as glamorous, and certainly not right in the heart of the city. That began to change, beginning with some groundbreaking (and money losing) projects that came out of the restoration work around Pike Place Market and Pioneer Square. Gradually, the idea of living near downtown took hold, and new buildings started to spring up, first in the Belltown neighborhood north of Downtown. But the most dramatic change happened in the South Lake Union neighborhood, where Paul Allen's Vulcan development company led the way with thousands of units of high-end housing, including high rises and lofts.

By the 2010 census, close to 30,000 people lived in the downtown-Belltown-South Lake Union area, not including the heavily populated Lower Queen Anne and West Capitol Hill areas. Nearly all of this downtown housing has come on-line in the past 25 years, introducing to the heart of the city a population equivalent to that of Issaquah.

As this new generation rediscovered high density urban living in Seattle, a similar pattern emerged in several suburban cities. Renton, Kirkland and Redmond all saw major apartment and condominium developments in their downtown cores, beginning in the 1990s. But the real action was in Bellevue, starting in the 1980s but accelerating rapidly in the 2000s. Unlike the projects in other suburban downtowns, which consisted mostly of mid-rise wood frame buildings, high-rise concrete construction dominated the building boom in Bellevue, introducing luxury urban living to an area best known for leafy neighborhoods and expansive back yards.

We should not, however, read too much into these trends. Even with this flurry of urban living—those Gen X and Gen Y kids watching having all those episodes of *Seinfeld* and *Friends* and wanting in on the action—the region's basic pattern of settlement did not change. The shift came not in the overall appeal of multi-family housing but in its location. (As noted below, suburban living remains popular.) The big national developers and investors shifted their emphasis toward mid-rise and high-rise buildings in urban settings and away from the suburban and exurban "garden" style walk-ups that had been so prevalent in the 1970s and 1980s. So the Growth Management Act, which had as its core, a return to dense urban living, got half its wish: new urban settings could lure those who would live in apartments or condominiums anyway, but those who prefer detached houses resolutely stayed in them.

These shifts, along with changes in the settlement patterns of immigrants, are part of a larger reshaping of urban America, as described by Alan Ehrenhalt in *The Great Inversion*.[14] One important consequence will be the increased segregation of lower income households into outlying areas. Seattle's urban and inner suburban neighborhoods, with their plentiful alternatives to driving, are becoming increasingly expensive places, forcing high transportation costs on those least able to afford them.

From louche to locavore

If you are old enough, recall the scene you would encounter walking down First Avenue in Seattle in the 1960s. The stretch from Broad Street to Yesler Street consisted of alternating establishments: pawn shops, peep shows, dirty book stores and taverns. Before containerization, cargo ships stayed at the docks a week at a time and their crews went out looking for the sorts of entertainment that sailors are supposed to look for. And in Seattle they would find plenty of it. But not anymore. With the lamented demise of the Lusty Lady in 2010, First Avenue is now almost completely devoid of the seedy behavior that defined the downtown areas near the waterfront for decades.

A stroll down First Avenue today reveals a string of boutiques, restaurants, bars and swanky hotels. What pass for taverns are inhabited by hipsters in search of irony. Highrises have replaced most of the old welfare hotels of Belltown, and those older residential buildings that remain now have fashionable restaurants at their base and pricy apartments above. The streets of the downtown area are mostly clean and, with the exception of a few well-known street corners, safe. The riffraff just cannot afford the high price of downtown real estate.

Some may romanticize the old days of Seattle and decry the loss of the original Skid Road—the "open city" south of Yesler Street—but the fact is that the retail and entertainment environment of a city reflects the rest of its economy and its workforce. When Seattle hosted the merchant marine and a huge fishing fleet, the old First Avenue served its purpose. But today the downtown workforce sits down to expensive locally-grown-organic-fair-trade-sustainable lunches and hangs out in sleek bars. And with thousands of people living in the urban core and stiff competition for retail and tourist dollars, city government feels pressure to keep the downtown clean and safe, if a bit less colorful.

From building to rebuilding

In the late-1950s, the region had poorly developed infrastructure. Decades of slow growth, the Depression and World War II had all put a damper on enthusiasm for large projects. The Denny Regrade was completed in 1930, the same year the Aurora Bridge opened, but a long dry spell followed, with only a few notable exceptions, such as the Mercer Island floating bridge, which opened in 1940, and the Alaskan Way Viaduct, which opened in 1953.

Then, beginning with the Metro sewer program, the region went on a building binge for the next thirty years. Metro finished its wastewater treatment system, the state built the Interstate freeways and the SR-520 bridge. The World's Fair gave us the Opera House, Coliseum, Pacific Science Center and Seattle Repertory Theater and through the Forward Thrust program, King County built pools, regional parks and, finally, the Kingdome. The last major piece of civic infrastructure that had no antecedent, the Washington State Convention Center, opened in 1988.

These investments added new facilities where before there had been no or only very limited capacity. This dramatic increase in infrastructure and facilities caused brand new or significantly expanded things to happen. Freeways and sewers gave rise to new communities. Elegant new performance spaces allowed the Seattle Symphony to grow into a major organization and enabled creation of the Seattle Opera, the Pacific Northwest Ballet and the Seattle Rep. The Kingdome brought Major League Baseball and the NFL to town, and the convention center brought tens of thousands of badge-wearing visitors.

Then the process of building wound down, and a process of rebuilding and replacing began. Rather than opening up entirely new travel corridors or allowing creation of new institutions, we began to upgrade and replace existing infrastructure, sometimes adding new capacity, but sometimes not. The West Seattle and Interstate 90 bridges added capacity as they replaced existing structures, but the configuration of the new SR-520 bridge adds no new general purpose capacity, and the tunnel replacing the Alaskan Way Viaduct will have less capacity than the existing structure. Safeco Field has less capacity than the old Kingdome. McCaw Hall represents a major upgrade for the Seattle Opera, but the season has not expanded. And the list goes on.

With the exception of new buildings on the University of Washington campus (many of which have been privately funded) and Sound Transit's light rail line, the community has added little in the way of brand new capacity to the region's infrastructure over the past 25 years, and has created very few new arts, cultural or civic institutions. This seems like a significant change from the 1960s and 1970s. I can't argue with the general principle that a community should take care of the things it has before rushing off to add new things. But at the same time, I cannot help wondering if we really have all of the core infrastructure and institutions we need. Has no vital need or compelling opportunity arisen in the past few decades? The world around us and the regional economy have certainly changed a great deal during that time, yet in the public sphere we seem content with a basic framework carved out in the 1960s.

A nagging suspicion lurks in the back of my head that the shift from building to preserving coincides with the aging of the region's leadership. The leaders who really shaped this region from the 1950s into the 1970s—Gordon Clinton, Jim Ellis, Eddie Carlson, Dan Evans, Wes Uhlman, Charles Royer, George Duff—all started making their marks while still in their thirties. Leaders today do not get a chance to drive the bus until they reach their fifties, and maybe not even then. The Boomers who took over in the 1970s as the young Turks still run things (as someone slightly younger than those Turks, I still often find myself the youngest person in the room during discussions of civic affairs). At the risk of indulging in a broad stereotype, the young think about building, and the middle aged think about saving for retirement. So maybe our reluctance to launch brand new initiatives stems from both the natural caution of older leaders and the fact that the region itself is no longer in the blush of youth.

Then we have the more political explanation. The infrastructure and institutions that originated in the 1960s have gradually built up strong constituencies that have a stake in preservation and enhancement. Bond repayments for brand new infrastructure take money from funds that would otherwise go to maintenance. When the big arts organizations undertake a capital campaign in excess of a hundred million dollars, they can suck all the oxygen out of the fundraising room. Anything that sells memberships, season tickets or luxury boxes, or holds an annual auction or gala, competes with the existing organizations doing the same thing.

A third possibility is that we have effectively privatized our investments in public goods. Some of the most successful urban spaces in the region have been created not as parks or public facilities, but as part of the private developments of Kemper Freeman in downtown Bellevue and Paul Allen in South Lake Union. In fact, redevelopment of South Lake Union started out as a public initiative, the Seattle Commons, and devolved into a mostly private undertaking. The new "town centers" in places like Kent, Redmond and Mill Creek have been largely private ventures. The Experience Music Project, love it or hate it, is the only new, large cultural institution built in Seattle since the Museum of Flight, and Mr. Allen paid for the big blob with no public money, as did the backers of the Chihuly Museum at Seattle Center. The LeMay car museum in Tacoma and the new Museum of History and Industry in Seattle have been largely privately funded as well.

I would never suggest we not take care of our existing physical and civic infrastructure, but I have to believe that in a region so dedicated to innovation, the current generation can leave some lasting mark on the public sphere.

A branch office town

While the region grew some very impressive headquarters over the past fifty years, it lost some older ones, especially in the retailing and banking sectors. This has come about as part of the general national and international trend in consolidations of service businesses and retail, but it does have an impact.

In 1962 a businessperson looking to expand a factory, build an apartment complex or simply finance an inventory could choose from several sturdy locally owned banks that would have the capacity to meet their credit needs. The businessperson probably had a long relationship with the bank and would see the top management regularly at the Washington Athletic Club or at weekly Rotary Club lunches. Loan decisions took into account that business owner's reputation and history of success.

Then all that changed. The liberalization of federal banking regulations that began in the 1970s allowed banks to operate across state lines, and this, in turn, led to the string of mergers and acquisitions that continues to this day. One-by-one, regional and state banks got swallowed up by the big banks, with Bank of America buying Seafirst in 1983 and Security Pacific buying Rainier Bank in 1987. The one big bank that became the eater rather than the lunch, Washington Mutual, finally met its demise in 2008, taken over by Chase. The state has some remaining regional banks and thrifts, but these cannot provide the loans and lines of credit needed by large businesses. The big banks, meanwhile, have their headquarters in far off places, and cycle executives through Seattle, making it difficult for businesspeople to establish strong working relationships.

The retail industry has experienced the same phenomenon, with local chains like the Bon Marche and QFC becoming part of large national chains. Regional grocery and drug stores have mostly disappeared, and chain restaurants dot the urban and suburban arterials.

So although Seattle has its share of headquarters of national chains, like Nordstrom, Costco and Starbucks, the business community has become dominated by branch offices. The practical impact of this trend varies. Some businesses will have a harder time getting credit when decisions get made in Charlotte, and some local manufacturers may have a harder time selling to national chains than to local retailers. But the bigger impact has been on the civic life of the region. These service businesses had always formed the heart of the economic development establishment. Along with local utilities and newspapers, these "place bound" businesses could grow only in tandem with the regional economy. Thus, they had a stake in the underlying factors that determine growth and would support their enhancement. Now, getting a bank or one of the national utility companies interested in an economic development project is a real challenge. They may see a zero-sum game, since what one region of the country wins another region loses, and they likely have operations in both the winning and losing locations.

In the end, this sort of change probably falls into the category of civic spilled milk—no use crying over it. Plus, we have benefitted from the trend by hosting our own set of corporate headquarters of national firms. But the organizations and institutions that used to rely on the now-national businesses to take up their local concerns will have to work a bit harder.

From "cultural dustbin" to arts and culture trend setter

When Sir Thomas Beecham famously described Seattle as an "aesthetic dustbin" he was referring not to a personal view of his own but to his perception of how others thought of Seattle.[15] He meant, sincerely, I imagine, to urge civic leaders to improve the cultural life of the city. Not an easy task. He made his remark in 1941, but by the eve of the World's Fair things had not improved much. The Seattle Symphony, which he had conducted, still played at the Civic Auditorium, a dingy space that would later become the Opera House. Otherwise, the highbrow culture of Seattle left a lot to be desired, and the avant garde element stirring up trouble at the Cornish College of the Arts had not reached enough of a critical mass to create a West Coast Greenwich Village.

Pulling Seattle out of its dustbin stands as perhaps the most important legacy of the 1962 World's Fair. Construction of the Opera House and the Seattle Reparatory Theater (now the Intiman) building finally gave arts organizations suitable places to work. Things moved quickly enough that when Jim Bouton was keeping his diary of the 1969 season of the Seattle Pilots, he could blame the team's failure on the "cosmopolitans" of Seattle who seemed to care more about the arts than about baseball.[16]

Over the next decades the Big Three—symphony, ballet, opera—would build themselves into very respectable regional organizations, with the symphony getting more than its share of recording contracts. But it was Seattle Opera's successful 1975 staging of Wagner's Ring Cycle that finally put Seattle on the highbrow cultural map. It would have both shocked and pleased Sir Thomas to see Seattle overrun with opera fans from all over the world, enjoying not only the mysteries of the Nibelungenlied, but also some lovely August weather.

As the region gained wealth, all the major arts organizations, and some of the minor ones, built themselves new homes. A glance through the back of their programs at the list of board members and major funders shows a gradual increase in names familiar to those following the region's technology boom. Yes, the nerds (or at least their bosses) had finally become respectable and joined in the establishment practice of funding and governing traditional arts organizations, gaining respectability the same way that steel and railroad barons had done a century earlier.

But as good as these organizations and the many smaller theater and music groups became, they remained mostly just fine examples of what one might expect in a city the size of Seattle. With mostly local audiences and funding they had to limit their programming. Efforts to foster "cultural tourism" did not produce results large enough to allow more aggressive scheduling. So while Seattle's highbrow scene would draw enthusiastic local audiences it would never rise to the level found in the major cultural capitals. This would be less a matter of quality—few people can hear the difference between a performance by the Seattle Symphony and the New York Philharmonic, and the Seattle Opera draws its singers from the international circuit—than tradition and perception. In a variation on Zipf's law, seen in Chapter 1, the world can support only a limited number of cultural capitals, and Seattle would not number among them.

Seattle would achieve global prominence in popular culture, however. The region had produced its share of nationally recognized acts, but they tended to be *from* Seattle: Jimi Hendrix and Quincy Jones never returned to the area after they began to tour nationally. We would hear of local bands heading to New York or Los Angeles, recognizing that to get anywhere in the music business meant leaving town.

Grunge changed that. Not only were the signature bands largely from the Seattle area (Aberdeen, in the case of Nirvana) they tended to stay here. Sub Pop records brought local bands to prominence, and although the successful ones got recording contracts with major labels, they maintained their Seattle roots. But most important for this story, Seattle became globally recognized as the home of something big and important. That had not happened before. A young women I worked with had been part of the early Grunge scene and came back from a trip to London gushing about how everyone she met there knew all about Seattle—a far cry from my own experiences in London in the late 1970s.

Seattle's second big pop culture splash came through the region's business success. Seattle companies began to have a noticeable impact on the culture as a whole, whether through Microsoft products, Starbucks and Nordstrom stores or the growing clout of Amazon. Each of these brands is strongly identified with Seattle, and the cumulative impact of their presence helped define the brand of Seattle itself. By the mid-1990s Seattle began to be viewed as a place where interesting things happened and where people lived enviable lifestyles.

The lifestyle thing then drew the attention of scriptwriters looking for TV and movie setting that would lend an attractive atmosphere to their stories. *Sleepless in Seattle,* released in 1993, offered the world a pretty and hopelessly romantic view of the city: a big star, playing an architect, living on a houseboat, taking evening boat trips with his son, about to pull his new love away from the corrupt and tired East to the clean and energetic Northwest. *Disclosure,* released in 1994, featured the obligatory ferry ride across Puget Sound, but also emphasized Seattle's technology industries. *Frasier* went on the air in 1993, and although the main characters are a bunch of complete nincompoops, they carry out their antics in very refined ways.

The big cultural coming out for Seattle happened in the 1990s, and, as noted in Chapter 3, the shine had faded by the end of the decade. But by then the image had stuck, and the cascade of negative events of the late 1990s and early 2000s did not seem to diminish the city's image. *Grey's Anatomy*, set in the fictional Seattle Grace Hospital, premiered in 2005 and became the top-rated adult drama on TV. *iCarly,* set in a Seattle loft apartment, premiered in 2007 and became the highest rated children's show on TV. Although neither of these shows has ever been filmed in Seattle (except for a few token outdoor scenes) the city still works as a setting.

While it will never rival the major cultural capitals of the country, Seattle has, over the past fifty years, carved out for itself an attractive image and served as a platform for several notable cultural trends. The importance of this positioning goes far beyond local pride. It comes back to the region's need to attract large numbers of highly skilled, highly sought-after people. When deciding where to move, these migrants will first look at job prospects, but they will also consider the image of a place they may put down roots. A job offer in Seattle no longer feels like an invitation to a career in Siberia.

Minor league to major league (sort of)

Seattle often receives totally justified recognition as the worst place in America for professional sports. The city boasts just one major national championship team, the 1979 Supersonics, and three second place finishes, the 1978 and 1996 Sonics and the 2005 Seahawks. Far more common have been cellar-dwelling franchises that dash the pre-season hopes of the faithful year after year. It's always a rebuilding year in Seattle.

But dismal as sports can be here, at least we have teams in the big leagues. In 1962 Seattle had no major league professional teams. Sports fans mostly turned their attention to the University of Washington Huskies, who had won the Rose Bowl the two previous years. Baseball fans had to content themselves with the Seattle Rainiers (also known at various times as the Angels and Indians), of the Pacific Coast League, playing in Sick's Stadium in Rainier Valley. At the time, cities comparable in size to Seattle had big league teams, but a remote location and the lack of a large stadium kept the city in the minors.

The first break came in 1967, when Seattle received an expansion franchise in the National Basketball Association. The Supersonics, named after the ill-fated plane that Boeing had begun to design, played in the Seattle Center Coliseum, a multi-purpose facility built for the World's Fair. The Sonics only broke .500 three times in their first 10 seasons. They finally hit their stride in their 11th season, losing in the NBA finals to the Washington Bullets in 1978 but coming back to beat them in the finals in 1979. The Sonics would make it to the NBA finals one more time, losing to the Chicago Bulls in 1996. After the usual wrangling over facilities, and with a series of increasingly unpopular ownership changes, the team moved to Oklahoma City for the 2008-2009 season, renaming themselves the Thunder.

Seattle's more comical entry into the big leagues came in the form of the Seattle Pilots, a Major League Baseball franchise that played exactly one miserable season in 1969 at Sick's Stadium. The franchise owners had originally wanted to suit up first for the 1971 season and play in the new stadium that voters had approved the previous year as part of the Forward Thrust bond campaign. But the stadium got delayed and the opening season moved up, putting the new franchise in a very challenging position. A poor record, poor attendance and undercapitalization doomed the team, which moved to Milwaukee to become the Brewers. But the season did live on in infamy through Bouton's diary, as presented in that classic of sports literature, *Ball Four*.[17]

The sudden departure of the Pilots had led to a lawsuit against Major League Baseball, brought by King County prosecutor and future Senator Slade Gorton, that resulted in the promise of a team once an appropriate stadium was built. In 1974 the National Football League also agreed to provide an expansion franchise. The key to both was completion of the new King County stadium. After years of protests, committees, meetings, studies and general Seattle-style process, the county picked the site south of Pioneer Square and got construction underway in November, 1972.

Both the Seahawks and Mariners had poor to mediocre success during their time in the Kingdome, with the notable exception of the Mariners magical season of 1995 when they improbably made it to the American League championship series. The Kingdome suffered from the same problems the Sonics had found in Key Arena: lack of amenities. In addition, the bright lights, still air, Astroturf playing surface and general lack of ambiance made for a less than thrilling "fan experience" for either baseball or football.

But from an economic development point of view, that never mattered. The Kingdome and its tenants delivered what Seattle desperately needed. With three franchises, the name "Seattle" got mentioned in national sports news most days of the year, reminding the country that the city existed and now swam in the same ponds as New York, Chicago and Los Angeles. As an added benefit, the teams drew fans from throughout the region and the Northwest, providing a welcome infusion of cash into the city's restaurants, bars and hotels. Draw a line from San Francisco through Denver to Minneapolis, and you will find that Seattle has the only NFL and MLB teams northwest of that arc. So despite their spotty records, the Mariners and Seahawks developed a loyal fan base from Alaska through Montana, Idaho and Oregon.

Eventually, though, both franchises threatened to leave if they did not get new venues that would provide a better fan experience and give the teams more opportunities to earn game-day revenue. And in both cases they got their wish. The Mariners moved into Safeco Field in the middle of the 1999 season, and the Seahawks opened their new stadium, now CenturyLink Field (the Clink!), for the 2002 season. Although both facilities are quite wonderful, state-of-the-art sports venues, they regrettably, have not improved team performance a great deal. But the teams continue to have loyal followings, despite their lack of consistent success. Both have very strong ownership and have elevated themselves from the "small market" category into the middle class of the leagues.

The Sonics were not quite so fortunate, though. Something interesting happened in the ten years between approval of the ballot measure for the new Seahawks stadium and the unsuccessful attempts to build a new arena that would keep the Sonics in town. Flurries of legislative activity in 1995, on behalf of the Mariners, and in 1997, on behalf of the Seahawks, reflected intense public fear about the loss of those two teams. Fast forward to the 2000s, and even blue chip local groups could not get enough enthusiasm from the public or the state legislature to put a measure before voters for a new arena. It is not clear whether this reflected a poor economy, a lack of enthusiasm for NBA basketball or a generally diminished fear of the impact of the departure of a franchise.

Let's consider the third of these possibilities. The comings and goings of professional sports franchises in mid- and small-market cities reflect two ends of the economic development arc. On one end, newly ascendant cities see sports franchises, especially the big-venue football and baseball teams, as a signal to the world that that city has arrived. At the other end, cities that have seen their fortunes wane and their populations and industrial bases shrink, want desperately to hang onto their teams so the nation will remember they still exist: even if your city does not show up in the business, lifestyle or travel news, at least it can show up in the sports news and on Sunday afternoon TV. In the pecking order of metro areas, professional sports provides the only real bright line of prominence: you are a major league city or you are not.

So, maybe in the ten years between 1997 and 2007 Seattle realized that it had already arrived and did not need as many mentions on the sports news. And the region certainly did not find itself on the economic downslope. With the Huskies putting on a great show over at Hec Edmundson Pavilion, Seattle University returning to Division 1 and gunning for Gonzaga-like status, and the Seattle Storm of the WNBA filling in the summer schedule, basketball fans had plenty of game to watch. As I write, a new deep-pocketed group is making a run at the NBA, looking to pick off a suffering franchise in another mid-market city and to build a new arena for them. In doing so, this group will confront a level of indifference not seen in the 1990s.

Meanwhile, the region found a new team to fall in love with: the Sounders. Soccer had taken root in the region in the 1960s, and by the time the original Sounders, of the North American Soccer League (NASL) arrived in 1974, they were able to build a substantial fan base, regularly selling out 17,000 seats in Memorial Stadium and then selling upwards of 30,000 seats in the Kingdome (the Kingdome's first event was a Sounders game—and I was there!). The NASL collapsed, and the Sounders resurfaced in Major League Soccer, first playing in the 2009 season. Unlike the old NASL which was populated mostly by minor league European players, MSL plays at a top international level. And the Sounders can draw the crowds, consistently selling out the lower bowl of the Clink with fans who drink heavily, march to the game in a parade from the bars of Pioneer Square, stand (or wobble) for the entire game, sing loudly and generally try to be as European as possible.

Evolving environmental consciousness

Residents of the region long ago recognized the unique natural beauty of the area. Approaches to preserving and enhancing the environment have changed significantly over the past fifty years, however. Environmental regulation, in turn, has had a major impact on growth and development of the region.

The 1960s and early 1970s were a golden age for the Northwest Republican conservationists. Governors Dan Evans, of Washington, Tom McCall of Oregon and Cecil Andrus of Idaho embodied a nearly forgotten approach to environmental stewardship that was motivated by a true affinity for their native land. They were not radicals, but rather people who enjoyed being outdoors and valued the opportunities that the Northwest provided to do so. Joining them, and following in the boot-steps of the Mountaineers, were similarly-wired upper middle class professional and old-money men and women who both voted Republican and cared a great deal about the environment.

This group led the charge to create natural areas and to purchase park land in urban settings. Many of them helped get the Metro sewer system built and participated in the anti-freeway movements of the 1960s that killed the R.H. Thompson Expressway and other proposed urban freeways. They eventually became the core of groups such as the Nature Conservancy and the Mountains to Sound Greenway Trust.

The environmental movement that grew out of the 1960s, heralded by *Silent Spring*, took a different approach, tending toward more aggressive and often radical action.[18] Instead of focusing on how humans can enjoy their natural surroundings, this new movement emphasized how humans have damaged the land, air and water. The big federal regulatory structures of the 1970s—Clean Air Act, Clean Water Act, Endangered Species Act—gave them their modus operandi.

Whereas the conservationists tried to figure out how to make resource-based industries more responsible, but still viable, the new crowd looked down on logging, fishing and mining as damaging to the environment and invented ingenious ways to stop them. Whereas the conservationists favored purchasing land to save it, the new environmentalists used regulatory measures to shape what could happen on private land.

Whether Congress and the Nixon Administration knew it or not, they had created a set of very powerful tools. Environmentalism no longer centered on public education, persuasion and funding. Now it meant litigation. Environmental groups that had started out as grassroots activists gradually oriented themselves to the federal regulatory and court systems. While this strategy proved effective in many ways, it tended to diminish the popular support that the conservationists of the 1960s built up. By painting mankind as the enemy of nature, rather than a participant in it, the new environmentalism set up an us-versus-them dynamic that persists to this day.

What hasn't changed?

The World's Fair invited its guests to look ahead and think about how the future might look different from the vantage point of 1962. And, as just described, the region did change in many important ways over the subsequent fifty years. But in many ways it did not change much at all. Let's have a look at some of the ways the region has stayed the same.

Risk-reward profile

News reports in Seattle media outlets regularly profile new technology start-up businesses, and, although less regularly, describe businesses that have crashed. Seattle remains a place where a larger than average share of industry operates within a high-risk-high-reward environment.

Henry Yesler opened a sawmill in a very remote and hostile environment, hoping to cash in on the burgeoning lumber market of San Francisco. He succeeded, but the timber businesses has had its ups and downs ever since. Mills that had processed 6.6 billion board feet of timber in 1929 cut only two billion board feet in 1932. By 1941 they got back up to 4.6 billion board feet, but dropped again to 3 billion by 1945.[19]

Boeing has always exemplified the high-risk-high-reward profile. It jumped into the jet business, betting the entire company on the Dash-80, at a time when passengers happily flew propeller airplanes. It nearly bankrupted itself with the 747, but ultimately used that plane to dominate the market for large, intercontinental aircraft. It threw the company into turmoil with the 787 Dreamliner, and then sold record numbers of them.

But perhaps the ultimate expression of the high-risk-high-reward ethos came from Amazon and the dot-com start-ups. "Get big or go home" became the motto, as internet retailers spent massive amounts of money to gain market share and mind share among newly on-line consumers. Investors took huge risks, and most lost big. But those that invested in Amazon have reaped large rewards.

Hand-in-hand with high risk business strategies come the aggressive tactics needed to vanquish the competition: a hell-for-leather style of capitalism hides just beneath Seattle's crunchy Birkenstock personality. Microsoft, then Amazon, got so aggressive they raised anti-trust concerns and accusations of unfairly squishing the competition and creating illegal concentrations of influence over markets. They may not have known it, but Bill Gates and Jeff Bezos had simply followed in the footsteps of Erastus Brainerd, the chamber of commerce PR man who had tried to monopolize the Klondike Gold Rush supply business for Seattle. Or John Considine and Alexander Pantages who started in the entertainment business in Seattle and ended up taking over vaudeville circuits across the country.

We still make things

From an economics perspective, this observation is axiomatic. As this book points out, Seattle's distance from major domestic markets has meant that few consumer products get made here. Seattle has no factories making cars or appliances, and most food and household goods come from elsewhere. So, for Seattle residents to buy such things they need money earned by selling something outside the region.

Mostly this means manufacturing things for sale in national and international markets. Things like airplanes. But also things like heavy duty trucks, construction lifts, paper, defibrillators, multimeters, luxury yachts and Almond Roca. In all, manufacturing makes up about 12 percent of GDP and employs about 14 percent of the workforce.[20]

By a quirk in the North American Industrial Classification System (NAICS) used in economic statistics, "software publishing" gets categorized as a service and not a product. A programmer working for a medical instrument maker gets classified as a manufacturing employee, whereas a programmer designing software for inclusion in hardware made by another firm falls under the service category. So if we snap our fingers and declare that the software industry makes "products," we can increase the manufacturing share of GDP to about 19 percent.

Aerospace still rules

In mid-2012, about 90,000 people worked in the aerospace sector in the Puget Sound area, constituting about 5.3 percent of the regional workforce.[21] This is somewhat smaller in numbers and quite a bit smaller in employment share than the industry of the mid-1960s, but aerospace remains the largest employer in the area, and one that can still rock the region's fortunes, for better or worse. With an employment multiplier of 3.96, aerospace supports over 350,000 area workers, or about 20 percent of the workforce.

As we will see later in the book, this is not a bad thing: if we have to put that many eggs in one basket, aerospace is a very good basket. But we need to hold onto that basket tightly, which we have not always done. In the rush to get to the Next Big Thing, we have often neglected the Really Big Thing in our midst. At the risk of metaphorical overreach, if a bird in the hand is worth two in the bush, we have had an ostrich in our hands while chasing quail in the bush.

In a 1991 speech to the Greater Seattle Chamber of Commerce annual meeting, Boeing CEO Frank Shrontz said:

> In my judgment the number one enemy of Boeing today is complacency. If management, our workforce—and the larger community—start to take the continued success of this company for granted, we are in serious trouble. Could Puget Sound turn into an aerospace rust-belt in the 21st Century—complete with padlocked factories, unemployment lines and urban blight? Yes it could.[22]

A warning does not get much clearer than that. Yet, a decade later, state and regional leaders found themselves scrambling to compete for the first 787 assembly facility, which we won, the second 787 line, which we lost, and the 737MAX, which, to our great relief, we won. Fortunately, the political and civic leadership woke up in time to make sure that we held onto the best industrial basket in the world.

Changed but powerful role of organized labor

Washington State has always had very high rates of unionization. In fact, from 1967 through 1969 Washington had the highest rate of union membership in the country, fluctuating between 40 and 45 percent, and held second place, behind Michigan, through the mid-1970s.[23] The major employers in the state—aerospace, forest products, ports, aluminum refining—had long been unionized, and aggressive organizing, especially on the part of the Teamsters under Dave Beck, had led to unionization of many other employers. Whether the moderate Beck or the more radical Harry Bridges, of the International Longshore and Warehouse Union, labor leaders had a large influence over politics and business in the region.[24]

And as in the rest of the country, that influence has waned, especially in the Seattle area. Industries that had been unionized in the early 1960s tended to remain so (the Brown and Haley plant in Tacoma is still unionized), but those industries gradually became less prominent parts of the regional economy. Meanwhile, employees at new technology and service industries have not embraced the union movement. As a result, union membership in the Seattle area has fallen from 28 percent of the workforce in 1986 (the first year that metro area data is available) to about 17 percent today. And an increasing share of unionized workers are in the public sector: about 11 percent of private sector workers belong to unions, while 53 percent of the public sector workforce does.[25]

Even with these lower numbers, however, labor still holds two very important cards. The first is the threat of strikes at Boeing. Aerospace Machinists struck in 1989, 1995, 2005 and 2008, each time wreaking havoc with both the company and the local economy. Boeing even acknowledged that they opened their plant in Charleston, South Carolina, a "right to work" state, in order to avoid strikes (an admission that generated a major complaint to the National Labor Relations Board). In 2011, however, knowing they both had a lot to lose by not cooperating, Boeing and the Machinists reached a major accord that paved the way for keeping 737 assembly in Renton.

The second card stems from the very high rates of unionization among public employees. Unions and their members participate heavily in elections for state and local office, turning out the foot soldiers and contributions that drive the campaigns of many Democrat politicians in Legislative races or in races for nominally non-partisan local offices. This political clout can, however, cut different ways. Government reformers, whether targeting education, employment taxes or workers compensation programs will always bump up against powerful labor interests. At the same time, labor has played critical roles in gaining political support for infrastructure funding.

Washington still has the fourth highest rate of unionization in the country, behind New York, Alaska and Hawaii, and at the metro level, only two regions with more than a million employees—New York City and Riverside—have higher unionization rates.[26]

Gateway to Alaska

Alaska has changed quite a lot, but the Puget Sound region continues to have a strong business relationship with it. Even before the Klondike and Nome gold rushes, Seattle had a lively commerce with Alaska. After all, the "ton of gold" came down on a steamer that had been making regular calls in Alaskan waters. But with the Gold Rush and the growth in mineral, fishing and timber businesses in Alaska, Seattle continued to be the shoving off point. This, in turn, led Seattle businesses to create ongoing relationships in Alaska to provide goods and services. If Seattle had location problems and seemed colonial, Alaska's location problems have always been an order of magnitude larger.

As Seattle grew into the hub for the North Pacific fishing fleet it also became home base for the canning industries that spread throughout Southeast and Western Alaska. Spending summers on fishing boats or working in Alaska canneries has long been a rite of passage for many young people growing up in Seattle.

Seventy years after the gold rush, the next big rush hit: oil. The oil mostly lay under the tundra in the north, and getting it to the year-round ports in the south required a long pipeline. The Alyeska Pipeline Company, a consortium of oil producers, received permission to build the pipeline in 1974 and completed it in 1977. A large part of the drilling and pipeline equipment and materials came through the ports of Puget Sound, and giant modules assembled in the region were towed to the North Slope.

Pipeline construction had a short term economic impact on the region (very welcome at the time) but the larger impact came from the economic growth that the oil industry brought to Alaska, a large part of which made its way back down to Seattle and Tacoma. Nearly everything consumed in Alaska comes from the Lower 48—on barges, container and roll-on-roll-off ships—and the vast majority of those goods come through Puget Sound ports, mostly the Port of Tacoma. In addition, service businesses based in the Seattle area, such as financial services and engineering, do an important part of their business in Alaska. Seattle has always served as a jumping off point for tourists heading north, and with cruise lines having shifted some of their business from Vancouver to Seattle, the region's role in Alaska tourism has grown substantially.

The Seattle and Tacoma chambers commissioned a series of studies of the economic impact of Alaska trade on the Puget Sound economy, and the latest iteration found that firms in the Puget Sound area exported $3.8 billion worth of goods and services to Alaska in 2003. Those exports of goods and, especially, services, supported 45,000 direct jobs in the region, and another 60,000 indirect and induced jobs. And the relationship keeps growing, with the jobs impact expanding 18 percent between a 1994 study and the 2003 study.[27]

These are big numbers. But because business with Alaska gets spread out through the entire economy of the region it doesn't tend to stick out. When I worked for the Seattle Chamber I participated in an annual trip to attend the Alaska State Chamber of Commerce convention, where we received regular reminders not to take our commerce with Alaska for granted. But I am afraid we do take that business for granted, not out of any purposeful neglect, but because Puget Sound and Alaska have been handcuffed together for so long we stopped noticing.

Military presence

The Puget Sound region may be remote from a commercial perspective, but from a military perspective it has important strategic advantages. As a result, the region has long hosted large military installations. And as the Pentagon began rationalizing its base structure, starting in the 1980s, Puget Sound actually gained personnel and operations. In all, Western Washington has among the highest concentration of military assets in the country, with about 90,000 uniformed personnel and civilian employees.[28]

But as you sit on the Seattle waterfront, gazing out at the placid waters, you would not have any idea of the awesome firepower within fifty miles. Due west from your table, as the crow (or the F-14) flies, lies the Bangor submarine base, home to the Pacific fleet of Trident nuclear submarines. Southeast of Bangor, in Bremerton, is the giant Puget Sound Naval Shipyard, one of the largest in the country, and the Bremerton Naval base, home to an aircraft carrier group. Sticking with the navy theme for the moment, turning to the north, another aircraft carrier group has its home in Everett, and both carrier groups base their aircraft at the Whidbey Island Naval Air Station. Still not feeling well protected? Then turn to the south, and head to Joint Base Lewis McChord, a recently merged Army and Air Force base with around 47,000 uniformed and civilian personnel.

As of 1991 the military has become almost completely absent from King County, however. The Army ceased all regular operations at Fort Lawton, just northwest of Downtown Seattle, in 1972, turning the land over to the city, which created Discovery Park. The Navy stopped landing planes at the Sand Point Naval Air Station in 1970, turning much of the land over to NOAA and the City of Seattle. After steadily ramping down operations, the Navy closed the entire base in 1991, turning the remaining land over to the city for parks and other uses.

Suburban living

Despite almost universal derision by the cultural elite, low density sub-urban living has maintained a broad appeal and just keeps on oozing outward. The centerpiece of Washington's Growth Management Act is an urban growth boundary (UGB) that forms a hard line outside of which new development is banned. The Act, and the UGB have, however, failed to change the basic demand for detached suburban style housing.

The UGB that stretches continuously from north of Everett, in Snohomish County, to Dupont, in Pierce County, accomplished one positive thing but also resulted in one decidedly negative outcome. By limiting the amount of land available for housing construction, land developers carved their subdivisions into smaller parcels. Whereas the old standard suburban lots ran between 7,200 and 10,000 square feet, developers began laying out lots in the 5,000 to 6,000 square foot range, and even smaller in master planned communities. So, from the perspective of limiting sprawl, that was good.

But the GMA provided no tools at all to change the employment patterns in the region, and the heaviest job growth took place in King County, which also had the tightest urban growth boundary. So, with tens of thousands of new jobs in King County and not enough moderately priced housing, middle income households with jobs in King County fled to Pierce and Snohomish Counties in search of affordable neighborhoods. The migration data from the IRS clearly shows this trend, with King County experiencing net positive in-migration from out of state, but net negative migration with respect to the adjacent counties.[29] Hence the horrible traffic along I-5, I-405 and SR-167.

The reason for this pattern is simple: the preference for detached housing has not changed. Gentrification and the shift of multi-family housing toward urban centers, noted earlier in the chapter, did not do anything to change the underlying demand of households to live in detached houses with yards. From 1990, when the GMA came into effect, to 2010, the share of the regional population living in detached housing remained frozen at 60 percent.[30] In King County the share of detached housing fell a bit, but it actually grew in Pierce and Snohomish Counties as families hit the freeway in the real estate game of "drive to qualify."

Quality of life

No need to dwell too much on this, but quality of life, especially the natural environment and the opportunity to get out and enjoy it, has served as a centerpiece to Puget Sound's identity since the first settlers arrived. Every profile of the region written by an outsider begins with a rapturous description of Mount Rainier and describes the region's residents' struggle to squeeze some actual work into their hiking-biking-kayaking-rock climbing-REI-infused lifestyle.

The lead of the 1992 *Fortune* cover story on Seattle as the best place to do business described a sign seen outside a store on the way to Mount Rainier: "Espresso and Live Bait." That pretty well sums up both our own self-image and the image the country, and increasingly the world, has of us.

This has not changed in fifty years. Or longer. A Kroll map printed in the 1930s, entitled "Evergreen Playground" says in its legend: "Neither Europe nor Asia nor South America has a prospect in which sea and woods and snow mountains are so united in a landscape." And recall the name of the *Seattle Times* Sunday magazine: *The Charmed Land*.

As noted, quality of life is a very subjective thing, and Seattle's version will not appeal to everyone. But for those looking for the combination cultural sophistication and an active lifestyle, Seattle seems to offer a pretty good package.

*   *   *

Would the World's Fair committee like it here?

I think they would. While many long-time residents lament the loss of the "big small town" atmosphere created by Seattle's isolation, civic leaders from Arthur Denny and Doc Maynard up to the present have always seen the region as something bigger. The founders of Seattle worked hard to ensure that it became more than just another mill town, and the World's Fair organizers continued that tradition. And whatever you might think about Seattle today, it is not just another mill town.

Chapter 5

Bridges, Brains, Bureaucracy
and Bistros

Seattle's first settlers had one excellent piece of infrastructure at their disposal—a deep, protected natural harbor—and absolutely nothing else. The economic history of the Seattle area since then has closely followed the development of the physical, institutional and human infrastructure required for a modern, globally connected region. This chapter describes these factors and how they have evolved to meet the needs of today's employers and residents.

The basics of infrastructure, K-12 education and the tax and regulatory climate, while necessary for economic progress, are far from sufficient for a region to prosper. After all, many struggling metropolitan areas of the country have excellent infrastructure and schools and are easy places to do business. And as the "Region on Trial" story in the introduction suggests, the Seattle area has prospered in spite of many failings in its basic business climate. So although we take it for granted that economic fundamentals are key to success, we need to understand why Seattle has grown and prospered in the face of mediocre performance in those fundamentals.

But before we begin, I will note that this chapter will not cover a number of important topics, including K-12 education, healthcare, crime and most environmental concerns. This is not to imply that these are unimportant factors in the regional economy. It seems to me, however, that there is little about them that is so unique in Seattle or elsewhere that they will make a difference in critical decisions made by employers and talented individuals. In addition, factors like education and crime vary widely across a metropolitan area, such that averages do not mean much.

We'll start with physical infrastructure. Don't yawn. This is actually pretty interesting stuff. The physical geography of the Puget Sound region presents challenges that have made infrastructure investments problematic. And while Seattle's image may have gravitated toward that of a brain-driven economy, the region remains a major manufacturing center and hosts some of the largest port and distribution complexes in the country. So while we like to talk about movement of ideas, business in the region still move a lot of freight on roads and rails.

Freeways

It is no exaggeration to say that freeways in general, and the Interstate highway program in particular, made the modern American metropolitan area possible. The Seattle region's limited freeway system has shaped settlement patterns, opening areas for residential, commercial and industrial development that previously had limited accessibility. In the late 1950s the Seattle area had only two real pieces of freeway. A ten mile stretch of the old US Route 99 ran uninterrupted from about North 80th Street in Seattle (in front of the Twin Teepees), across the Aurora (George Washington) Bridge, south through the Battery Street Tunnel, onto the Alaskan Way Viaduct, touching down on East Marginal Way. The old US Route 10 ran uninterrupted across the Lacey V. Murrow floating bridge, but became a more conventional highway at Eastgate.

By today's standards these "freeways" were pretty poor. Narrow lanes, lack of shoulders and center barriers, tight turning radii and short on-ramps severely limited their throughput. Although no one likes to merge northbound into the Battery Street tunnel from Western Avenue, even that experience cannot compare to the famous "bulge" on the original floating bridge span which, when combined with a reversible lane, made for utterly terrifying driving.

But President Eisenhower came to the rescue with the National Interstate and Defense Highways Act of 1956. The feds provided strict design standards and 90 percent of the money, but left routing of the system up to the individual state highway departments. This proved relatively easy in rural areas, but not so easy within cities.

Seattle sits on an isthmus, the narrowest part of which was heavily developed in 1956, leaving little space to squeeze in a freeway. So like many cities in similar predicaments, planners made compromises and Seattle ended up with a suboptimal design. In the end, while eight lanes of Interstate 5 approach downtown Seattle from the north, and four lanes from the south, just two lanes travel in each direction all the way through downtown. And measures to further reduce the freeway's footprint included several left lane on-ramps and off-ramps, which created dangerous merges and weaves. So, in spite of some recent improvements downtown, a major bottleneck remains on the freeway that runs from the Canadian to the Mexican border.

The other north-south interstate route, Interstate 405, wrapped around the east side of Lake Washington from Tukwila through Renton, Bellevue and Kirkland to Lynnwood. When completed, the Eastside was still relatively lightly populated, and the new freeway worked well as a bypass route. Most notably, it provided access to Boeing's massive plant in Renton, fueling the housing boom on the Eastside. Another design problem, the famous Renton S-curves, created a choke point once the freeway began to move toward capacity, and two major upgrades later, traffic still bunches up there.

Interstate 90, which begins in Seattle and runs all the way to Boston, follows the original U.S. Route 10 across Lake Washington, via Mercer Island. Since this corridor already existed as a four-lane limited access highway, it took a back seat to the higher priority stretches where no freeways existed at all. But as designers got to work on it and actually began construction of a new bridge, communities on Mercer Island and in Seattle openly revolted and stopped the project for ten years. The original plan called for a massive swath of freeway across Mercer Island and a deep cut through the Mount Baker neighborhood of Seattle. Lengthy negotiations with Mercer Island resulted in heavy mitigation of impacts and some very expensive lids. On the Seattle side, engineers designed one of the largest soft-earth tunnels ever built and combined it with a refit of the existing tunnels to avoid cutting the Mount Baker neighborhood in two.

But by the time Seattle and Mercer Island approved these new designs, money had gotten tight. A major civic effort in the early 1980s finally resulted in funding and the Interstate 90 corridor project got underway—the most expensive stretch of Interstate in the country up to that point. The new, double-deck tunnel went through smoothly, but things did not go so well over the water. The new floating bridge section opened as planned, but while the original floating span was under renovation, a terrible thing happened: it sank in a storm. The state scrambled and built a new span, delaying final opening of the project.

The Lacey V. Murrow bridge across Lake Washington had opened in 1940, and within 10 years discussions had begun about a second bridge. The Eastside had grown rapidly in the post-war housing boom, creating a need for more lanes across Lake Washington. More cross-lake capacity fell outside the scope of the Interstate system plan, however, so the state would have to fund the entire project itself. After considering the usual options—a bridge parallel to the existing bridge across Mercer Island, a bridge from Sand Point to Kirkland—the state settled on the Montlake to Medina route that became the SR-520 corridor. This new toll bridge opened in 1963 and linked the newly built Interstates 5 and 405, completing a Seattle-Eastside loop. SR-520 would see two extensions, once to 148th Avenue in the early 1970s and all the way to Redmond by 1979.

The final major piece of freeway, the SR-167-SR-512 corridor, provides a second north-south route, stretching from Renton, in the south part of King County, through Pierce County and hooking up to Interstate 5 south of Tacoma. This corridor serves the large industrial/ warehouse districts of the Kent-Auburn Valley, Sumner and Puyallup and provides access to attractive neighborhoods that provide much-needed lower cost housing. But it also has one of the region's missing links, since the SR-167 freeway does not get all the way to the Port of Tacoma.

The unpleasantness of freeway construction in Seattle, and the emerging national backlash against the violence that freeways had done to urban neighborhoods, gave rise to movements that caused cancellation of three major freeway projects in Seattle. The "ramps to nowhere" in the Montlake neighborhood, remnants of the never-built and now largely forgotten R.H. Thompson Expressway, provide diving platforms for those swimming around Foster Island, and also provide a reminder of the power of citizen action.

As one would expect, the development of the region followed along the major freeway corridors. Suburban growth moved up and down Interstate 5, filling the space between Seattle and Everett to the north, and Tacoma to the south. Growth spread across the Interstate 90 and SR-520 corridors, filling in Bellevue, Kirkland and Redmond, and climbing past Redmond and Issaquah to the Sammamish Plateau. Then, consistent with a national pattern, jobs and industries followed that housing. As this pattern unfolded in the 1970s, the region experienced a major surge in population growth, nearly all of which took place in the suburbs. At the same time, Baby Boomers and women hit the workforce in record numbers, straining the freeway system badly, and rendering parts of it nearly dysfunctional for much of the day. By the early 1990s the Texas Transportation Institute had ranked Seattle metro area traffic congestion second worst in the country.[1]

If this had been Dallas or Atlanta, clogged freeways would have given rise to a major move to expand those freeways. But this was Seattle. The view of freeway congestion that emerged had two basic parts. The first, following the theories promoted by Anthony Downs, a frequent visitor to the region, says that expanding freeway capacity will only generate more travel demand and fill the new capacity to the point where congestion is no better than before.[2] In other words, expanding freeways is futile. The second part of the emerging consensus suggests that public transit will provide the solution to the region's transportation needs.

This prevailing view of freeway congestion has produced a consistent result. Voters overwhelmingly approved the Sound Transit program of light and commuter rail and regional bus service in 1996, and voted for a second phase of that program in 2008. Meanwhile, the basic freeway network remains largely unchanged, with long-planned links, such as the completions of SR 509 and SR-167, still un-built. Freeway improvements have centered on construction of high occupancy vehicle lanes, elimination of choke points and use of management tools like ramp meters. These techniques have certainly improved things, but in all of this work, the state DOT has added very few long stretches of new general purpose capacity. Transit ridership has risen, but not nearly enough to offset the growth in travel demand that continues to land on top of a freeway system already badly congested.

The fact that a lack of freeway capacity has not brought the region to a complete halt stands as a testament to the adaptability of residents. Those who can afford it, adjust their lifestyles to live closer to work and avoid freeways. This has had the benefit of keeping the older, inner-ring suburbs in high demand, but has also made life difficult for those who cannot afford to live close in. The desire, on the part of wealthier residents, to avoid traffic congestion, has helped drive the gentrification discussed in Chapter 4.

Many, perhaps most, people in the region approve of the disinclination of the state to expand the freeway system, and the lack of capacity has not resulted in any easily identifiable economic impacts. But with steady growth in the region and no new capacity on the horizon, congestion will only get worse, and communities will become increasingly stratified economically as the wealthy can afford to live close in and the less wealthy must commute from great distances.

Limits on freeway capacity also reflect limits on the money available for major expansion projects. All infrastructure has a useful life, beyond which it becomes a maintenance headache or, in the worst case, collapses. Lightly used city streets can last almost indefinitely, but heavily used freeways and bridges may last only thirty to fifty years. Infrastructure building in the Seattle area began in earnest about one hundred years ago but really picked up steam in the high growth years of the 1950s and 1960s. That means that large parts of the region's infrastructure have reached or exceeded their useful life and require replacement. And even if a facility does not need replacing, anything built prior to the 1970s will need retrofitting to bring it up to current safety and environmental standards.

In Chapter 4 I noted the shift from building to rebuilding, and that certainly applies to the road and freeway system. The three Rs—repair, retrofit, replace—can soak up all the money available for infrastructure investment, leaving little for capacity expansion. Furthermore, the state's main source of financing for roads, the per-gallon fuel tax, declines in purchasing power due to inflation and improving fuel economy of vehicles. So, I hope I am right that infrastructure problems are not our biggest economic concern because I do not see much hope for future major freeway system expansions.

Anything other than roads and cars

In spite of the fact that well over 80 percent of trips taken in the region involve cars, substantial civic energy and funding goes into "anything but cars." These efforts have resulted in a slight shift away from cars, but at a cost.

In the 1960s the region's transit service was a mess. Voters twice rejected a rail transit system in Seattle, in spite of a very generous federal funding package (the money earmarked for Seattle's system eventually went to Atlanta to build MARTA). An extensive but ancient bus system served residents of Seattle itself. Suburban riders had limited choices of privately operated transit that served routes into Seattle. Then, in 1972 voters authorized Metro, which then operated the regional wastewater system, to create a county-wide transit system based on the existing Seattle routes and new suburban routes. It would be funded with a dedicated local sales tax. Snohomish County created Community Transit in 1976, a long distance service that supplements Everett Transit, and Pierce County created an integrated countywide system in 1979. Bolstered by relatively generous sales tax funding and successful appeals for federal assistance, these transit agencies modernized and expanded their fleets, and by the end of the 1970s, the region had greatly improved transit coverage.

Then, in the mid-1980s, the region got the itch to take another run at rail transit, this time on a three-county basis. King County got the ball rolling in 1988 with a non-binding advisory ballot measure to "accelerate rail planning." It passed with nearly 70 percent of the vote. That vote helped convince the state legislature to enable creation of an agency to build a rail transit and express bus system covering the urbanized parts of the three-county metro area. With voter approval, the agency would have authority to levy sales and car tab taxes to pay for construction and operation of the new system.

After an initial failed vote in 1995, voters approved the program that became Sound Transit in 1996. Sound Transit's service has three components: light rail radiating from downtown Seattle and a short line serving downtown Tacoma, commuter rail on freight tracks stretching from Lakewood to Everett, and a network of 25 express bus lines. The first section of Link light rail, from downtown Seattle to Sea-Tac Airport opened in 2009, and the line to the University of Washington is expected to open in 2016.

By the late 1990s, the three-county region had five transit agencies, with service frequently overlapping. For example, a commuter traveling from Everett to Seattle could choose Sound Transit commuter rail, Sound Transit express bus or Community Transit express bus. Efforts to combine agencies have always met with fierce resistance.

While expensive for taxpayers—the share of operating costs covered by fares ranges from six percent in Everett to 26 percent for King County Metro—the Puget Sound area does have relatively high transit ridership, especially for a Western region. But compared to cars, transit still accounts for a small share of travel. According to the Puget Sound Regional Council, in 2006, 87 percent of all trips in the region involved a car, and only 3.3 percent of trips consisted of passengers walking to a transit stop. In fact, more children walked to a school bus that year than transit riders walked to their stop.[3]

I do not mean to be critical of transit. I am a lifelong transit user and advocated for transit systems for many years, even serving as treasurer for the 1996 Sound Transit campaign. But I am dismayed by the degree to which transit is expected to meet a large part of the region's mobility needs; whatever the transportation question, transit always seems to be the answer. Transit does a couple of things very well: mobility for the transit-dependent and cost-effective commuting to areas with high parking costs. Beyond these two essential functions, transit struggles to match the convenience of driving, and we simply need to be realistic about that.

Adding new transit riders—the marginal cost of service —is very expensive since the most productive service presumably already exists. To lure new riders, agencies will need to expand service to low density areas or to increase service at off-peak times—two strategies that tend to result in sparsely occupied buses. Voters, however, seem disinclined to provide funding for any substantial new service expansion beyond Sound Transit's second phase, so we will not likely see major system expansion. Agencies need to accept the limits of what transit can do and shift service to the most productive routes.

An even bigger dose of realism is needed when it comes to bicycling. I love biking and have spent time as a bike commuter: what a nice way to begin and end a day. But from a regional transportation perspective, biking is just too small to factor into planning. The PSRC's 2006 survey showed it as comprising slightly less than one percent of all trips, making it smaller than the margin of error of the survey and certainly smaller than the variation in travel demand during the winter flu season.[4] Weather and topography will keep biking to the margins of the larger transportation picture, but because bicycle advocates are a very powerful constituency in the Seattle area, its political position will remain prominent. As an example of the clout of the bicycle lobby, Seattle has undertaken program of "road diets" that substitute bike lanes for general purpose lanes on some four-lane arterials.

The most promising anything-but-cars alternative is the oldest: walking. The resurgence of downtown housing over the past couple of decades has made it not just possible, but very attractive, for thousands of people to walk to work and to take care of errands in their neighborhood. The 2006 PSRC survey showed that walking comprised over eight percent of all trips in the region, and about four percent of commutes. While walking has not increased quite as much as transit over the past 20 years, it has the advantage of costing little or nothing.[5]

Water and sewer—keeping the region flowing

For the first of these utilities, water, we can cover the story for the past fifty years quickly, thanks to the foresight of the legendary R.H. Thompson, who served as Seattle City Engineer from 1884 to 1914. Thompson identified the Cedar River, coming out of the Cascade Mountains southeast of the city, as the best source of water, and succeeded in acquiring the water rights and, after protracted battles, most of the land in the watershed.[6] This system, combined with the Tolt River reservoir, has provided clean, safe, abundant water not only to Seattle but to many of the city's suburbs. In the 1990s, cities on the Eastside created the Cascade Water Alliance to meet their needs and enable them to have long term alternatives to the Seattle system. Although a few years with low snowpack have led to lawn watering restrictions, water supply has remained a minor concern.

Sewers, on the other hand, have been a major concern for the region. In the 1950s Seattle and its burgeoning suburbs had totally inadequate sewage treatment capacity, and, as a result, Lake Washington had turned into a cesspool. The region's greatest natural asset had become unusable much of the year, and something had to be done. Along came another legend, attorney Jim Ellis, whose tireless efforts led to creation of the Municipality of Metropolitan Seattle (the same agency that took over transit service in 1972) and its massive sewage collection and treatment system. By the 1960s Lake Washington was on its way toward cleanliness and the system had room for growth. Metro expanded the West Point treatment plant in the early 1990s, and opened the very expensive new Brightwater plant in 2011.

Unsexy as they may be, these utilities often hold the key to a region's capacity to grow: we all need to flush. The state Growth Management Act has a feature, "concurrency," which requires that infrastructure capacity precede construction, and in particular, every application to build a new home or commercial building must come with a "certificate of water availability." Localized lack of water system capacity has led to building moratoria in several areas. Other areas ripe for development or redevelopment still lack sewers. While roads can always squeeze in one more car, water and sewer pipes have definite capacity limits.

Ports and airport—connecting to the world

Seattle and Tacoma began their lives as port cities, and they continue to be major conduits for imports and exports. The Port of Seattle helped pioneer containerized shipping in the 1960s, leading to dramatic cuts in cost and increases in security of cargo. Handfuls of skilled crane operators replaced the armies of workers loading ships by hand that we saw in *On The Waterfront.* The port and its tenants managed to come to agreements with the powerful longshore unions which faced membership losses as a result of containerization.

The Port of Seattle operates Seattle-Tacoma International Airport (SeaTac), the 15th busiest airport in the country.[7] The airport opened in 1947, and saw a major expansion in the late 1960s. SeaTac was among the first airports in the country to centralize all operations in one large main terminal. In the days of regulated air service, passengers rarely changed airlines, so carrier often had their own terminals. SeaTac's design anticipated deregulation and the emerging pattern of transfers between airlines. The addition of a third runway, completed in 2008 provided the airside capacity needed to serve a growing region.

Airports do not do much good, however, without air carriers. Being tucked up in the northwest corner of the country means that SeaTac will never be a major domestic hub. Carriers have opened non-stop service to most major destinations in the U.S., but the real action is attracting and keeping direct international service. SeaTac has always had several non-stop polar routes to Europe and has had reasonable success in attracting routes to Asia. In all, SeaTac has an adequate portfolio of international routes, but trails San Francisco, Los Angeles and Vancouver in offering its globetrotting businesspeople non-stop service to a wide range of international destinations.

Forward Thrust and the power of bonding

Big infrastructure projects come with big price tags and require some combination of federal grants and long term bond financing. Borrowing for infrastructure makes sense since future generations of users should contribute to the facilities from which they will benefit. But bonding requires a large base of taxpayers around which to spread the repayments, usually levied on real property. As Seattle and the communities around it grew in the Postwar years they needed new infrastructure, but lacked the bonding capacity to get projects going.

The creation of Metro and its sewer system were the first example of aggregating property values in a large enough pool to float bonds for big projects. Ten years after the creation of Metro, the same forward thinking civic leader, Jim Ellis, came up with a more elaborate plan to raise infrastructure funds for a wide variety of purposes. The Forward Thrust campaign developed a series of bond proposals, with 13 appearing on the ballot in 1968, and four on the ballot in 1970. Seven of the 1968 measures passed, including funding for the Kingdome, the Seattle Aquarium, Marymoor and Luther Burbank parks and swimming pools throughout the county. The most notable failure was the local match for the large federal commitment for a rail transit system. None of the four measures proposed in 1970, which included a second run at rail transit, passed due to the severe downturn in the economy.

In Washington state, general obligation bonds backed by property tax require a 60 percent majority to pass, which presents a major hurdle. The fact that so many of the Forward Thrust issues did clear that hurdle stands as a testament to both the optimism of the time and the skill of the organizers. The Kingdome is long gone, but the region still benefits not only from the parks and pools, but from the less glamorous highway and sewer projects also funded that year.

Overloaded infrastructure points to economic vitality

One of C. Northcote Parkinson's lesser known laws says that an institution that has achieved perfection in its physical surroundings is on the verge of collapse. Conversely, growing, thriving organizations often squeeze themselves into shabby, undersized facilities.[8] At a larger scale, it seems that crowded, overloaded infrastructure signals a place too busy to catch up. Business grows far faster and less predictably than the glacial pace of road and rail line building.

Just ask yourself: Do I really want to be in a place that *doesn't* have traffic jams?

The Seattle area has done reasonably well keeping up with the infrastructure investments central to global competitiveness and connectivity: SeaTac Airport works well and the marine terminals can hold their own against the competition. Average commute times, while not especially short, are not too punishing and potholes don't appear more regularly than anywhere else. Since I have never heard of a case of a business declining to locate in the Seattle area solely because of a lack of infrastructure, I suppose what we have is good enough. So long as we keep pace with upgrades, fix the remaining design mistakes and complete the missing links, especially those like highways 167 and 509 that link to the ports, our current infrastructure should be adequate to the task. Put another way, if we are looking for the best place for the next incremental dollar of investment in our region's global competitiveness, the returns might be higher elsewhere.

Taxes and regulation

A favorite, although possibly apocryphal, quote about the local business climate is attributed to the Roosevelt Administration's Postmaster General, James Farley: "There are 47 states in the Union, and the Soviet of Washington."[9] This sentiment exaggerates the role of Communists in the state's history, but it does capture the truth that the state and the Puget Sound region have leaned to the left since the early twentieth century. The region's historically dominant industries —aerospace, wood products, shipping—are heavily unionized, and very aggressive work by the Teamsters and other unions made sure that other industries got unionized too.

Then, in the 1960s, left-leaning environmental groups arrived on the scene, seizing the initiative from the state's longstanding Republican conservationist establishment. While the old guard did not see any particular conflict between supporting logging and then enjoying a hike through the remaining forests, the new environmental groups took a far harder position on regulation of resource industries and anything else that might damage the environment.

By the 1970s, the inclinations toward regulation seen at the national level had arrived in this Washington. Although Seattle has always had its share of firms known to have very conservative leadership—Safeco and Paccar come to mind—it has been a long time since business dominated the political environment at either the state or the local level in ways that would make the tax and regulatory environment especially "business friendly." Weak push-back against the power of labor and environmental interests stems, in part, from the fact that the dominant businesses in the region have never been primarily cost driven. Business often finds it easier to make peace with the labor, tax and regulatory climate, carve out whatever exemptions and exceptions the state might grant, and get on to more important things. (As we'll see later, this point of view does not work well for local service businesses or consumers.)

Overall, Washington has among the highest business tax burdens in the country. Ernst and Young, with the Council on State Taxation, conducts regular studies comparing state and local tax burdens on business, and Washington does not come away looking very good. In their study of business taxes as a share of total business activity, Washington ranked thirty-seventh out of fifty states, with state and local taxes soaking up 5.4 percent of private sector output. This compares poorly to states that Washington considers its peers in attracting knowledge based industries. Tax burdens were 3.7 percent in Maryland, 4.0 percent in Virginia and 4.4 percent in Colorado. Even the tax-happy states of Massachusetts (4.3 percent) and California (5.2 percent) place less of a tax burden on business.[10]

A second study looks at the impact of state and local taxes on new capital investment. Washington does even worse, placing fortieth out of fifty states, with an effective tax rate of 9.4 percent, versus a median of 7.3 percent. Peer states all performed better on this measure, with Virginia at 5.4 percent, Maryland at 6.3 percent, Colorado at 6.8 percent, California at 7.7 percent and Massachusetts at 8.2 percent. In both studies, most of the states that measured up worse than Washington have large, and heavily taxed, oil and mining industries.[11]

Washington has enacted some tax breaks for investment in R&D and in plant and equipment, and specifically for the aerospace industry, but the real burden comes from the state and local business and occupation (B&O) tax. This tax applies to gross receipts, whether the business made a profit or not, and thus hits start up and some low margin businesses hard. Because the state has no corporate income tax, many high margin businesses prefer the B&O, and over the years, large taxpayers have worked out various special rates and exemptions that help them live with the tax. But those accommodations have weakened concern about the system and made it very difficult to promote any sort of tax reform for business: the devil they know is better than the devil they don't.

I was involved in an effort to reform business taxes in 2008. We developed an excellent plan designed to be revenue neutral in the first year, deal with some significant unfairness and shift the tax burden slightly from business to high income households. But in the end we could not generate enough enthusiasm within the business community to move it forward. In spite of the high tax burden on business in Washington, other issues seem to take precedence.

While the state tax environment may not be optimal for business, the absence of a state income tax certainly works well for high income households. The resultant reliance on high sales and sin taxes does make the state's entire tax system quite regressive, however. Poor people in Washington pay a higher share of their income in state and local taxes than wealthier people because they spend more of their income on taxable things.[12] About every decade some individual or group tries valiantly to get an income tax adopted and each time the effort gets clobbered. As progressive as Washington thinks it is, its voters will not accept an income tax and just do not seem all that worried about regressive taxation.

On the regulatory front, Washington State and many of its local governments have reputations as difficult places to get things done. Layers of land use and environmental regulation, and a deep love of process, combine to make commercial and residential development difficult. In addition, Washington has among the most expensive workers compensation systems and most generous unemployment insurance programs in the country. Among the thousands of things that the state regulates, it is difficult to find examples of "business friendly" approaches.

Task forces, commissions and blue ribbon panels convene every few years to tackle regulatory reform of one sort or another, but little seems to come of these efforts. Any regulation, no matter how nonsensical it may seem to one interest group, will be vigorously defended by another, and the stakes are rarely large enough to justify protracted battles.

In the end, as much as developers, industrialists, farmers and large employers complain —often justifiably—about the difficulty of Washington's regulatory environment, these problems seem not to have a very large an impact on actual economic development. I suspect this is the case for a couple of reasons. For high impact, high stakes projects—a Boeing plant, a data center, a composites factory—state and local governments send in SWAT teams to clear the way and make sure that the project gets the best treatment from regulators and, if necessary, special legislative relief.[13] The political atmosphere has changed dramatically from 1991, when the City of Everett hit Boeing with a $50 million mitigation fee when it expanded its plant to accommodate the 777. No government would dare send such a bill to an expanding industry today.

But SWAT teams are often not necessary. Much of the economic growth of the region happens in leased space in high rises and office parks where the few environmental burdens that might arise fall on the developer, not the tenant.

These dynamics do, however, leave out important parts of the economy that are, indeed affected by regulation. A food processor competing against low-margin producers in other states has to absorb Washington's employment tax burden. An equipment dealer faces rising stormwater fees levied on her storage yard. A dairyman must reduce his herd because of large stream setbacks.

The business climate situation in Washington State and the Seattle area reflects the divide taking place as we evolve toward a boutique economy. Fast growing, high margin businesses can treat tax and regulatory burdens as minor irritants, far less important than talent attraction and market development. On the other side of the divide, mature, lower margin, cost-conscious industries need to assess whether they can afford stay in the area.

Higher education

If infrastructure is overrated as a driver of economic progress, then higher education is often underrated. Most of the recent work in urban economics that examines metropolitan success ends up with a focus on higher education. With the exception of the Boeing Company, no institution has had a larger impact on the evolution of the Seattle region than the University of Washington.

The UW has benefitted the region through several distinct channels.

Graduating students. As the flagship campus of the state's higher education system, the UW attracts top high school graduates from across the state and provides them with the opportunity for an outstanding undergraduate and professional education. All universities do this, of course, but the trick is in keeping those newly minted university graduates in the area. We are fortunate that the UW has the highest graduate retention rate of any major university in the country, meaning that many of the state's best and brightest stay around the area and provide the next generation of talent. Many regions with fine colleges and universities struggle to keep their graduates from moving on to cities with better prospects.[14]

Relationships with research institutions. Seattle has a large and growing presence of independent research institutions in the life sciences and global health. Many of the scientists who work at those institutions have joint appointments with the UW. And, graduate students at the UW provide a ready and cost effective workforce for these institutions.

Applied research. Although many believe the UW underperforms in this area, it does engage in applied research for industry in the state. Boeing has long used the UW for research projects, and Lamborghini, the Italian sports car maker, has funded a composite materials laboratory there. Microsoft and other IT firms have active research relationships with the UW Computer Science department. The Washington Technology Center, now part of Innovate Washington, brings UW resources to the challenges of moving new technologies into the marketplace.

Arts, culture and sports. The UW is more than technology, and the university's large arts programs feed into the region's cultural assets. The UW drama department has long enjoyed a strong national reputation, and its graduates help make Seattle's thriving theater scene hum. Performances, lectures, libraries and a beautiful campus are all important amenities in the region. The Huskies provided big-time sports programs long before the professional leagues ever discovered Seattle and continue to have loyal followings through their ups and downs.

Spin-off businesses. Although scientific breakthroughs at a university tend to be made available to the public, research has shown that businesses will more likely take root near the place of discovery.[15]

Stable employment. The UW is the largest employer in the Seattle city limits and the third largest employer in the state. It has well over 30,000 people on staff, most of whom do something other than help educate students. The research enterprise, in particular, has a major impact on the regional economy, bringing in over $1 billion per year, providing steady employment for thousands of scientists, technicians and staff. UW Medicine staffs four major hospitals in the region.

The University of Washington is not the only four-year higher education institution in the area. Seattle University and Seattle Pacific University are located within the city, and University of Puget Sound and Pacific Lutheran University are in Tacoma. The UW has branch campuses in Bothell and Tacoma. Washington State University, on the other side of the state, educates many students from the Seattle area and has launched a major presence in Everett.

But even with these fine institutions, plus the four other state campuses and several other private colleges, Washington state remains woefully short of seats in its higher education system. To some degree, the state's large community college system makes up for the lack of openings for freshman, but the upper divisions of the state's colleges and universities still lack capacity. As noted in Chapter 2, the state ranks near the bottom of all states in providing education opportunities.[16] This creates some big problems for those aspiring to higher education. Many families cannot afford to send students out of state for their education. And for those students who do venture to other states, there is no assurance they will come back to enrich the Puget Sound workforce.

The story of higher education and the UW really has two pieces, one very positive and successful, the other problematic. The university's research enterprise and massive healthcare arms continue to grow and prosper. Meanwhile, the state starves the undergraduate side of its higher education system, having imposed disproportionately large cuts during the budget crises of 2007-2012. This, in turn, forced the UW and other state schools to raise tuition and to give more slots to those paying out-of-state rates.

Unfortunately, I cannot idenfity an obvious feedback loop to correct this situation. Although rhetoric seems to suggest that the shortfall of state funding for undergraduate education will come back to bite the rest of the university, it is not clear just how this would happen. The medical and research enterprises, which make up two thirds of UW operations, are self-funding and therefore insulated from state budget problems. Underfunding will weaken the teaching mission, but no one knows the point at which the loss of highly regarded faculty in the English or sociology departments leads to an inexorable decline of the entire institution. I am pretty sure, though, that by the time we figure that out, it will be too late. In the meantime, because the UW and other state universities fail to exhibit obvious signs of distress, they appear to be crying wolf, and important decision-makers stop listening.

Attraction of talent

The world-leading industries that drive the Seattle area economy consume talent at a very high rate. Even if we found the money for substantial growth in our higher education system we could not come close to providing the educated workforce the region needs. Moreover, these firms will not take just anyone with an engineering, computer science, biology or design degree. They demand the best, and fortunately, the best are often willing to move to the Seattle area.

Because the U.S. has no national residential registration system, as exists in other countries, we have a difficult time keeping track of migration. But using data from the Census Bureau, the Internal Revenue Service and the Washington State Department of Licensing, we can learn a few things. In-migrants tend to be:

Young and single. This makes intuitive sense. Young people are more mobile in general, and single people do not have to manage two career transitions. The Census Bureau's American Community Survey shows that while the 20 to 29 year old age group makes up about 15 percent of the overall population, 35 percent of in-migrants fall into that category and that while 31 percent of all residents have never married, 44 percent of in-migrants have never married.[17]

Well-educated. For people with high level skills, the payoff from a long distance move will be much larger than the payoff for a person whose skills are commonly used across the country. Well-educated people, especially those early in their careers, are more likely to scan the country looking for the place that offers the best career prospects. In the Seattle area, 37 percent of all adults have at least a bachelor's degree while 52 percent of in-migrants arrive with one. As noted in Chapter 2, the persistent in-migration of well-educated people has pushed the overall education level of the region far higher than it would be through just the graduates of local colleges and universities.[18]

From all over the U.S. When Seattle natives feel overrun, they generally blame the Californians—and with good reason. Our neighbor to the south has historically been our largest source of new residents, accounting for nearly a quarter of all migrants to the Seattle area between 2002 and 2011. Given the complementarity of industries between the two states—aerospace, software, Navy—this should come as no surprise. What is more surprising is the number of people who move to the Seattle area from much farther away: 6 percent of migrants, about 3,900 per year, come from Texas, 5 percent from Florida, and about 3 percent each from Illinois, Michigan and New York. Only one state, West Virginia, sent fewer than one hundred people per year to Seattle during those ten years.[19]

From all over the world. The Seattle area has, from the beginning, attracted its share of migrants from other countries: in 1890, over one third of King County's population was foreign-born.[20] Scandinavians dominated the timber and fishing industries, and Seattle had a large Chinese population in its early days. A wave of Southeast Asian immigrants in the 1970s was followed by the current wave of South Asian immigration tied to the region's technology industries. With this latest technology-driven immigration, 17 percent of people in the region are foreign-born, but as we saw in Chapter 4, the foreign born share is very high in some suburban cities.[21]

As I have asserted before, and will again, in-migration of highly skilled people from elsewhere in the U.S. and abroad constitutes the single most important factor that will determine the future success of the Seattle economy. And as I will continually gripe, I do not find this dimension of our success as a prominent feature in any economic development strategy, and it appears only tangentially in discussions about the future of the regional economy. To the extent that talent migration does come up, it is usually within the context of amenities thought to be important to talent attraction, yet even this issue does not receive much analysis.

Economic strategies assume, I suppose, that businesses and institutions will take care of talent attraction through their national and international recruiting processes. But that underplays the phenomenon of "talent clusters": pools of talented people who gather in metropolitan areas and feed the needs of the resident industry clusters over time. A talent cluster should be more than just the sum of the people recruited by businesses. I can think of many ways that public and civic efforts could provide a more strategic platform from which regional employers can compete for the limited pool of high skill, mobile talent and then help ensure that those people remain in the area and populate the regional talent clusters. It will probably always be the job of Boeing, Microsoft or the Fred Hutchinson Cancer Research Center to scout the world for talent, but we all have a stake in making sure those recruits accept the offer and then stay around for their entire careers.

The "Mount Rainier factor" certainly plays a part, but we need to remember that we compete for talent with some very attractive places like the San Francisco Bay area, San Diego, Denver, Boston, Washington D.C., Raleigh and Austin. And, as noted in Chapter 1, smaller markets like Seattle do not have the depth of employers that large regions have, and therefore cannot offer quite as many varied opportunities and career paths.[22]

Like every other place, we have organizations dedicated to attracting physical investment, like factories and distribution centers. But we have no comparable effort to attract intellectual capital, which we know is far more important.

Let's look next at one of the main factors in talent attraction.

Amenities and quality of life

In their 2008 paper, economists Yong Chen and Stuart Rosenthal ask a seemingly frivolous but actually highly important question: Do people move for jobs or fun?[23] Their work followed a flurry of activity among urban economists who had been trying to determine the role that amenities and quality of life play in relocation decisions. This particular paper concluded that high skill individuals choose cities with strong economies, but it is no accident that cities with strong economies also tend to offer an attractive amenity package. Regions that have strong business fundamentals and a high quality of life can set up a virtuous cycle in which high value enterprises attract productive people who, in turn, support even more amenities.

Each year about seven million Americans move from one state to another, and of those, about 100,000 move to the Seattle area.[24] A large number of these migrants have the luxury of choosing a new place to live based on the quality of life, and if Seattle is to maintain a steady flow of talented people that its leading edge industries require, we need to pay attention to the same things that potential migrants do. Recall that weather is the single most important factor in migration, and that Seattle's weather falls into the lowest category of attractiveness. So, because we start with such a severe weather handicap in trying to attract mobile talent, the rest of the amenity package had better be awfully good.

The notion of quality of life covers far more than snowshoe trips and nightlife. When considering the challenge of attracting mobile people, we cannot just see them as young, single hipsters. Remember, the talent attraction challenge is to make sure that these recruits put down roots and become part of the regional talent pool. They will age, like all of us, and most will form families, stand on the sidelines of soccer games, chaperone senior proms and send their own children out in to the world. Quality of life factors need to address all of these stages of life.

The stickiness of a high quality of life has an added benefit: keeping good people around when times get tough. Seattle learned this lesson, in a positive way, after the Boeing Bust. As we saw, the famous billboard that read "Will the Last Person Leaving Seattle Please Turn Out The Lights" missed the point. A large number of the engineers laid off by Boeing in the late 1960s actually stayed around the region, providing the talent for the technology sectors that would emerge in the 1970s.

In his book *Seattle*, written in the immediate aftermath of the Bust, Gerald Nelson chastises businesses in the region for luring people in, allowing them to settle down, and then pulling the rug out from under them. But, he concedes that:

> *Many of those who cling to Seattle, middle–class, fired and broke, do so not out of masochism but because they love it. They want the mountains, the lakes, the Sound. They want the peace that the last remnants of the land can offer even the penniless.*[25]

The factors that define the quality of life can be grouped into several categories.

Natural environment

This is the hand that Mother Nature deals us, and Seattle holds some good cards. The combination of water and mountains is unmatched in North America, save for Vancouver, and hilly terrain offers many opportunities for views of the region's undeniable natural beauty. Residents can easily access these natural features for recreation. An outdoor enthusiast might skip out of work at 2:30 and be sailing on Puget Sound by 3:00 or skiing on lighted slopes by 3:30.

So much for the good parts. This category also includes the weather, which, as noted before, is the most important factor in decisions about where to move. While relatively mild year round—temperatures rarely get above 90 degrees or below 20 degrees—the marine weather systems that flow in from the Pacific Ocean keep a cloud cover over the region much of the year. Persistent gray, drippy weather really does take its toll on the regional psyche, and even long-time residents run around in their shirtsleeves when the sun makes one of its rare appearances in February.

Seattle's weather is no secret, however, so the steady in-migration to the region indicates that people do make their peace with the climate. Moreover, the mildness of the climate means that outdoor activities can be pursued comfortably year-round. Golf, biking, sailing, running and other sports rarely get interrupted by excessive cold, snow, heat or humidity.

Social environment

Here is gets complicated. Seattle has always been a very tolerant place. In the early days of the "open city," leaders turned a blind eye to the vices that the loggers, fisherman, dockworkers and sailors engaged in. But they made darned sure those activities stayed south of Yesler Street (and also made darned sure that authorities were properly compensated for their cooperation). As the bawdy frontier town matured it still made room for what the establishment would have considered the fringe. In the 1930s Seattle had a thriving jazz scene centered on Jackson Street. A couple of decades later the Beats found a friendly reception in Seattle as did hippies in the 1960s. In addition, Seattle has long had among the largest and most open gay and lesbian communities in the country.

Not that the "respectable" crowd embraced any of this transgressive behavior too much—I don't recall Seattle's active Black Panther Party attending upscale cocktail parties, as in Tom Wolfe's *Radical Chic*—but there was never much pressure to enforce conservative social norms. Seattle is the least-churched part of the country, and to the extent that the establishment belonged to any organized religion, it tended to be the more tolerant branches of mainline Protestant churches and not the more conservative evangelical ones. And Seattle's Catholic Archdiocese and Jewish leadership have been notably liberal.

Seattle is not only open and tolerant, it is also very polite. People hold doors and let others merge into traffic. We wait at least ten seconds at a green light before gently making a small, apologetic, bump on the horn to wake up the snoozing driver in front of us. No one ever wants to offend anyone in public, which leads to frustrating, and at times comic, discourse.

But this polite tolerance masks a dirty little secret: we are not very friendly. Social warmth sits on the surface, and below that comes the Seattle chill—a bit like swimming in Lake Washington in the summer. You might have a delightful chat with a coworker in the break room, but don't count on being invited to lunch, a ballgame or, heaven forbid, dinner at their home. A really ambitious social climber (usually new to town) might host a holiday open house, but it will be buttoned up by eight o'clock, the curtains drawn, and everyone sent back home. My father, who grew up in a gregarious Portuguese family, always chaffed under this feature of Seattle social life, and attributed it to the dominant Scandinavian culture of the area. Whatever the explanation, Seattleites will always love and embrace their neighbors in the abstract, but not so much as individuals.

Built environment

Not a whole lot to brag about here, at least among the signature structures of the city. Architecture critics have long noted the paucity of outstanding buildings in Seattle and its surrounding areas. With a few noted exceptions—the downtown library and the Chapel of St. Ignatius at Seattle University—architecture and public spaces tend to be practical but not very interesting. Things have gotten somewhat better in recent decades, most of the truly dreadful buildings—the Kingdome, Seattle Municipal Building, King County Administration Building, Seig Hall at the UW—having been products of the 1960s and 1970s.

Residential areas fare much better. Seattle never experienced the trauma in its inner city neighborhoods that many cities lived through, and never had the large public housing complexes that so much of that trauma centered on. So even areas that were traditionally low income never went too far down hill and now, as noted in Chapter 4, find themselves facing gentrification.

Suburban areas have developed in a pretty standard fashion, offering a variety of neighborhood choices. The high quality of city and inner-ring suburban neighborhoods, combined with a clogged freeway system, have resulted in price gradients that move consistently out from the job centers in the Seattle-Bellevue-Redmond axis.

The major change of the past 20 years has been the steady emergence of new "urban" neighborhoods. Growth management plans of the early

1990s anticipated the creation of dozens of new urban centers, and while most of those have not gotten very far, a few areas have undergone remarkable transformations.

Services and entertainment

Now we find ourselves in the territory of Richard Florida and others who argue for the importance of things to do outside of home and work. The early techies prided themselves on working 80 hour weeks, sleeping under their desks and subsisting on ramen and peanut butter. Thankfully those days have passed.

We presume that the high skill individuals who drive economies today have sophisticated tastes and the desire for quality, excitement and "authenticity," and have the ability to pay for these things. When they come in from cycling or yoga or some fitness fashion-of-the-day they will venture out to chic restaurants, trendy nightclubs and bars that pour exotic new drinks, in search of others like themselves. As they move into family life they may cut their evenings shorter, but their sophisticated tastes do not change. A region that wants to attract a high value workforce had better offer more than TGI Friday's, the Olive Garden and a few old-school "special occasion" white tablecloth restaurants.

Seattle has developed a very sophisticated culinary and entertainment scene that seems to keep pace with the tastes of its residents. It boasts award-winning restaurants and, while the state's long-standing 2:00 am cutoff for bars keeps the city from having a true 24-hour life, those looking for action will find it not only in Seattle but, increasingly, in Bellevue and other suburbs.

Traditional cultural institutions—museums, theaters, galleries, classical music—do not seem to play as large a role in perceptions of quality of life for in-migrants. Seattle certainly has an excellent set of these institutions, but so do all large cities. Like basic infrastructure, they are only a starting point, and advanced economies are presumed to have them.

Places like Seattle have a particular challenge since they compete for talent with regions like Boston, San Francisco and New York City that have long histories of cultural sophistication. Seattle will never match the offerings of these places, but it needs to be in the ballpark. I think it is.

The capitalization studies cited in Chapter 2 that impute a value to a region's quality of life give the Seattle area a fairly high rating, meaning that people will pay a price in terms of lower earnings, unfavorable housing costs and commutes in order to live here. This is a good thing, because, as noted, Seattle will never be able to offer as many career opportunities as larger regions. After local employers attract high skilled people for their first job, the region needs to offer an outstanding set of amenities and quality of life features to keep them here.

Innovation ecosystems

Like infrastructure, the presence of a strong research university is a necessary, but still not sufficient condition for an innovation-driven, knowledge economy. We can easily think of top research universities located in regions that struggle economically, so the mere presence of top-ranked programs, legions of scientists and millions of federal research dollars does not guarantee that economic benefits will spin out. Commercializing the output of a research university is extremely difficult, and although the University of Washington has served the Seattle region well, the untapped potential is huge and frustratingly hard to realize. A former UW President told me once that the University of Washington's technology transfer operation is among the best in the country, but still badly underperforms relative to the university's research output.

Several years ago I did some work for an international consortium of ten cities comparable to Seattle, that wanted to know how to build their "knowledge economies." These metro regions all have well-regarded research universities, and some had built incubators, accelerators, office parks and other institutions designed to promote technology transfer, but many of them were looking for better results.[26]

The starting point for my work was the European concept of the "triple helix" of business, government and research institutions, which presumably work together to promote technology-based economic development. But what I came to realize is that these three actors do not connect very much in ways that promote entrepreneurial activity: they often look like a Venn diagram with no overlaps. Furthermore, although each has something to gain by turning university research into new companies none are in a position to lead the process.

The helix metaphor never made much sense. A better biological met-aphor is the ecosystem. If an idea or new scientific discovery is a seed, the ecosystem consists of the environmental factors that help that seed sprout and grow. Just as a plant needs soil, water, sun and nutrients, an idea needs a risk-taking entrepreneur, product developers, financing, legal and business advice and marketing support. We can say that a healthy innovation ecosystem exists when anyone with a good idea can find these services in abundance locally.

Silicon Valley is the ultimate innovation ecosystem. In *The Social Network* the Sean Parker character demands that Mark Zuckerberg take his new company, Facebook, to Silicon Valley, knowing that all the pieces exist there for success in a way they might not, even in Boston.

So, how might we characterize the innovation ecosystems of Seattle? Like so many parts of the regional economy, they might best be de-scribed as the top of the second tier. All the pieces are in place, they are just not as abundant and deep as in the top tier regions. In regular list-ings of venture capital placement, for example, the Seattle area and Washington state generally show up in fourth or fifth place. This seems admirable, except that the numbers show a very large difference between the first three places—the San Francisco area, New York City and Boston—and the next tier. Although it certainly has all the right elements in its innovation ecosystems, many believe that the soil is still a bit thin and the water too scarce.

Federal government

The Northwest is all about independence and rugged individualism, right? Well, not entirely. Without the assistance of the federal govern-ment on many levels from almost the beginning of settlement, the Northwest would be a very different place. The federally-sponsored Lewis and Clark Expedition first mapped the area, and federal policies and programs have had a major influence ever since. Consider:

Railroads. Prior to the arrival of federally subsidized railroads in the 1870s Puget Sound was a lonely outpost accessible by wagon from Port-land or by water from San Francisco. Seattle's great transformative event, serving as the launch point for the Klondike Gold Rush, would never have happened without direct rail connections to the East, nor would the city have grown as the largest U.S. port serving Asian markets.

Ports and waterways. The Army Corps of Engineers and the Coast Guard have played a central role in the evolution of the ports on Puget Sound, and the Corps built the Lake Washington Ship Canal that created miles of accessible, fresh water industrial and recreational shoreline in Seattle. The Corps also undertook projects to reduce regular flooding in the Green River Valley, making that area useable for agriculture, and now for industry.

Hydropower and irrigation. This is the great gift of the federal government to the Northwest. The federally funded dams on the Columbia and Snake Rivers provide abundant, inexpensive, clean energy to the Northwest. Those dams, along with other federally funded reservoirs in the state provide irrigation water to millions of acres of highly productive farmland. No federal dams, no potatoes.

Military spending. Most of Boeing's output prior to World War II consisted of specialized airmail and military planes, and war production caused it to grow dramatically. After the War, Boeing continued to produce bombers, and the Pentagon's need for a jet powered refueling tanker for those bombers led directly to the 707 and Boeing's dominance of commercial aircraft. Shipyards on Puget Sound have always relied on Navy and Coast Guard work for a large share of their business.

Military bases. Pierce County hosts the massive Army-Air Force Joint Base Lewis-McChord and Puget Sound has five navy installations, all of which combine for a total of about 90,000 military and civilian personnel in the region.

Federal research funding. For many years the University of Washington has been the second largest recipient of federal research dollars (after Johns Hopkins University), at over $1 billion per year. Major federal funding at the Fred Hutchinson Cancer Research Center and other life sciences and global health institutions, plus the West Coast headquarters for NOAA add up to a very large federally supported scientific presence.

I do not mean to characterize Seattle and the Northwest as monuments to federal pork. On the contrary, the nation has received a very good return on these investments. If, by funding projects and research the federal government aims to stimulate the creation of productive economies, it has, by all accounts, succeeded in the Northwest. Much of the federal activity in the area began through the efforts of two very powerful senators, Warren Magnuson and Henry "Scoop" Jackson. Yet when both of these senators passed from the scene in the early 1980s, the flow of federal dollars and programs continued to grow, which stands as a testament to the quality of outcomes on federally funded activities in the region.

The "Seattle Spirit"

Now comes the part that is, shall we say, somewhat less objective. Can we identify unique cultural attributes, shaped by history, that have defined the Seattle area and contributed meaningfully to its economic progress? We do this with other cities. Chicago is the muscular, nononsense capital of the Midwest. Miami is the capital of Latin America. Los Angeles is both Raymond Chandler and Disney. Philadelphia is Ben Franklin and Rocky. Dallas—well, just watch the old TV series. Behind these broad images lies a certain amount of truth, and while I am not entirely certain how an outside observer of Seattle would characterize the city, we can see a few important features of the local culture that help drive the economy.

To begin with, residents and businesses have an above average appetite for risk. Historically, Seattle has been a bit unsafe. The city began with logging and fishing, among the most dangerous industries in the world. The Klondike Gold Rush was a collective act of lunacy, and a large number of the lunatics who participated in it settled in Seattle, adding to the already edgy local DNA. Everyone's favorite Seattle business story is the one about test pilot Tex Johnston's stunt of barrel rolling a Boeing Dash 80 prototype over the Lake Washington hydroplane racecourse in 1955: although Johnston claimed the maneuver was totally safe, a crash would likely have destroyed the company. Seattle has been home to some of the nation's greatest mountain climbers and, of course, the sport of hydroplane racing itself always had a very high mortality rate.

The appetite for personal risk is an essential ingredient in fostering an entrepreneurial culture. Most business ventures fail, and entrepreneurs and their financial backers know this and yet pursue them anyway. While Seattle is not quite as blasé about failure as Silicon Valley, entrepreneurs in Seattle can get out on a limb and know that their entire career is not at risk.

As noted in Chapter 2, Seattle businesses tend to focus on quality, not price. Two signature companies, Nordstrom and Alaska Airlines, have always positioned themselves first as purveyors of high quality products and services. Costco distinguishes itself by offering top quality merchandise, and by making premium brands available at lower prices. Starbucks introduced premium coffee to middle America, Seattle start-ups brewed some of the nation's first craft beers, and a pair of Seattle restaurateurs invented the premium cinnamon roll, the Cinnabon. Being a relatively affluent region, people can afford to pay more for quality, and strong local support allowed these companies to expand beyond local markets.

As discussed several places in this book, the region tends to have a more international outlook. Because so many people get exposed to international business in a positive way, Seattle residents will more likely embrace globalization than will people in regions that have suffered due to import competition. The region and state have enough successful exporters that businesspeople are more apt to see international markets as viable places to explore.

Comfort with international connections extends beyond business. High levels of immigration, especially to the suburbs of Seattle, mean that schools have very diverse populations, as do daycares, sports leagues and other community activities. Families in the region get direct exposure to other cultures on a daily basis. Now, like any attribute this one is a question of degrees, and we certainly have our share of xenophobes, but overall, the region seems comfortable with the idea of growing as a global hub.

The curious thing about local cultures is just how enduring they can be, even in the face of population turnover through migration: in spite of the huge numbers of Californians moving to Seattle it does not feel like an extension of Santa Monica or the Embarcadero. I will leave it to the anthropologists to figure out how a melting pot can keep the same flavor after tossing in dozens of different cheeses.

In the late 1800s, when Seattle was still quite young, we begin to see references to the "Seattle Spirit," an idea that promised success to those who would work hard, bounce back from adversity, take chances and cast off their tired old past. Seattle saw itself as a land for a new start, a place of limitless possibilities for those willing to head out to the edge and be captured by the Spirit. The indolent, the shiftless, the weak-willed, the quitters need not apply. Well, does a twenty-first century version of the Seattle Spirit live on? I'll let you decide when you get to the end of the book.

Is the Seattle region globally competitive?

The growth and income metrics discussed in Chapter 2 suggest the answer is yes, overall. But the answer will vary by industry. The factors discussed in this chapter affect the business prospects of sectors differently.

Mature, low margin firms tend to worry about cost factors like taxes and regulation that can put them at a disadvantage vis-a-vis competitors in other states. At an even finer grain, Washington's B&O tax will favor some industries over others when compared to corporate income taxes. Firms that build facilities and operate outdoors will feel differently about environmental regulations than firms working in downtown high-rises. Industrial operations with complex supply chains will feel the pinch of traffic congestion more than operations that deal strictly in paper and electronic transactions.

Newer, technology-based businesses tend to feel less strongly about cost issues and more strongly about talent. They need the right people and they need them now. They want more of those right people coming out of local colleges and universities, or, failing that, they need to lure them from somewhere else with the promise of a great career and an enviable lifestyle.

When business magazines publish their annual rankings of the best places to do business, the criteria they use indicate which type of firms they are thinking of. Magazines like *Site Selection* focus on the concerns of manufacturers, distributors and other real estate-intensive businesses and tend to rank the Seattle area fairly low. Rankings such as *Bloomberg-Business Week*, that focus on new businesses and lifestyles tend to rank Seattle fairly high. The State New Economy Index ranks Washington second, behind Massachusetts, as a platform for innovation.[27]

The characterization of Seattle as a boutique economy—quality, but at a price—seems on target. Because this makes the Seattle area a relatively unattractive place for cost-conscious firms we run the risk of creating (to shift imagery) the hourglass economy, with lots of highly paid, high-skill jobs at the top, lots of service jobs at the bottom, and few mid-skill, high productivity jobs in the middle. We'll come back to the hourglass later in the book.

But the region does have one mitigating factor that can overcome its high costs: a highly skilled manufacturing workforce. Boeing's main reason for committing to build the 737MAX at its Renton plant was the daunting prospect of trying to recreate its workforce somewhere else. The Puget Sound workboat industry had enough skill to make a strategic pivot and capture a large share of the luxury yacht business. The region's medical device industry produces very sophisticated instruments for worldwide export. Although these businesses do need to keep a close eye on costs and will be sensitive to taxes and regulations, the productivity of the workforce and quality of the output makes the Seattle area an advantageous place to locate.

Recall the story of the "Region on Trial" exercise back in the introduction. In 1991, regional leaders could not see past obvious failings in many of the factors discussed in this chapter in order to recognize the success about to descend on the Seattle area. What did the prosecutors miss in the exercise that would have reversed the guilty verdict?

The obvious answer is the collection of top talent that had assembled itself in Seattle. Instead of fleeing *from* the area to more exciting places as in the past, highly capable and ambitious people came *to* Seattle. And those born here, like Bill Gates and Paul Allen, decided to return home and build their companies here. I am sure that every entrepreneur, scientist, engineer, musician or chef who chose Seattle over other equally compelling places had their own personal reasons for doing so. But I would bet that their reasoning had little to do with the quality of roads and schools and the tax and regulatory environment. As important as those things are, addressing them will never be enough.

Chapter 6

Drivers of the Seattle Economy in 2012

N ow that we have wandered through the business biosphere of the Seattle area we can take a look at some of the wildlife that inhabits that space. We covered the evolution of the various businesses and industries in a cursory fashion in previous chapters, and now we can look a bit more closely at how the major industries developed and how they fit into the larger picture of the regional economy.

This chapter will profile industries that definitely play an important role in the economic base of the region. The choice of which to profile at some point becomes arbitrary, but I hope to provide some flavor for what industries got us to where we are now, and which would seem to have promise for carrying the region into the future. But before we start poking away at these critters, we should take a short detour through the concept of the economic base.

The economic base

The industries described in this chapter all belong to the "economic base" of the region, also known as the "traded sector," and sometimes as "primary industries." As described before, the economic base consists of activities that result in sales of goods and services to buyers outside the region. This brings in money used to purchase goods and services made somewhere else. When we think of "trade" we tend to think about international commerce, but the same principles apply within a country. We cannot buy things from outside the region unless we sell things of an equal value. And the Puget Sound region's remote location means that most consumer products will be made somewhere else, requiring us to make products for sale nationally and internationally for which a remote location does not present a disadvantage.

Identifying the industries that make up the economic base is not so straightforward, however. For example, we would not tend to think of a local hair salon as part of the economic base. Yet when a businessperson visiting from Los Angeles, whose coif has just been ruined in the rain and who needs a quick fix before a big presentation, steps into that salon, it suddenly becomes part of the economic base. The money for the touch-up came from Los Angeles, and the salon owner has just exported a service to an Angelino. Most industries, however local they may seem, do export some amount of value from the region, often through tourism and increasingly through the tools the internet provides for small businesses to sell worldwide. And what might seem like totally export-oriented firms sell some products locally.

One way to identify the economic base is to look at the Washington Input-Output (I/O) model. This data comes from studies that describe the state's entire economy and estimate the amount of goods and services that businesses buy and sell from each other. The model also indicates the degree to which businesses purchase inputs from and sell goods and services outside the state. I/O models provide those magical multipliers, referred to throughout this book, that determine how many jobs in the non-traded sector get supported by a job in the traded sector.[1] (One important thing to remember: don't confuse the multiplier effect with the pejorative concept of "trickle down." I won't take the time to go into it here, but, while related, they are not the same thing.)

Using the I/O spreadsheet we can calculate the share of industry output that gets sold in the rest of the U.S. or internationally versus how much is sold in the state. Eighteen of the fifty industry groups in the model show export shares in excess of 80 percent, and these industries make up about 26 percent of the state's economy. In all, about 48 percent of all the goods and services that that do not get purchased by another Washington business get sold out of state.[2]

Economists use another method to identify industries important to the region: employment location quotients (LQs). The LQ for an industry is calculated by dividing the percentage of all employment represented by that industry at the regional level by the employment percentage at the national level. For example, if an industry comprised 4 percent of the regional workforce and 2 percent of the national workforce, it would have an LQ of 2.0. Or, if an industry comprised 4 percent of the regional workforce and 5 percent of the national workforce, it would have an LQ of 0.8. An LQ of 1.0 indicates that the region has exactly the same proportion of its workforce in that industry as the nation, and therefore has about the right size of industry to serve local needs. An LQ of more than 1.0 indicates that the industry serves more than just the local area, presumably making it part of the economic base, and an LQ of less than 1.0 points to products and services that the region must import.

For its 2012 Regional Economic Strategy, the Prosperity Partnership identified 10 sectors in its "portfolio of clusters" for the region. The LQs for these are revealing. Not surprisingly, aerospace has an LQ of 6.2, meaning that the region has over six times the aerospace employment that the average region would have. Maritime industries came in at 3.0, military at 1.9, and tourism at 1.0. Information technology had an LQ of 2.28, but the analysis appears to have cast a pretty wide net, diluting the impact of the software industry itself.[3]

Now, having described these two ways to define the economic base, what follows is my own take on what industries shape and will shape the region.

Aerospace

Did you expect to start with anything else? You gotta dance with the one who brung you, and whether we like it or not, aerospace brung us to the high tech, globalized hootenanny. Boeing and its chain of suppliers dragged Seattle out of its colonial past of hewing logs and gutting fish, and continues to have the most wide ranging impact of any sector in the region.

And most people have no idea how insanely fortunate the region is to have aerospace powering its economy, even with the volatility described in Chapter 3. As an engine for regional development, there is simply no better industry in the world. None. Put another way, if an economic strategist set out to design, from scratch, the perfect industry around which to build a metropolitan economy, the result would look an awful lot like aerospace, and, more specifically, the design and production of large commercial jetliners.

I am not unbiased in this judgment. Like everyone who grew up in the Seattle area in the 1960s I have a few drops of kerosene in my veins. Even so, think about the following characteristics of this industry.

High barrier to entry. Right now, all of the commercial aircraft over 150 seats sold in the world come from two companies: Boeing and Airbus. Brazilian builder Embraer has stayed away from larger jets and Canadian builder Bombardier has a 145-seat jet on the market, but has sold few. Plane makers in China and Russia have been trying to get into the business, but even if these firms succeed in developing commercially viable products with over 150 seats, they will make little dent in the market. The current duopoly owns this industry for the next two decades, at least.

Huge growth prospects. Boeing estimates that global air travel will grow at a rate of five percent per year, and that world airlines will buy 34,000 commercial airplanes between 2012 and 2031. Airbus has a slightly less bullish projection of 27,000 planes over that period, but even that lower figure represent a major increase in production over today's levels.[4]

Stable customer relationships. Airlines do not like to shift from one make of plane to another due to high training and maintenance costs, so Boeing and Airbus tend to keep their customers. Most open competition between the firms takes place at the margins, involving new airlines or mergers between airlines that result in mixed fleets.

Long product life cycles. The lives of airplane designs and plant investments are measured in decades. When Boeing commits to an assembly facility, that factory will operate for a very long time: the 737 line in Renton and the 747 line in Everett will operate for at least *seventy years.* In an era when manufacturing operations seem to be getting more and more "flexible," an aircraft plant represents a welcome solidity.

Large high tech workforce. Boeing employs tens of thousands of top level engineers and scientists in almost every conceivable field and pays them very well. As a place that builds perhaps the most complex commercial products in the world, Boeing can attract the best talent to the region, helping fill the larger technical talent pool that other industries can draw upon.

Large high-skill blue collar workforce. Those "flexible" manufacturing operations around the country often employ very few people. But at Boeing, the shop floors still swarm with union machinists who take home very nice pay and benefit packages. And, importantly, these men and women are not just cogs in a machine; they carry with them key tacit knowledge that they leverage into job security.

And finally, well, everyone loves airplanes. Having a close association with a very cool product and a very recognizable and prestigious brand does wonders for a region's overall positioning. Seattle used to call itself the "Jet City" and should perhaps start doing so again.

As of this writing, Boeing has about 85,000 employees in the Puget Sound region, and its 600 suppliers in the region have another 5,000 employees. About 44,000 Boeing and other aerospace employees work in Snohomish County, about 44,000 work in King County and about 2,000 work in Pierce County.[5]

Those thousands of workers produce two basic types of aircraft: transcontinental and intercontinental.[6]

Transcontinental, or single-aisle planes, such as the Boeing 737 and the Airbus A320, are designed to travel frequently within continental markets. None of these markets, anywhere in the world, has a route longer than 3,000 miles, so that serves as the outer bound for the range of these planes and sets the fuel capacity requirements. The 737 and A320 come in families with seating capacity ranging from about 100 seats to about 200. Most airlines find that the 150 to 175 seat range works best, providing good economics for fuel use and crew size, while keeping the turn-around time at the gate to a minimum. The travel market clearly prefers frequency of flights and fast loading and unloading, so as demand increases, airlines add more flights rather than using larger aircraft. Boeing estimates that world airlines will buy over 23,000 single-aisle planes between 2012 and 2032.

Intercontinental twin aisle aircraft come in two types. The "large" planes include the Boeing 767, 777 and 787, and the Airbus A330 and

A350, which range from 200 to 400 seats. The "very large" plane catego-ry has just two products, the Boeing 747 and the Airbus A380, which range from 400 to 600 seats. Twin aisle planes have ranges from 6,000 to over 9,000 miles. While airlines can easily estimate ranges for transcon-tinental routes, they have more difficulty determining appropriate ranges for intercontinental routes, since there are so many possible city pairs. But adding range increases costs significantly: more fuel means more weight which means less payload, more structure and heavier landing gear, etc. So when ordering planes airlines need a good idea of what routes they intend to fly so they do not over-spend on range. Newly emergent airlines based in the Persian Gulf have pushed routes to greater lengths in recent years and have urged Boeing and Airbus to extend the range of their planes.

In the 1990s, Boeing and Airbus had very different views of the future of intercontinental air travel markets. Airbus took the view that the fat routes between big airports—New York to London or Los Angeles to Tokyo—would form a large share of the market, and since those airports could not grow, aircraft themselves would need to grow. Based on this assumption, Airbus committed to the enormous A380. At the same time, Boeing took the opposite view, believing that the traveling public would rather have more point-to-point routes to choose from and, if given an option, would prefer not to transfer at Heathrow, JFK or Narita. Hence, Boeing committed to the smaller, fuel-efficient 787 Dreamliner. It appears that Boeing won that bet. Having sold only about 200 A380s in its first five years, Airbus had no choice but to launch the A350 to compete with the 787, which had sold over 700 planes in its first five years. And Airbus has still not convinced many customers that the stretched A350-1000 is a real competitor to the Boeing 777, a very profitable plane that continues to rule the large, long-haul market.

Once the twin-aisle intercontinental market settled out by the mid-2000s, the action moved to the single-aisle market where both the 737 and A320 were getting a bit long in the tooth. The planes, after several upgrades each, still performed well, but airlines were demanding greater fuel efficiency and engine-makers had figured out how to provide it. Airbus moved first, declining to offer a brand new plane and simply putting new, more fuel efficient engines on the A320. Once Airbus made that decision, in early 2011, Boeing had no choice but to respond. It explored building a brand new plane, but in the end, decided to follow Airbus' move and put new engines on the 737, calling it the MAX.

I have meandered through this look at the commercial airplane business first because I think it is really interesting, and anyone who wants to understand the Seattle area needs to understand what Boeing does. But mainly I wanted to highlight the industrial footprint that Boeing will have in the region in the future. With their commitment in 2011 to build the 737MAX in Renton and significantly step up production, the Boeing presence in King County will only grow. The 787, with its ambitious outsourcing program, does not have a large employment impact in Everett, but that plant continues to operate three other assembly lines. The 767 will stay in production for the new Air Force refueling tanker, as a freighter and as a less expensive alternative to the 787. The 747 has become something of a niche product on the passenger side (private jets for very rich customers!), but is still the largest freighter in the air (Airbus decided not to build a freighter version of the A380). The 777, Boeing's highly successful big plane, has a large backlog and is due for a makeover in the next decade.

Boeing went through some very tough times in the 2000s, trying to get the 787 and the latest version of the 747 launched and fending off aggressive competition from Airbus. Then, in 2011 the news started to get better. Boeing had won the competition for the new Air Force refueling tanker, had gotten final FAA sign-off on the 787 and 747-8 and delivered the first units to their customers. A hard-fought agreement with the Machinist Union meant labor peace for some years, and with that agreement in hand, the company made the commitment to build the 737MAX in Renton.

All good. Except for one difficulty: finding enough people to build all these airplanes.

Boeing faces major workforce shortages in the next decade due to upcoming retirements. The average age on the factory floor is relatively high, due to the way layoffs get managed. Rules negotiated with the Machinists require that layoffs take place on a "last in, first out" basis. This has tended to wash out the younger workers, with the older workers staying around. But those older workers have generous retirement plans that they can start cashing in, and the flow of younger employees to take their place has not caught up.

I still find these workforce issues weird and ironic. We go to great lengths to get Boeing to commit to building an airplane here so people can get good jobs in the factory (the engineers are not going anywhere) and yet we need to devise all sorts of ways to get local people to qualify for those jobs. But studies have shown that absent some intervention, new jobs created in an economy tend to go overwhelmingly to new residents.[7] So, if we do not work hard to get the underemployed living around us onto the factory floor, Boeing will happily send word out to St. Louis, Long Beach, Huntsville and other places with lots of skilled aerospace workers. If I were working in one of those places I might be nervous about the future of military and space programs and start thinking about a move to the Puget Sound area and a long career on the far more stable commercial side of the industry.

Ports and trade

Boeing may have brought the region out of its colonial era, but it was the ports that kept Seattle from complete isolation for its first hundred years. Today they still provide that connectivity, while directly supporting a critical piece of the region's economic base and enabling other segments.

While we take it for granted that ports are public infrastructure, that was not always the case. Until 1911, facilities on the Seattle and Tacoma waterfronts were privately owned, mostly by the railroads, with which the public had a love-hate relationship: love the convenience, hate the pernicious influence. The state legislature authorized public port districts in 1911 and voters approved creation of the Port of Seattle that fall, along with a $3 million bond issue to fund acquisition and development of terminals.[8] Pierce County voters created the Port of Tacoma in 1918 and approved a $2.5 million bond issue in 1919.

Seattle and Tacoma have two of the finest natural, deep water ports in North America.[9] From the earliest days of loading logs and fish on sailing ships, vessels have pulled right up to piers on the waterfront, protected from harsh weather and not in danger of running aground. By the late nineteenth century these ports had critical rail connections directly to markets in the east. But the real advantage lay in location. For once, being in the upper corner of the map helped.

Try this exercise. Find a globe and a piece of string. Hold one end of the string on Tokyo and, stretching the string tight, lower it down so it touches Seattle (or Tacoma, if you'd like). Make a mark on the string to show the Tokyo-Seattle distance. Now hold the string in the same place for Tokyo and pull it to Los Angeles. These are the "great circle" routes that ships and airplanes follow, and represent the shortest distance between two points on the globe. You will note that the distance from Tokyo to Seattle is shorter—about 600 nautical miles—than the distance from Tokyo to Los Angeles. That difference translates into about a full day of sailing time for a container ship. And since costs are proportional to time and distance, the voyage to Seattle or Tacoma costs about 15 percent less than the voyage to Los Angeles/Long Beach.

Now, as long as you have the globe out, note that Chicago is slightly closer to Puget Sound than to Los Angeles. Rails and highways do not go in straight lines, of course, but you get the picture: the ports of Seattle and Tacoma offer faster and more cost effective shipping from Asia to markets in the central and eastern U.S. In the late nineteenth century, when steamships first started plying North Pacific routes, this shorter distance made a very large difference, thereby making Puget Sound ports highly attractive. Steamers traveled more slowly then, so the advantage over California ports would have been two days or more, and because those ships ran on coal, a bulky, heavy fuel, a shorter trip meant less fuel cost and more tonnage and space for cargo.

By 1917, the Port of Seattle was the third largest load center in the country, behind New York and Philadelphia, dominating West Coast shipping. And back then, sources of exports and markets for imports were almost entirely in the Eastern part of the country, so getting cargo onto the northern tier rail lines made sense.

All of those advantages have eroded over the past hundred years. But before we get to the challenging competitive environment for the Puget Sound ports, let's look at the role that the ports play in the regional economy today.

The Port of Seattle's most recent economic impact study, based on data from 2007, found that the port's maritime operations supported about 23,000 jobs, including 5,600 people who work with the fishing fleet based at port facilities, and about 1,900 who work at the cruise ship terminals. A recent Port of Tacoma study tallies up a total of about

11,000 jobs statewide. So the two ports, between them, generate about 34,000 jobs in their maritime operations (the Port of Seattle also operates Sea-Tac Airport). Using appropriate multipliers, the port studies show an additional 11,000 indirect jobs with suppliers around the state, and 32,000 induced jobs that result from household spending by those working around the ports. So, altogether, the maritime operations of the ports of Seattle and Tacoma support somewhere in the neighborhood of 75,000 jobs in the region.[10]

And like the workers at Boeing, jobs at the ports tend to pay quite well. The deals made back in the 1960s, when containerization displaced thousands of longshore workers who used to load ships by hand, ensured high pay for those still on the waterfront. (It should be noted that the independent, non-union truck drivers providing drayage to and from the docks often earn far less than longshore workers.)

Ports are not, of course, an end in themselves, but transfer points in the process of moving goods from producer to user. From the perspective of the economy of the Puget Sound region we can think of two types of cargo, that which starts or ends inside the area and that which passes through, on its way to or from somewhere else in North America.

About 30 percent of inbound cargo through the two ports stays in the Northwest. The 14 million people in the five Northwest states may not constitute a California-sized market, but the area does consume a lot of stuff, and those goods head from the ships directly to warehouses throughout the region. On the outbound side, manufacturers in the area have convenient access to the ports, and the growers of Central and Eastern Washington rely heavily on the ports to ship apples and other produce to lucrative Asian markets.

A subset of the cargo that stays in the region heads to the warehouses of firms like REI, Zumiez, Sur la Table, and other national specialty retailers that distribute from the area. While we hear a lot about the economic impact of exports, we need to remember that the Puget Sound region has substantial economic activity related to imports. The products may get assembled overseas, but Seattle area firms undertake the design, marketing, distribution and retail management for those products, which, together, constitute the majority of the value in them. Convenient port access allows these firms to operate from the Seattle area and serve national markets.

The other 70 percent of cargo going through the ports starts or ends beyond the Northwest. This cargo tends to arrive or depart by train. Corn and soybeans arrive by railcar to the port grain elevators, as do pieces of heavy equipment too big to travel on the roads. Containers on double-stack cars travel across the Cascades and Rockies, to and from the ports.

That 70 percent figure keeps port managers up at night. It represents discretionary cargo that could go through any port, and make its way to its final destination. None of that cargo has to go through the Puget Sound ports, whose natural advantages make less of a difference today than they did one hundred years ago. Ships have become much faster and more fuel efficient, reducing Puget Sound's time and cost advantage. But more importantly, California has grown from a sparsely populated agricultural and mining state into the largest population center in the country, and, therefore, the largest destination market for products from Asia. A large share of what comes into the ports of Oakland, Los Angeles and Long Beach stays in California, or heads just east to the booming markets of the Southeast, making those ports convenient places for shippers to set up West Coast operations.

Now, the Puget Sound ports have one remaining advantage over the Southern California ports: they are not in California. Shippers want to have alternatives to avoid monopoly situations on the part of ports, unions, railroads, truckers and other participants in the shipping process. The Puget Sound ports serve that role. But other ports want that role too.

So, get that string out again, and measure the distance from Tokyo to Prince Rupert, British Columbia (if Prince Rupert does not show up on your globe, stick your finger on the southern tip of the Alaska Panhandle). You will see that Prince Rupert is quite a bit closer to Tokyo than Seattle is. The Canadian government has been aggressively building port facilities and rail lines there with an eye toward diverting cargo from the Puget Sound ports.

The other development that worries port leaders is the widening of the Panama Canal. Twenty-five years ago the shipping industry decided it did not need the canal, and could design ships wider than it could accommodate—the "post-panamax" ships. Now, however, the government of Panama has undertaken a project to widen the canal to fit these larger, more efficient ships, providing direct access from Asia to Gulf Coast and East Coast ports. This makes for a much longer trip, but one that bypasses western railroads and get directly to inexpensive distribution hubs in the Southeast.

The ports of Seattle and Tacoma cannot change the geography of the planet or the population distribution of the country to improve the security of their cargo flows. But they can undertake a larger strategic effort that would improve their attractiveness. Recall the discussion of the "global city," defined as a business hub where complex international transactions take place. These hubs have service providers that cater to importers and exporters and offer specialized capabilities that those companies will not have in-house and will not have even near their base of operations. While Seattle and Tacoma can offer some of these services to businesses, the region does not have the capacity found in San Francisco, Los Angeles or Vancouver.

One study broke cities out according to their strengths both as ports and as international service centers.[11] It labeled those places with heavy shipping concentrations but lower service concentrations "load centers" and those with lower shipping capacity but high service capacity "service centers." Those rare places with high concentrations in both are "world port cities." Turning the Puget Sound region into more of a world port city would seem an attractive goal. So, as a way to solidify the ports' position we need to build up the service capacity of the region and not defer so much to the capacities in Vancouver or in California. The Puget Sound ports' natural advantages no longer play such a big role, and discretionary cargo could easily move to the north and south, leaving the ports of Seattle and Tacoma fighting over the much smaller volume of cargo that starts or ends in the Northwest.

Any discussion of the future of the ports raises the always-uncomfortable question: why do we have two separate and competing port agencies operating harbors within thirty miles of each other? Every time a shipping line shifts from one port to another (usually from Seattle to Tacoma) outside observers shake their heads, wondering why the ports compete with one another when the real competition is up and down the West Coast. But like most regional governance questions, this one never gets any traction. We may be one big metropolitan region, but some things just don't cross Hylebos Creek very well.

Software

Remember back when no one had ever heard of software? Difficult, isn't it? But not too long ago this industry simply did not exist in the public consciousness. *Washington Works Worldwide*, the economic strategy released in 1988 by the state Economic Development Board, that declared itself "ambitious . . . not for the faint-hearted . . . rethink[ing] the future" made no mention of software at all. When the board began its work in 1986, Microsoft had just become a public company, creating a new cadre of millionaires. But apparently this did not catch the eye of the economic development establishment of the time.

Today we cannot think about the regional economy without putting software in the inner circle. The most recent figures put employment in software somewhere in the 53,000 range in the state.[12] The majority of these people work at Microsoft, but quite a number of other software firms have located either headquarters or engineering offices in the area. Google set up shop in Kirkland in 2004, Yahoo arrived in 2007, Facebook opened an office in Seattle in 2010 and Zynga followed in 2011. Seattle now has among the largest concentrations of software employment in the country. The big Silicon Valley firms set up offices in the area to poach talent from Microsoft, and, eventually, each other.

In addition to the big software and internet companies, the region has become host to a large and thriving "interactive media" industry. Building on Nintendo and some early independent game producers, the local industry has grown to include hundreds of firms, and now is the second largest center for game design in the country.

Fifth-three thousand employees certainly makes for a large industry, and Microsoft ranks as the second largest private sector employer in the state after Boeing. But the impact of software goes far beyond these direct employment numbers. Microsoft's employment multiplier of 6.8 means that the company, and its industry colleagues, support a large part of the regional economy.[13] Assuming that the Microsoft multiplier would apply to other software firms (and since they compete for the same employees, this seems a plausible assumption) software would support 360,000 jobs in the state. If we assume, for discussion sake, that 95 percent of these jobs are in the Puget Sound region, software would support about 20 percent of the regional economy. Aerospace supports about the same share (higher employment, lower multiplier), so between the two, they support about 40 percent of the economy of the three-county region.

Narrowing the impact down to King County, the concentration gets even higher. The 2008 Microsoft Economic Impact Study found that all but a handful of Microsoft employees worked in King County, and 93 percent lived in King County. So, it might be safe to bet that at least 93 percent of the impact of the company falls in King County. If so, and if numbers are similar for the other software companies, software would support 29 percent of county employment.

Even with all the legendary high living by software employees, that multiplier of 6.8 seems astonishingly high. What do Microsoft and its employees buy that generates all those other jobs? To begin with, the company purchases quite a lot within the regional economy—the "indirect" impact. Microsoft reported purchasing $2.15 billion worth of goods and services in the Washington economy in 2008, which would support between 15,000 and 20,000 additional jobs, many of which would be high paying positions in technical, legal and financial services. Then, all of the employees of Microsoft and its suppliers spend money in the economy. And since they get paid quite a lot—an average of $152,000 per year in 2008—they can afford lots of goods and services. Next, every store clerk, nanny, architect, estate planner, waiter or other individual who benefits from the free spending habits of software employees, spends their own paycheck in the economy, circulating those dollars again and again. So, the bigger the initial spending, the more dollars get to circulate through multiple hands before eventually leaking out of the area.

On a marginal basis, over the past decades, the impact gets even more pronounced. The total economic impact of software in 1990 was about 31,000 jobs. By 2011 that had grown to about 350,000 statewide, and if, again, we assume that 95 percent of the job growth generated by software took place in the Puget Sound area, the net growth from 1990 to 2011 in jobs supported by the software industry in the Puget Sound region would total just about 300,000. In that same time period, the job base of the three county region grew by about 370,000, so software accounted for all but 70,000 of the region's net job gain over 20 years.[14]

I find this quite remarkable. If the rest of the economy had just bumped along as it did, and software had not come along, job growth in the region from 1990 to 2011 would have amounted to an anemic 0.25 percent per year. Rather than having robust in-migration over that period we would have had out-migration, as job growth would have been slower than the natural growth rate of the workforce (school graduates minus retirees).

Let's go back to the purchases that Microsoft and other software firms make in the local economy, the business-to-business or "B2B" spending. Microsoft reported to the researchers doing the economic impact study that the company purchased $2.15 billion worth of goods and services in the state economy in 2008. The Washington Input-Output (I/O) model found that the "software publishers and internet service provider" category purchased $4.6 billion worth of goods and services in Washington in 2002. I won't try to unravel the discrepancy, but we can use the I/O analysis to identify where the B2B spending by the software industry lands within the rest of the economy. The input-output study shows that only seven percent of that spending went to the goods producing sector, and half of that went to construction. Another 17 percent of expenditures went to the utilities and transportation sectors (mostly telecommunications) and 11 percent went for leasing of real estate. After all that, the remaining half of B2B spending by the software industry went to purchase financial, legal, administrative and other services.

The contrast with aerospace is particularly striking. Although Boeing has some suppliers in the state, 70 percent of the value of a Boeing airplane comes from out of state, and much of its in-state B2B purchases are for manufactured goods, which themselves will have a lot of out-of-state value. With software, the in-state B2B purchases lean heavily toward services provided by people working in the area, so most of the dollars stay in the local economy: the lawyers buy computers and paperclips, but most of their spending goes to compensate themselves and their support staff. That is why the multiplier is so high and software ends up supporting so much of the regional economy: the B2B spending gets more cycles before it leaks out of the area.

Is all of this a good thing? For years the regional economy rested on one big pillar, aerospace, a few medium sized pillars like the ports, and a bunch of smaller ones. Now, a much larger economy rests on two big pillars—aerospace is about the same size it has been for decades, and software matches it—a few more medium sized ones like ports, military and now life sciences, and the same assortment of smaller ones. Two big pillars certainly feels safer than just one. But how durable is the software pillar?

Here is the concern—you knew there would be one. Recall from Chapter 3 that during the Boeing Bust of 1969 the service sector of the economy did not shrink much. The household spending multiplier did not seem to work in reverse, so even if households lost their main source of income, they continued to muddle through and kept spending enough to maintain service sector employment. But with software, much of the impact comes from B2B spending which would evaporate instantly if the industry ran into trouble. A lot of suddenly unemployed lawyers, financiers and product designers would stop their own spending, and the economy would take a huge hit. Software, with its large multipliers and B2B purchasing, would seem to expose the region to a higher level of economic risk than aerospace does.

Should we worry? Yes and no. Some day when you are out and about in the Seattle area, drive by Boeing's Renton or Everett plants, and then meander along I-405 to Bellevue and Redmond and drive by the many tendrils of Microsoft. The two enterprises feel a bit different, no? The mass and uniqueness of the Boeing plant and the machinery inside and the huge investment in equipment and training that will pay off only over many years, provide some comfort. While we may not know the fate of the next airplane, we do know that the current assembly lines will continue to roll out planes for decades.

Microsoft is . . . a bunch of office buildings full of computer equipment that gets depreciated over five years. The staff we see wandering the campus look like they could decide any day to quit and try their hand at craft distilling or become missionaries in Africa. That solid feel one gets from a Boeing plant seems harder to conjure up around the software industry. Software is entirely about people, and unlike giant riveting machines, people have options in life. So the capital structure of software—nearly all human—leads to worry about its long-term future.

But we know exactly what we need to do to secure the future of that industry: keep people here. The future footprint of software will be determined by the quality of the talent pool available to it. The industry itself fills that pool by recruiting locally and from around the world, and the diversity of the industry will determine the depth of career options that those recruits will have over their working lives. Public policy will, in many respects, determine whether those people enjoy living here enough to put down deep roots.

So, continue your drive past the Microsoft campus, down Bel-Red Road to Marymoor Park. Watch kids playing soccer and baseball, South Asians playing cricket, canine lovers romping through the dog run and cyclists heading up the Sammamish River trail. Take the pulse of the place. If we look for solidity in a Boeing plant we need to look for community vibrancy in software-land. If we have created a region where really smart people want to spend their lives, we can worry less.

Life sciences

The life sciences have an obvious appeal as a part of the regional economic base. The flip side of the huge growth in the healthcare sector is that those on the receiving end of all those expenditures will do very well.

The growth in health spending does have a logic. The developed world and much of the developing world is already awash in stuff, and stuff just keeps getting cheaper. As incomes increase and the cost of stuff decreases, what do we do with all the money? We spend it on services, healthcare in particular. After all, what is more important to most people than living a long, healthy life? (Actually, we mostly pay for other people to have longer lives, but that's another subject.) 80 years ago, food and clothing accounted for 34 percent of personal consumption expenditures, while healthcare accounted for 4 percent of expenditures. Today, food and clothing account for just 12 percent of expenditures, and most of that additional spending power has gone into healthcare, which now soaks up 19 percent of expenditures.[15]

The life sciences, most of which involves the health of humans, has big bucks behind it. This has not gone unnoticed, however. Just about every economic development strategy in the world targets this large swath of activity, and unlike sectors such as aerospace and software, many places have plausible reasons to believe they can get in on the action. Some states, like Florida, have poured hundreds of millions of dollars into initiatives to create major life sciences centers.

Fortunately, Seattle has more than its share of catalytic institutions at the core of its life sciences sector. But before describing them, we need to understand just what we mean by the "life sciences." To a large degree this is an artificial category cobbled together from activities in a number of settings. Broadly, the life sciences center on understanding biological processes and looking for solutions to health, environmental and energy problems. What makes the sector unique is that these activities can take place in a variety of settings, from government and university laboratories to non-profit research centers to private companies. Sometimes an idea will pass through multiple settings on its way from basic research to a commercial product. (Most conventional healthcare operations are not counted in the life sciences sector, since they serve almost entirely local clients. As noted, though, many hospitals have research arms, and these do get counted.)

When bioengineering first emerged as a possibility in the 1970s, much of the economic development action focused on for-profit biotechnology companies. New diagnostics and treatments emerged that not only addressed longstanding medical challenges, but also had the power to make enormous amounts of money for those who owned the patents and got regulatory approval for products based on them. By the 1990s biotech had become the favorite centerpiece of economic strategies. Seattle joined this bandwagon, and did indeed have some successes, with firms like Immunex, Zymogenetics and Icos.

But few of these private sector firms ever scaled up to become large employers, and many of the biotech firms started in the region got purchased by larger pharmaceutical companies. Immunex, the region's largest biotech firm, got up to several hundred employees before being acquired by Amgen. Icos got up to 700 employees before being purchased and dismantled. A few others got past one hundred employees, but altogether, the for-profit biotech sector never became a major force in the regional economy.

As things turned out, however, that did not matter a great deal. The life sciences sector became dominated by university and non-profit research, as well as medical device makers, and these employers got big. A Washington Research Council study from 2011 found that in 2010, 33,500 people worked in the life sciences sector (excluding hospitals and other healthcare providers). Of these, only about 2,000 work in biotechnology and other pharmaceutical firms. Another 8,000 work in the medical device industry—hardware and the associated software—long established in the region. The balance, about 22,500 people, work in the university and non-profit laboratories of the "research industry."[16]

In a very real sense, university and non-profit research has become an industry in itself, an industry that forms an important part of the economic base of the region. Like other parts of the economic base, life sciences research brings money in from outside the region, in this case mostly from the federal government. Whereas economic strategists once considered research as a means to an end—feeding knowledge into the pharmaceutical and medical device industries so they could create products, jobs and wealth—they now recognize research as an economic end in itself.

The emergence of the region as a center of life sciences research began with the University of Washington, which has not only attracted top scientists, but created a culture that encourages the pursuit of grant funding for research. In 2010 the UW brought in $450 million in grants from the National Institutes of Health (NIH) alone, and performed $518 million in life sciences research.[17]

The other big player is the Fred Hutchinson Cancer Research Center. The Hutch brings in over $200 million in NIH grants per year and ranks among the largest independent medical research institutions in the country. Although its name says "cancer research," work at the Hutch goes well beyond that field, managing major national health research projects.

A large and growing group of institutions work in the field broadly known as global health. Organizations like the Program for Appropriate Technologies in Health (PATH) and the Seattle Biomedical Research Institute specialize in research on health problems particularly associated with developing countries. The emergence of the Gates Foundation as one of the world's largest funders of such research has given a major boost to the region's global health institutions.

Other health-related life sciences research takes place all over the region. Non-profits like the Institute for Systems Biology and the Allen Brain Research Institute bring in major grant funding for specialized research. Hospitals, notably Seattle Children's, Group Health and Virginia Mason, have stand-alone research arms.

For the life sciences research industry to thrive in the region it needs three things.

It all starts with money, of course. This is a service export business and it needs customers. The region's institutions have had substantial success securing federal grant dollars, but like anything to do with the federal government, we cannot assume the continued existence of those funding programs. The Gates Foundation and other private funders have stepped in, but in any case, these groups must prove themselves year after year to continue to attract funds.

Next, researchers need laboratory space. Unlike software companies that can locate almost anywhere, life sciences research requires specialized laboratory facilities. "Wet labs" need to have all the plumbing, wiring and ventilation needed for complex operations, and must be flexible enough for easy reconfiguration. Look closely at a lab building and you may see more than the usual ten feet between floors: the "interstitial spaces" house pipes, wires and ducts that serve the labs. These are very expensive and unique buildings, and their existence can serve as the most important constraint on the expansion of the research industry. Several new laboratory buildings have been built in the South Lake Union area by the UW and various non-profits, making it the hub of much of the region's research activity.

And like any technology-based enterprise, these institutions need the right people. This is perhaps the biggest challenge of all. Chapter 1 describes the problem mid-sized regions can have in attracting top talent, and this comes into play in the life sciences. As impressive as Seattle's assets may be, the region is still not in the ranks of Boston and San Francisco when it comes to the life sciences. Both of these regions have major research facilities and major commercial biotechnology companies, and have much larger life sciences workforces. Seattle may sit at the top of the second tier—a very good place to be, considering the global competition for this activity—but the region still must lure highly sought after scientists who may not see the best long-term career prospects in Seattle.

If the life sciences have a downside it is the relatively low employment multipliers for some segments of the industry. Recall that aerospace has a multiplier of 3.9 and software has a multiplier of 6.8, allowing these industries to support a wide swath of the local service economy. The life sciences sector has a composite multiplier of 2.7, and within that, the largest segment, research laboratories, has a multiplier of just 2.3. So, as the many non-profit laboratories in the region grow and thrive, they will not generate a great deal of additional employment in the region. The laboratories themselves purchase relatively little in the local economy (indirect effects) and tend to employ many part-time and student laboratory assistants who do not get paid lavishly. The pharmaceutical industry has a higher multiplier of 4.6, but, as noted, does not have a very large employment presence in the region.[18]

National retail

This sector flies completely in the face of the location theories discussed in Chapter 3. Under those theories, a remote place like Seattle should host only those industries that exploit the region's geographic position or natural resources, or those industries that just happened to blossom here and that are indifferent to shipping costs. It might make sense for one or maybe two large retailers from the region to gain a national presence, but for a large number of national and international retailing headquarters to emerge in the Seattle area defies easy explanation.

Two of the largest of these, Amazon and Starbucks, are not retailers in the most traditional sense, but each has defined or redefined the retailing landscape in its sector, leading to major changes in how the world shops and uses its time. Amazon has thrown the competitive environment for nearly all consumer goods into turmoil, as traditional retailers learn how to operate across channels. Starbucks created an entirely new category of restaurant-retail experience that has spread across the country and internationally. We can see the power of the Starbucks concept in the many successful local and regional coffee chains that have sprung up all over the country whenever Starbucks has entered a market.

Costco, started by a former executive of the original California-based Price Club, which it later bought, combines low prices with high quality in a way that customers find irresistible. Very careful buying and inventory management allow Costco to offer middle and premium brand products at reasonable prices, often to upscale customers. Costco successfully bucks the conventional wisdom that American consumers need endless choices—at least 75 different breakfast cereals on the shelf—by instead offering just one or two brands of a product. This greatly simplifies inventory and increases buying power. And they *know* that you will leave with far more than you planned to buy when you came in!

Before any of these three upstarts existed, Nordstrom had redefined customer service, empowering sales staff in ways that the traditional department stores had never tried. The result was startling, as Nordstrom spread across the country, starting in the 1980s, with per-square-foot sales figures far beyond what its competitors could generate. Although in a less dramatic fashion than Amazon, Nordstrom, too, redefined a segment of retailing.

The Seattle area has been home to important players in the active outdoor and sportswear segment. Recreational Equipment Inc., the funky store on Capitol Hill where we got our hiking gear in the 1970s, expanded into a wider range of outdoor sports. "The CoOp" was started by mountaineers pooling their purchases of European equipment. It later went national, with 130 stores in 2012, including a new store in Manhattan. It remains member-owned. Everett-based Zumiez corralled all the "board" sports into one place, offering year-round gear and apparel for snow, wake and skate boarders and other "action sports" enthusiasts. Founded in 1978 the company now has 445 stores nationwide, purchasing a European chain in 2012. Eddie Bauer, an old Seattle brand started in 1920, has struggled with its identity, but continues to operate 370 stores nationally from its Bellevue headquarters.

That is an impressive roster of traditional and leading edge retailers that all got their start here and found their particular brand of service in demand around the country and the world. Can we find any explanation for this assemblage of firms? We could go back to the gold rush and the aggressive merchant activity generated by thousands of ill-equipped miners, but that ignores the decades in which nothing of note happened on the retailing scene.

Maybe it's just luck. Sometimes, in the random distribution of good ideas, fortuitous timing, capable individuals and smart organizations, a flock of success happens in one place for no discernible reason. Can we find commonality between the natty Nordstrom family and the nubby-socks crowd at REI? The green-eyeshade guys at Costco and such *sui generis* characters as Howard Schultz and Jeff Bezos? The Bobos who shop at Sur la Table and the slackers who shop at Zumiez? It certainly taxes the imagination. So let's not try.

Instead, how about considering this good fortune as something the region can build on. These companies may have little in common in their origins, but they have one big thing in common now: a keen understanding of how to serve customers. Retailing, no matter the channel, is an art form, and those who master it know some very important things; they form a talent cluster just as distinct as that of software, aerospace or the life sciences. And a strong talent cluster presents the opportunity to bring in or grow more firms that want to take advantage of it.

The region should include this industry and talent cluster in its strategies for a couple of reasons. The obvious one is that it will grow. Retailing will continue to change, and those that have found success in the current challenging environment have a good chance of finding success through the next round of evolution. Second, this industry offers careers that do not require a scientific or technical background. Rather, it relies on artistic and creative capabilities and knowledge of the social sciences. The arts and commerce have always intersected at interesting points, and a large and vibrant retail headquarters industry will enable those kinds of synergies with the region's impressive arts community: copywriter by day, aspiring novelist by night; art director by day, painter by night; jingles by day, indie songwriter by night. . .

But first, we need to recognize that this industry exists as a distinct cluster. While internet commerce shows up as an element in economic strategies, other retailing does not, despite its visibility. We tend to think that industries worth targeting must center around technology, but that misses important activities. All of these retailers use technology heavily, but their business is about humans and satisfying their age-old need to buy things and enjoy doing it. That process will never go away.

What local retailer will go national next? Here's a hint for where to look: Starbucks and Sur la Table (96 stores in 28 states) had their first stores in the Pike Place Market. So, next time you are at the Market, look around—perhaps a hot investment opportunity awaits.

"Other" manufacturing

Manufacturing forms the heart of the economic base of most regions. With Boeing casting such a long shadow we can easily forget that lots of other things get produced in the Seattle area. Some manufacturing activities have a strongly local component, like bakeries, printers and beverage makers. But most manufacturing serves regional, national and international markets.

In 2012, about 182,000 people worked in manufacturing businesses in the three-county region, and about 90,000, or about 49 percent, worked in aerospace.[19] What did the other 92,000 manufacturing employees make? Well, the categories given in the employment statistics do not tell us much. The largest categories after aerospace and food processing are computer and electronic equipment, fabricated metal products, machinery and miscellaneous.

I will spare you, gentle reader, a laundry list of manufacturing companies that employ all these people. Like the region's collection of national retailing firms, these "diversified manufacturers" are just that, diversified. Some clusters exist, such as boat building and medical devices, but overall, it's a mixed bag. What many of these firms do have in common, as you should expect by now, is a relatively high ratio of value to weight, such that shipping costs do not factor in very highly. Others, such as boatbuilding, rely on skills that have historically resided in the region.

And I cannot fail to mention that most important contribution to the world of male fashion, the Utilikilt, designed and sewn right here in Seattle, and adding an important dimension to the diversified manufacturing sector. Gentlemen, you owe it to yourself to check it out.

The main thing is that 92,000 is a very big number, and one that has fallen recently. Between 1990 and 2007, regional employment in non-aerospace manufacturing fluctuated between 103,000 and 134,000, averaging 116,000. It fell to 91,000 in 2011 and bounced back slightly in 2012. But as the overall workforce has grown over the past 22 years, non-aerospace manufacturing employment fell from nine percent of all jobs in 1990 to five percent in 2012.[20]

But 92,000 is still a big number. Jobs multipliers for manufacturing vary quite a bit, with most between 2.5 and 4.0.[21] If we assume a jobs multiplier of 2.75 across the diversified manufacturing sector that would mean it accounts for about 250,000 jobs in the region, or about 15 percent of total employment. That puts it in the same general ballpark as aerospace and software as an underpinning of the regional economy. The trouble is, though, that "diversified" does not tell us much about what we need to do to keep the 3,600 manufacturing businesses in the region healthy. When it comes to the definition of a good business environment, a medical device manufacturer will have more in common with a software company than it will with a maker of concrete blocks. Sure, every manufacturer would like to have lower business taxes and, especially, lower unemployment and workers compensation costs. But do we know what the top priorities are? I suspect they vary as much as the businesses that fall under the "diversified manufacturing" category itself.

Travel and tourism

Always the under-performer. Seattle will never be Orlando or Honolulu or even San Diego. But considering its assets, the region consistently underperforms in visitor attraction. Those who work in the tourism business know this, but can never seem to get much traction around efforts to boost the visitor industry. When the state Legislature zeroed out the already-thin state tourism promotion budget in 2010, no one seemed very surprised. Despite the fact that it brings in billions of dollars of easy, clean money, tourism remains the Rodney Dangerfield of the economic base.

Perhaps the callous sophisticates grow faint at the thought of more pale-limbed families in shorts and tank tops standing on street corners staring at their incomprehensible visitor maps, in search of "Pikes Market." But we need to set aside our snobbery and consider the many benefits that the visitor industry bestows on the regional economy and the unique opportunities it presents.

The one thing ya gotta love: tourism keeps growing and growing. As societies become wealthier, the desire to travel increases. We can only own so many big screen TVs, but there is no limit to the number of interesting places we might visit. The U.S. Travel Association projects an annual growth rate of domestic tourism of over 4 percent in the next decade, and the U.S. Department of Commerce projects that international visits to the U.S. will increase between 4 and 5 percent per year between 2012 and 2016. The largest increases from outside North America will come from China, which the Commerce Department expects to increase from 1 million to 3 million visitors per year, and from Brazil, which should grow from 1.5 to 2.5 million visitors per year.[22]

Tourism provides a helpful part of the economic base because it offers employment opportunities to a lot of people with low skill levels, and face it, we will always have a layer of the workforce that cannot do very complicated things. As the general manager of one of Seattle's finest hostelries, told me, "we serve the top and employ the bottom." Whether in hotels, restaurants or amusements, the tourism business provides decent jobs for people who do not have a lot going for them.

Tourism also provides abundant opportunities for small business. Enterprising entrepreneurs can always find new and unique ways to legally separate visitors from some cash. Sure, we cringe at the sleazier characters, but in general, small operators provide services that add value to the visitor experience. Most of us, when we travel, like to eat at the local restaurants and food carts, ride a pedicab, buy things on the street and sometimes take our chances on a dodgy but enthusiastic local tour guide. Tourism rewards hustle and imagination.

Much of the visitor industry is not very glamorous, but it adds a needed diversity to the region's economic portfolio.

And beyond its direct economic benefits, tourism, especially international tourism, is still among the best ways to increase the visibility of the region. If we have as a goal to become a stronger node in the global web of business and interpersonal relationships, what better way to accomplish that than to have people from around the world enjoying themselves here. And you never know when a person on a pleasure trip will stumble upon an opportunity to do business.

Measuring the economic impact of tourism is tricky, since most of the businesses that serve visitors also serve local customers. A study sponsored by the Washington State Department of Commerce found that in 2009, travel spending in the three county region totaled $8.6 billion and supported 69,000 direct jobs and $2.6 billion in payroll.[23] Multipliers in this industry are low, at about 1.45. So, if the jobs found in the study all reflect spending by people coming from outside the area, the visitor industry supports a total of about 100,000 jobs in the region. The average job in this industry does not pay very well, but remember, many of those jobs are available to people with low skills who do not have a lot of employment options.

The region seems to put up pretty good number when it comes to employment in the visitor related industries, but they are at best average by national standards. Seattle: "nice place to live, but you wouldn't want to visit there."

In its attempts to boost tourism, Seattle, it seems, suffers from challenges on both the domestic and international fronts. On the domestic side, we have the old upper-left-hand corner problem. Seattle is still out of the way, and although it makes sense to package Seattle along with Portland and Vancouver, the bundle still seems less than compelling, especially for those who still have not seen the Golden Gate Bridge. In keeping with the perception of isolation, Seattle lacks a really big, obvious draw. It will never be in the company of New York or Los Angeles, but even within the next tier of Western cities, Seattle does not have the perfect weather and family attractions of San Diego, the mythic scenes of San Francisco, the thrills of Las Vegas or the golf, spas and heat of Arizona.

Yes, we have all that natural beauty, but I am not sure that most potential visitors know quite what to do with it. Ecotourism is a lovely niche, but one with limited appeal: hard to imagine that family on the street corner booking a bird watching kayak trip through the Skagit delta. And in a way, selling the natural beauty of the region might work against Seattle itself, as caravans drive away from the city toward the North Cascades or the San Juan Islands, or head off to the Olympic Peninsula, searching for Bella, Edward and Jacob in Forks.

If potential domestic visitors can't quite move Seattle to the top of their list, potential international tourists simply have never heard of Seattle. And even if they have heard of Seattle, few images float out there on the global ether that might give them some reason to consider coming here. Ichiro Suzuki served as a one-man tourism promotion agency, but, as we learned after his departure in 2012, it is dangerous to pin a marketing strategy on a single celebrity.

To be fair, though, some good things have happened with the visitor industry in the past fifty years. The Washington State Convention Center in Seattle has provided a big bump in visitors, especially in the off-season when weather keeps the casual visitor away. Because of its location and configuration, the Convention Center has consistently attracted upscale meetings of doctors, dentists and other big spending professionals. The center expanded once, but has hit a snag in its efforts to grow again to provide capacity for even larger events.

Big league sports have also provided a boost to tourism. With the only NFL and MLB teams northwest of that arc drawn from San Francisco through Denver to Minneapolis, Seattle has a lot of potential fans. And the Mariners in particular, with Japanese ownership and prominent Japanese players, have drawn large numbers of visitors from Japan. Out-of-town ticket sales are so important to the Mariners that they insisted on a retractable roof for Safeco Field so no games would get rained out and disappoint fans who had traveled hundreds or thousands of miles for a game.

More recently, the arrival of cruise ships on the Seattle waterfront has brought thousands of visitors through the city. Many of the cruise ships that ply Caribbean and Mexican waters during the winter move to the Alaska market in the summer. Originally, because these ships fly a foreign flag, they had to operate out of Vancouver. Now, with faster ships the cruise lines can circumvent that problem. In 2012 Seattle had about 200 sailings from its three dock spaces. The Port of Seattle estimates that each sailing generates about $2 million in economic impact in the Seattle area, making this a nice bit of work—seasonal, but still a welcome addition.[24]

Military

Although hardly entrepreneurial enterprises, the military bases of the region constitute an important part of the economic fabric. We include military bases in the traded sector because the Department of Defense brings considerable money into the state to pay for operations at the bases, the benefits of which are "exported" to the rest of the country in the form of national security. Not quite like selling widgets on the world market, but the economic impact is the same.

All of the service branches have operations in Washington, although the Marine Corps presence is relatively small. An economic impact study conducted by the Washington State Economic Development Commission in 2010 found that the federal bases in the Puget Sound area (that is, excluding the National Guard) had a total of 90,000 uniformed and civilian personnel.[25] These are divided almost equally between the various naval bases around Puget Sound that make up Navy Region Northwest, and the massive Joint Base Lewis-McChord.

Starting with the Navy, it has four principal facilities on Puget Sound, and two smaller ones. The oldest facilities are found along Sinclair Inlet in Bremerton. The Navy has operated out of Bremerton since 1891, and although the ships have gotten much larger since then, fleets of tugboats do manage to maneuver aircraft carriers through the narrow gap of Rich Passage at high tide. The Navy presence at Bremerton has two components, the Puget Sound Naval Shipyard, with thousands of civilian employees, and the Bremerton Naval Base, which serves as homeport for a carrier group.

Not far from Bremerton, at Bangor, along Hood Canal, lies the Navy's Trident Submarine base. This base serves as the West Coast homeport for Trident nuclear submarines, which carry the most secure portion of the nation's nuclear deterrent. Built on the site of a former naval ammunition depot, this base opened in 1977 and has received periodic upgrades. Construction at Bangor turned the neighborhood of Silverdale from a wide spot in the road into a major urban center. The Bremerton and Bangor facilities both operate under the command of Naval Base Kitsap.

In an effort to diversify its economy away from such a strong reliance on Boeing's Paine Field operations, Snohomish County leaders pursued siting of a naval base in Everett. Everett was selected as a new homeport in 1984 and the base opened in 1994. Naval Station Everett, on the waterfront just below downtown, serves as the homeport for a carrier group.

When an aircraft carrier is not on deployment (which is the majority of the time) the air wing needs a home. The Whidbey Island Naval Air Station, in Oak Harbor, serves as the land base for the air wings of the carriers based in both Everett and Bremerton. It also has served as the base for the Navy's fleet of electronic jamming planes and some of its P-3 Orion submarine chasers.

Puget Sound is home to two lesser known bases. On Indian Island, just across from Port Townsend, lies Naval Magazine Indian Island, where the Navy stores and maintains munitions for its fleet. At Keyport, near Poulsbo, the Navy operates its Undersea Warfare Center, which maintains torpedoes and other underwater weapon systems.

The Army has operated out of Fort Lewis, in Pierce County, since 1917. This facility has grown over the years, coming out on the winning end of the various rounds of base closings that shuttered military facilities since the 1980s. As other Army bases in the west, like Fort Ord, in Monterey, closed, missions and personnel came to Fort Lewis. The base now has Ranger and Stryker armored units, and regularly sent large groups to the wars in Afghanistan and Iraq.

Back when the military's strategic air capacity still resided in the Army, the Pentagon decided it needed an air base to protect assets in the Puget Sound area, and the Army acquired Tacoma Field from Pierce County, creating McChord Field. Later, when the Air Force became a separate service, that base was renamed McChord Air Force Base. It lies immediately adjacent to Fort Lewis, next to the city of Lakewood in Pierce County. The base has always specialized in cargo and logistics, and the massive airlift planes can be seen flying over the south Sound area.

In 2005, during another round of base realignments, the Pentagon decided to put McChord back under the aegis of the Army, creating Joint Base Lewis-McChord. The merger took place in 2010, giving the combined operation a total of about 47,000 uniformed and civilian personnel.

In addition to the Army, Navy and Air Force, the Coast Guard has a substantial presence in the region. District 13 has over 2,500 personnel, patrolling waters, maintaining aids to navigation, and operating the nation's (diminishing) fleet of ice breakers.[26] The Coast Guard also operates the Vessel Traffic Control System on Puget Sound which maintains the safety of shipping lanes.

The Commission's study found that the 90,000 military personnel in the Puget Sound area (which does not include those serving in the Washington National Guard) command a total payroll of about $4.7 billion. The bases spent another $1.3 billion in the regional economy. The multipliers for military bases tend to be low, since most personnel are not highly paid, and much of the household spending by personnel and their families takes place on-base. Nonetheless, the total jobs impact for the bases in the Puget Sound area probably comes in at around 130,000.[27] That puts the military up in the company of the other major pillars of the region economy.

The impact of the military bases in the state goes beyond just the activities in those facilities, however. Although many soldiers, sailors and airmen go back to their hometowns after mustering out of their service, many stick around, adding to the region's skill base. An important component of regional economic strategies has been to figure out how to capture those skills most efficiently and get former military personnel into the workforce quickly. In addition to the younger veterans, many career military personnel retire in the region. Not only to they often go on to second careers, adding to the region's experienced skill pool, they enjoy pensions that contribute to the overall income of the region.

Capital of the Northwest

Although not an industry or a cluster in the strict sense, Seattle does owe a certain amount of its prosperity to its historic role as a regional service center for the northwest part of the country. Offices in Seattle provide a wide range of private and government services to residents and businesses in five states, and sometimes beyond.

The federal government operates regional offices, such as the Environmental Protection Agency Region 10, or the Federal Transit Administration Region 10. Foreign countries operate consular offices in Seattle.

As private services increase in sophistication, they become less and less available in smaller communities. People will come to the major hospitals in Seattle for highly specialized treatments. Retailers operate outlets in Seattle, and increasingly in Bellevue, that can be found nowhere else in the Northwest. Fans come from all over the Northwest to attend major league sports events, and the opera, symphony, ballet and theaters also draw audiences from well outside the region.

For any one organization, business with customers from out of the area may not amount to a very large share of their overall sales. But in the aggregate, spending in the Seattle area by customers from the rest of the Northwest does add up.

In search of balance and diversification

In 1957 Fred Haley pointed out the region's dependence on natural resource-based industries, and urged that leaders find new, more advanced ways to grow the economy. Little did Fred know that within a decade he would have his wish: by that point, half of the regional economy rested on the shoulders of the commercial aerospace industry. By 1970 no one needed reminding that industrial monoculture has large risks, and the quest for diversification began again. In the 1970s and 1980s some promising new industries, particularly in the "diversified manufacturing" segment, began to have an impact on the economy. The region grew well through the 1970s, and again after the recession of the early 1980s, all without much help from Boeing, which remained flat.

It appeared that maybe the region had achieved a level of diversification of its economic base that would shield it from another drubbing like it had taken in 1970 and 1980. Then came software, fueling a growth in population and wealth not seen since the gold rush, and vaulting the Seattle area to the highest ranks of average incomes. It seems that we had gone from having half of our eggs in one basket to having nearly half the eggs about evenly split between two baskets, aerospace and software.

What about the baskets with the other half of the eggs? Port and trade activity has done well, as has that catch-all of diversified manufacturing. The military remains a large presence, although one with limited impact off the bases. Life sciences certainly has a bright future, but like the military, it spins out limited impacts. National retail is intriguing, and we have the opportunity to build on our current assets and make that sector into a bigger part of the economy. The natural resource-based industries that built Seattle's economy are still alive and well in the state, although not a big presence in the Puget Sound area. And tourism continues to generate ardent ambivalence.

So overall, I think the region has made major progress toward diversification. But maybe that is the wrong way to look at it. Whatever industries arise in the future, through the Schumpeterian process of creative destruction, will grow up here because they find the right people living in the region. So, rather than just looking for a diversity of industries, we should look for a diversity of talent resident in the area.

Chapter 7

Who's In Charge Here?

conomic progress of the sort described in the preceding chapters
does not happen in a vacuum. All businesses rely to some degree
on the local infrastructure, services and regulatory systems
described in Chapter 5. The quality of those services is shaped, in turn,
by decisions made by local leaders.

As we will find out, however, leadership at the local level is far from
simple. The lines between the public, private and non-profit sectors can
blur in ways that would, at the state or federal level, cause great concern
but that raise few eyebrows at the local level. In discussing the leadership process at the local level we often talk about "governance" as
opposed to "government." The latter refers strictly to formal structures
whereas the former describes the larger, more complex arrangements
that provide public goods and services on the ground and give direction
to policymakers. Much of the activity in the public sphere at the local
level involves more than government agencies, so to describe just what
those agencies do gives an incomplete picture.

Local governments provide the majority of the public services we
experience on a daily basis: roads, schools, police, fire, water, sewer, etc.
This level of government remains, however, something of a mystery to
many. The U.S. Constitution does not mention local governments at all,
leaving them entirely up to states under the Tenth Amendment. Cities
and towns have their origins in the Middle Ages, and in the U.S. they

grew up and evolved organically as rural areas developed and urbanized areas expanded and generated a need for local services. The organic structures that worked adequately for 150 years have been challenged over the past fifty years as metropolitan areas developed large, integrated regional economies that transcend political boundaries.

Making matters even more complicated, local governments below the county level have a fundamentally different underpinning. They are "corporate" in nature, and not locked in mosaics or necessarily tied to specific territories like states or counties. Although local governments do have physical boundaries and must abide by federal and state constitutions, we can almost think of them as businesses or clubs or associations that exist to provide some specific services. For example, there is little practical difference between a public water district and a private homeowners association that manages a community water system. Unlike counties or states, local governments can be created, dissolved or merged, expanded or contracted, all with the approval of the "members." In fact, early city governments did take the form of legal corporations, and we still use the term "municipal corporation" and refer to areas covered by cities as "incorporated."

States authorize all local governments and have ultimate control over them. The U.S. Supreme Court made this clear in 1868 with the Dillon Rule:

> *Municipal corporations owe their origin to, and derive their powers and rights wholly from, the legislature. It breathes into them the breath of life, without which they cannot exist. As it creates, so may it destroy. If it may destroy, it may abridge and control.*[1]

Each state has its own particular rules for local governments and dictates what those governments can and cannot do, especially how they can raise revenue. Although they may impose requirements on cities and special purpose districts, for stormwater treatment or educational standards, for example, states are usually reluctant to be too heavy handed when dealing with local governments, especially when it comes to sensitive issues like land use.

According to the 2007 Census of Governments, the country has 36,011 cities, towns and townships, 13,051 independent school districts and 37,381 other special purpose districts.[2] These governments can overlap each other in service territory, such that one house might be covered by several at the same time, each performing its own specific service. Boundaries do not need to be coterminous in most cases, so it is common to have, for instance, two or more school districts serving a single city, a fire district spread across several cities or a transit district covering several counties.

The three counties that make up the greater Seattle area encompass 78 cities and towns, 48 school districts and 181 other special purpose districts, including nine port districts, 67 fire districts, 59 water and sewer districts, nine park districts and one cemetery district.[3] Altogether these local governments keep about 1,800 elected officials busy several evenings a month. Adding to this complexity, the region has a number of independent tribal governments that operate within an entirely different framework.

This book provides an economic history of the Seattle area, so while it might be interesting to delve into the broader political history of the area over the past fifty years, we'll stick to those parts of the story tied to Seattle's economic evolution. As such, we will not spend time on the fine grain of election outcomes nor will be we able to get into some important developments, such as Seattle's unique experience with school desegregation or the various police scandals that have rocked local governments. I will leave it to another, braver, author to write the complete political history of the post-Dave Beck era.

Understanding local politics

For local politics to make any sense, we need to move away from the divisions that shape politics at the national (and to a large extent the state) level. The big existential issues that tend to define "liberal" and "conservative" nationally—foreign policy and defense, social policy, church-state issues, national indebtedness—do not appear at all, or very prominently, at the local level. An entirely different set of issues defines life in local politics. The distinction between national and local politics is illustrated by the difficulty that Rudy Giuliani had getting traction as a presidential candidate: he had run a jurisdiction larger than all but 11 states, yet he struggled to seem a peer of even small-state governors, and wore his party label uncomfortably. National leaders tend to start out in state houses, not city halls. Although many local governments remain partisan, traditional ideological and party distinctions do not mean much in them.

So we need some other frame to understand local politics, especially as it affects local investment and economic development. Fortunately the sociologists have given us a useful one, the cosmopolitan/local continuum introduced in Chapter 1.[4] For our purposes, the cosmopolitan/local continuum is defined by the degree to which individuals perceive that they have a stake in the growth and development of the broader community—that is, the expansion of the economic base. This does not suggest some sort of moral virtue or selfishness: cosmopolitans and locals are equally self-interested but pursue that self-interest in different ways.

Cosmopolitans support public investments, services and growth-friendly regulatory approaches because such activities directly or indirectly enhance their well-being. A businessperson with a local customer base wants to see that customer base grow. The administrator of a charitable organization wants to see incomes, and therefore contributions, grow. A labor leader favors projects that provide high wage, union construction jobs. A panhandler will get more handouts if a booming economy puts more people on the sidewalk with more cash in their pockets. Cosmopolitans are not necessarily wealthier or more worldly, but simply occupy positions where economic growth has a pay-off for them.

Locals, on the other hand, do not need economic growth to guarantee their security. In fact, for many locals, economic growth brings negatives, in the form of higher housing prices, traffic, crowding, competition for jobs and a general threat to the charms of the place they enjoy living. A consultant with a national practice does not gain customers through local growth. A school teacher gets paid the same whether the parents of his students do well or not. A retiree on a fixed income would rather not see a property tax increase to pay for a civic improvement, no matter how attractive. Locals may or may not be wealthy and worldly, but whatever their status, they do not perceive that the quality of their lives will be enhanced, or their security protected, through local economic growth.

We can find perhaps the best illustration of the cosmopolitan/local divide in the matter of professional sports facilities. When local leaders ask taxpayers in a metropolitan area to pay all or part of the cost of building a new football stadium, baseball park or arena, attitudes fall out along predictable lines. The cosmopolitans, quite reasonably, call attention to the economic benefits of the facility, citing the revenue from visitors and the national media exposure. They also note that sporting events add to the quality of life that brings high-demand talent to the region—businesses find it much easier to recruit people to a "major league" city. The locals, also quite reasonably, say that sports are fine, but that the fans themselves can pay for the facilities. When the city has a shortage of affordable housing, threadbare parks and crumbling bridges, why should taxpayers fork over to build a palace for rich sports fans and ludicrously overpaid athletes?

Now, out in the political pasture, the cosmopolitans are easy to pick out of the herd, since they tend to make themselves visible and their preferences unambiguous. Locals are trickier. Many of the neighborhood activities and amenities they champion are quite wonderful and make the community a better place. But a healthy region must be more than just the sum of nice, unchanging neighborhoods, and when localism veers into opposition to essential projects and to responsible approaches to unavoidable change, it becomes troublesome. NIMBY[5] reactions can be helpful in calling attention to impacts that can be mitigated, but taken to extremes can be quite destructive.

Emergence of the Seattle progressive–cosmopolitan

For most of its history Seattle has leaned toward the cosmopolitan side. The region has always had plenty of people with a local orientation, but history suggests they have carried the day less often than the cosmopolitans. Seattle's earliest settlers were unrepentant boosters who pushed growth and change at every opportunity. A direct and continuous thread runs from the Denny party that named their settlement "New York one-of-these-days" all the way to the present leadership that travels the globe spreading the word about Seattle and the Puget Sound area.

Leaders have regularly received approval for major infrastructure investments from R.H. Thompson's water system to the floating bridges across Lake Washington to the Metro sewer system to Seattle's own Big Dig through downtown. If you have any reason to doubt Seattle's cosmopolitan roots, consider that the University of Washington opened in 1861 when Seattle had perhaps 1,000 souls, few of whom had finished high school. The locally-funded Territorial University building represented a totally irrational act of optimism about the future, promoted by cosmopolitans in cork boots.

Although one might expect a more local orientation on the part of suburban communities, that is far from the case. In a 1958 election, the proposed Metro sewage treatment system received a higher percentage of the vote in the suburbs than in Seattle. Bellevue and Kirkland have invested hugely in elaborate and expensive park systems that go well beyond the needs of local residents. And as we've seen, the King County suburban crescent has a larger international population than Seattle.

In reality, cosmopolitan/local is not a divide, but a continuum, with some die-hards at either end and most voters strung out along the line. The middle shifts with the times and the business cycle, and both ends of the continuum have had their successes in recent years. The cosmopolitans won the day in the 1990s when taxpayers ended up funding a rail transit system, a new ballpark for the Mariners, a new stadium for the Seahawks and Sounders, a symphony hall as well as an expensive downtown parking garage And during this time the Port of Seattle expanded terminals and the airport. But the 1990s also saw locals succeed with the CAP initiative to limit downtown building heights and efforts to kill a waterfront redevelopment plan, the Seattle Commons park project and an attempt to bid on the Olympic Games.

The overall cosmopolitan orientation of the region should come as no surprise. Political cultures are surprisingly sticky and durable. Seattle's culture began on an adventuresome note and gelled with the Klondike Gold Rush and the expansion of trade with Asia. Since then Seattle has attracted enough similarly oriented people to keep the underlying cosmopolitan outlook strong. Moreover, the mobility and fluidity of much of the population base tends to discourage the rootedness that engenders a more localist perspective. Migrants self-select, so people who move to Seattle today come with some expectation that they will work in growing, changing, unpredictable industries.

More than any other factor, though, the region's cosmopolitan outlook has been maintained by the presence of the Boeing Company. Boeing has always focused on new, risky ventures and has sought ways to capture more of the global aerospace marketplace. Boeing's long time horizons make optimism about the future a requirement for emotional survival. Furthermore, the company's up and down fortunes over the years have undermined the stability and predictability that a localist orientation requires. A strong cosmopolitan base grows out of the presence of a company that has had as many as 100,000 employees whose livelihoods are tied very directly to the vicissitudes of the global economy.

In the late 1960s and early 1970s Seattle underwent a political shift, with its cosmopolitan nature making a significant pivot. This shift manifested itself first in a change in the city charter to strengthen the mayor's office and bring some departments, notably City Light, under closer control. A group of reformers, working under the banner of Choose an Effective City Council (CHECC), successfully replaced most of the city council with new blood over the course of two elections. Then, in 1969, a 33-year old Democrat state senator easily defeated the establishment candidate for Mayor.

The old guard that had created the World's Fair and promoted the infrastructure investments of Metro and Forward Thrust seemed awkward and ill-suited to deal with the changes happening in urban America. Moreover, city government had become moribund at best, and downright corrupt in places. When the new young Turks took over, things happened quickly. A combination of the new crowd at City Hall and newly empowered citizen groups stopped urban renewal projects that would have demolished the Pike Place Market and much of Pioneer Square. Instead, both areas were successfully restored at public expense.

This new progressive crowd, coming out of CHECC, the Argus newspaper, the Seattle Weekly, and the offices of Senator Warren Magnusson and Mayor Wes Uhlman, came to dominate city politics. In working to clean up city government and save the Market and Pioneer Square, they may have viewed themselves as liberals, fighting the conservatives of the old line downtown business establishment. But in fact they were simply a new breed of cosmopolitan. They had no qualms about growth, as such, but saw the value of preserving and enhancing an attractive urban landscape. The leader of the Pike Place Market campaign was an architect, Victor Steinbrueck, and others in the movement had planning backgrounds. The ethos of the city had shifted from promoting a sort of generic economic expansion to promoting growth based on uniquely local

features and a high quality of life. This hybrid progressive cosmopolitan-
ism has defined the dominant political culture within the city limits of
Seattle for the past forty years, and the young radicals of 1969 are now
establishment figures in their own right.

Outside of Seattle, things have evolved differently. Newer suburban
cities, although cosmopolitan in their populations, have had fewer major
decisions across which we can evaluate their political cultures in terms
of the cosmopolitan/local continuum. Until the mid-1980s, Seattle's suburbs were predominantly bedroom communities with local concerns. The
Tiebout Hypothesis, mentioned in Chapter 1, makes the point that as
smaller suburban communities solidify their own particular identities,
the residents of those cities elect leaders committed to minimizing
change.[6] Most suburban elected officials view their job as dealing with
concerns of their small city. With the aversion to change that is evident
in most of those communities, many, if not most of their elected officials
would probably lean toward the local side of the spectrum, at least with
respect to their city.

But as will be discussed below, the Seattle area has always relied on
federated approaches to regional issues. A body of local elected officials
governed the original Metro until the early 1990s. A federated body governs Sound Transit, the region's rail transit and express bus system.
Local officials draft countywide planning policies and the Puget Sound
Regional Council, the region's metropolitan planning organization, is a
federated body. The work of these groups involves mostly planning and
infrastructure that accommodates and even encourages growth and
change, making that work essentially cosmopolitan in nature. Dozens of
elected officials in the region find themselves part of both locally focused
city councils and regionally focused federated bodies.

But before we get to those governments and elected officials, we will
take another detour through some back roads of political science and
sociology. Interesting stuff—don't skip it!

Who governs?

A century ago the answer to that question in most big cities would have
been easy: the Boss. Machine politics grew out of the rapid growth of
cities in the nineteenth century and the influx of waves of immigrants

who happily sold their political support. The machines were almost feu-dal in nature, with the bosses protecting their clients and providing patronage jobs and a safety net in exchange for unwavering political support and tolerance of high level corruption and poor services. Reforms in the Progressive Era took aim at machine politics and by the middle of the twentieth century most machines had faded away.

But it was not clear who, in the post-machine era, really ran cities. A series of studies in the 1950s, most notably those by Robert Dahl (whose book was titled *Who Governs?*) and Edward Banfield tried to discern exactly who has influence in cities and how they exercise that influence. These scholars concentrated on understanding two competing ideas about local politics: pluralism and elitism.[7]

Pluralism suggests a messy but essentially open local government that gets things done in a clean, but not necessarily organized way. The mayor and city council sit at the center of the process and all groups have more or less equal access to them. Elitism, as the term suggests, evokes the "ten rich white guys smoking cigars in a downtown club" image. Elitism holds that while a city government may appear open and accessible, powerful individuals operating behind the scenes manipulate outcomes to suit their financial and personal interests.[8] Dahl and Banfield fell on the pluralist side, observing that the cities they studied had more or less open processes. The optimism of the pluralist camp came under severe strain in the 1960s, though, when one city after another experienced severe crisis and governments seemed unresponsive to those affected. In this case the influence of shadowy elites seemed a plausible explanation.

But as academics and practitioners looked at cities more closely—the 1960s and 1970s was the golden era of urban studies—neither pluralism nor elitism seemed very satisfactory. Clearly not everyone had equal access to government, and real estate and other business interests wielded disproportionate influence, especially during the era of urban renewal. At the same time, no one has ever found a situation in which an unelected elite really pulled all the strings: elitism has a nice visceral feel for the unempowered, but no one ever proved it existed anywhere. With both competing concepts of urban governance failing to provide very good explanations for what was happening in cities, a new school of thought emerged and continues to prevail today: urban regime theory.[9]

Regime theory borrows from both pluralism and elitism, but begins from a different place. Rather than thinking of power and influence as abstractions or ends in themselves, regime theory focuses on the goals of governance, emphasizing the "power to" instead of the "power over." Economic development lies at the heart of regime theory, which assumes that local governments do not have the resources to build communities and must solicit private investment. Regime theory says that the public-private coalition efforts we have become accustomed to seeing around major local initiatives are not the exception, but rather the rule.

Articulated most comprehensively by political scientist Clarence Stone, regime theory holds that cities are run by semi-permanent coalitions of public and private actors that place an emphasis on economic outcomes. Like pluralism, regime theory suggests that the governing coalition is relatively open. Like elitism, it assumes that private parties use influence to advance their economic interests. They key is that in any city, some people who are in positions of institutional authority will find themselves part of the governing coalition and some will find themselves excluded. Admission to the governing coalition is available to just about any individual or organization provided they do two things.

To begin with, they must agree to the coalition's agenda. The agenda is critical because in defining the governing coalition by the "power to" we need to know what, specifically, the coalition has in mind to do. A healthy governing coalition has an overall point of view about what needs to be done, and some identifiable set of goals and objectives for improving the city and managing it competently. But many people in positions of authority will disagree with the prevailing agenda and, as a result, find themselves outside the coalition. For example, if the current governing coalition has a cosmopolitan orientation and promotes growth-inducing investments, a city councilmember with roots in locally-focused neighborhood concerns will not fit in.

Then, a prospective member of the coalition must bring resources to bear on the pursuit of the agenda. Resources may be very concrete, such as real estate investment and job creation. They may take the form of political power, such as delivering votes on referenda or the ability to raise campaign funds. Resources may be even less tangible, such as support by influential ethnic or community leaders. Whatever the nature of the resource, a coalition member must bring something to the party that advances the cause. Simply signing on to the agenda and attending meetings will not be enough.

This second requirement for a governing coalition explains why mayors rarely succeed in governing from a base of localist neighborhood support. As we'll see next, not all Seattle mayors in the past fifty years have assembled smoothly functioning governing coalitions, and one reason is their attempt to rely on neighborhood or community groups that cannot amass the resources the mayor needs to govern. Mayors who have gotten elected as the "neighborhood candidate" find themselves gravitating toward the business community and the civic and non-profit establishment, often to the disappointment of those who got them elected in the first place.

So who would we find as members of a typical governing coalition? Generally the mayor and a functioning majority of the city council will form the core of a healthy coalition, since little can get implemented without them. Some key bureaucrats who have discretionary authority for major programs might be considered coalition members. "Downtown business" leaders will usually be part of the coalition if they are on the same page as the mayor. Union leaders, university presidents, leaders of large non-profit organizations and leaders of religious and ethnic communities may also be coalition members if they can bring real resources to the table.

It is important to note that the governing coalition hangs together across issues. So, the president of the downtown merchants association will be expected to support expansion of port terminals, just as the head of the Teamsters local will be expected to support a parks levy. The coalition does not build itself for each issue that comes up, but relies on its members to support the entire agenda, or, if not actively support all parts of it, at least not oppose any part. Thus, the agenda from which the coalition operates cannot be too eccentric and cannot embrace truly fringe issues that will strain relationships.

Having read a description of what might constitute a governing coalition, don't go looking for a directory with a list of members; for the most part, governing coalitions do not know that they exist. Rather, do a thought exercise. Imagine that the mayor has a meeting one afternoon with a location consultant looking for a site for a new facility that will employ 1,000 people. The consultant lays out a long list of requirements, some quite expensive, and asks the mayor to respond within a week. When the meeting ends, which ten people does the mayor call first? Later, after the city wins the competition, and the CEO of the company comes to a private reception with the mayor at the old oak-paneled club, who is in the room? Who isn't? And which club member picks up the tab?

Urban regime theory answers Dahl's question of "who governs" by sketching out a recognizable pattern from contemporary American cities. The framework applies less in smaller suburban cities and needs some adaptation to explain regional leadership. Nonetheless, regime theory has become a widely accepted lens for viewing local governance. The line between the public and private sectors blurs because city governments cannot accomplish much on their own. Cities develop mostly through private investment, and that private investment, in turn, requires infrastructure and support from city government.

With the dialectic emergence of urban regime theory, have the elitists gone away? No. For some observers, regime theory is just as naive as pluralism and therefore insufficient to explain the obvious inequities visible in cities. These observers cannot imagine wealthy developers holding hands and singing Kumbaya with mayors, councilmembers, the United Way, the chamber of commerce the Urban League and the labor council. Elitism has morphed into the more sophisticated, and actually quite plausible, theory of the "growth machine."[10]

Like regime theory, growth machine theory concentrates on the "power to," but really only concerns itself with the power to develop land and build private buildings for private gain. In this view, local governments are manipulated by coalitions of mostly private actors that have a direct or indirect stake in real estate: developers, bankers, construction firms, unions, architects, engineers, suppliers, etc. Elected officials will embrace the growth machine because local governments rely on expanded property, sales and business tax revenues that come from increased building activity. Unlike more traditional elites of previous theory, growth machines have only one thing on their mind—making money by building things—and if they can do that, they will be indifferent to aspects of urban life that do not touch on the development process.

Although the academic proponents of urban regime and growth machine theories appear at odds with each other, the two ideas do not seem mutually exclusive. A poorly maintained urban regime can deteriorate to the point where it becomes a growth machine. It is not uncommon for city leaders to become so wrapped up in the need to promote development that they consciously or unconsciously exclude important players from their governing coalition and find themselves surrounded only by the forces of development and growth.

I hope that by sticking with this ramble through the question of Who Governs? you will gain a better understanding of how Seattle leadership has evolved over the past fifty years and who really runs things today.

Local government in Seattle since 1962

Now let's look over the past fifty years to see how, within the city of Seattle itself, governing coalitions have evolved to reflect the leadership styles of various mayors.[11]

In the early 1960s, as the World's Fair was taking shape, Gordon Clinton sat in the Seattle Mayor's office. Clinton was a young, energetic Republican who, like many of his fellow party members of that age, held views that today's Republicans might find far too liberal. Clinton was a major promoter of infrastructure investment, a key supporter of the creation of Metro and a negotiator of the route of Interstate 5 through Seattle. He was also a pioneer in housing desegregation and created Seattle's first Sister City arrangement with Kobe, Japan. And, significantly, Clinton actively promoted and facilitated the World's Fair, itself.

Clinton has been well regarded as a mayor. Major infrastructure projects, and the World's Fair itself, demonstrate that he had a strong governing coalition behind him. As a prominent Republican and Methodist, Clinton had natural affinities with the downtown business establishment. His work for fair housing and building relations with Japan gave him credibility with minority groups at a time when that was not necessarily something mayors sought. Although not without its faults and losses, the Clinton years would have gained the approval of Dahl and Banfield as an excellent example of the pluralism they observed in post-war cities.

James d'Orma "Dorm" Braman followed Clinton as mayor in 1964, serving until becoming Deputy Secretary of Transportation in the Nixon Administration. Like Clinton, Braman actively promoted infrastructure investment and he worked tirelessly on the Forward Thrust bond program and on the ultimately unsuccessful effort to build a rail transit system in Seattle. Perhaps because of his small town, small business background (he was a high school dropout from Bremerton who owned a lumber yard) Braman was ill at ease in dealing with the turmoil of the inner city in the 1960s. He was, however, considered a smart and successful mayor, able to exert leadership from the relatively weak mayor's position of the time.

Braman, like Clinton, enjoyed a positive relationship with the city's business community—he was a business owner himself—and used that relationship to build support for major investments, including the Kingdome. But he had no way of knowing that the governing coalition that had worked so well for the past generation was about to crumble under the weight of urban crisis and the economic strain of the Boeing Bust. Braman left for Washington D.C. six months before the election of 1969, with his term filled out by the council president, Floyd Miller.

With CHECC having already elected a reform slate of city council candidates and with the new city charter giving the mayor much more power, the 1969 mayoral election would bring further change. The usual power structure—the chamber of commerce and the Central Association—put up their favorite candidate, Mort Frayne. Frayne was from an old Seattle family that owned a printing business. He lived in Broadmoor, Seattle's oldest gated community, and had served in the state legislature. But he was not an able speaker and although he would have made a decent mayor, as a candidate he struggled. His opponent, emerging from a crowded primary, was Wes Uhlman, a Democrat state senator from North Seattle. The very young and articulate Uhlman contrasted sharply with the older, less polished Frayne, and Uhlman won election easily.

From the beginning Uhlman had his hands full, mostly with internal operations. Seattle may have accomplished some great things in the sixties, but the underlying city government was a mess, after generations of corruption, nepotism and absent oversight under the previous weak mayor system. Uhlman challenged public employee unions and bureaucratic fiefdoms throughout the city, restructured departments, hired minorities and aggressive reformers as department heads, and generally upset apple carts all over town. As a result, he faced a recall election—and survived. Even with all the struggles he did make permanent changes in city government that were badly needed, and paved the way for the new progressive-cosmopolitan crowd to gain ascendance in city politics. His support for the preservation of Pioneer Square and the Pike Place Market permanently changed the prevailing idea of what economic progress meant.

Uhlman's tenure was hobbled by an exceedingly weak regional economy, which made it difficult to undertake any major development initiatives. The Boeing Bust began just as Uhlman took office, cutting tax revenues and putting a strain on city services. A few new office buildings went up downtown during his time in office, and King County built the Kingdome, using proceeds from the 1968 Forward Thrust campaign. But otherwise it was a decade of recovery.

Although he came into the mayor's office as a Democrat having defeated the establishment candidate, Uhlman did made peace with the business community. To pursue his aggressive government reform program he needed support from outside City Hall, and he found it at the chamber of commerce and, especially, among the city's minority leadership. The fact that his reforms have stuck to this day is a testament to the effectiveness of his administration and ability to keep the reform coalition together through a recall.

After narrowly losing the primary election for governor in 1976, Uhlman declined to pursue a third term for mayor in 1977. The open mayoral primary attracted a large cast of characters, including Charles Royer, a reporter for KING TV. As often happens in a crowded primary with multiple establishment candidates (four city councilmembers appeared on the ballot) one off-beat candidate squirts through, and that was Royer. After defeating former Uhlman planning director, and future mayor Paul Schell, Royer began what would be considered, charitably, a challenging first term. With his outsider status he felt no need to hire establishment figures and ended up with an administration possessing very little experience.

But as insurgent mayoral candidates often learn, winning an election as an outsider is one thing, but trying to govern as one is an entirely different matter. Royer needed to rebuild relationships with city councilmembers, several of whom he had defeated and all of whom he had skewered as a TV news reporter. The business community kept its distance, showing little enthusiasm for Royer's ideas.

But Royer proved a savvy politician and gradually assembled a serviceable governing coalition. He began, along with the chamber of commerce, the Intercity Visit program, now in its thirtieth year. This program, described later in this chapter, is the quintessential regime-building activity, as it educates a wide cross section of top leadership in a variety of issues. He expanded Seattle's Sister City program from four to thirteen pairings, and instituted an Office of International Affairs. And although his relationship with the downtown establishment was generally good, he did run afoul of business in his third term when he pushed through an increase in the city's business taxes to fund public safety, a function that business leaders thought should be a general fund priority. And his final project, a proposed waterfront redevelopment, received only half-hearted support from the business community and failed at the ballot.

Royer was, in many ways, the perfect mayor for the 1980s, serving as a bridge between the turmoil and restructuring of the early 1970s and the smoother years of the 1990s. His own transformation from outsider to insider reflected the evolution of city politics.

In terms of regime stability, a high water mark for city government in Seattle came during the 1990s under the administration of Norm Rice. Rice, an African American politician in a mostly white city, had been a popular city councilmember with a background in banking. Rice did not come out of the city's black establishment, nor did he, like Royer, arrive as an outsider. Loose ties to "local" constituent groups make it relatively easy for him to forge strong links with the city's business and non-profit communities. "Mayor Nice," with the help of Deputy Mayor Bob Watt, shaved off the rough edges of the Royer administration and generally maintained a city council majority for his priorities.

Rice succeeded in building an effective governing coalition because he had a coherent agenda around which his coalition could rally. Royer had struggled with his early community-based agenda because the coalition he assembled around that agenda had few resources. Rice, on the other hand, built his coalition from the beginning around two agenda items that would easily attract resources: improving public schools and revitalizing the downtown retail core. The business community strongly supported both agenda items and remained receptive to other things that Rice wanted to do. Neighborhood and ethnic groups generally approved of the city's new involvement with public schools, which was centered on the Families and Education Levy, a fund devoted to non-academic school improvements. Some neighborhood groups opposed Rice on the most expensive of the downtown improvements, but this opposition never threatened the projects and Rice left office a popular mayor.

Rice's successor in 1998, Paul Schell, never succeeded in building a workable governing coalition. Schell came out of the progressive-cosmopolitan generation of the early 1970s—he had served as community development director under Wes Uhlman—and had spent time as the Dean of the University of Washington Architecture School, as a Port Commissioner and developer of downtown restoration properties and boutique resort hotels. The business community strongly backed Schell's candidacy, partly out of genuine enthusiasm, but also out of naked fear of his opponent, councilmember Charlie Chong. Chong, a neighborhood activist from West Seattle, had survived a crowded primary election by capturing most of the "local" vote and letting the mainstream candidates split up the "cosmopolitan" vote.

Once elected, Schell pursued an idiosyncratic agenda that failed to much enthusiasm beyond his fellow urban architecture fans. A plan to light the city's bridges for the Millennium fell flat and seemed to reinforce a sense of elitism within the administration (Seattle could be like Paris!). Schell did oversee a new city hall and police station, as well as the new downtown library, designed by Rem Koolhaus. While successful, these projects failed to bind the mayor to the important constituencies he needed. But it was two massive public safety failures—the WTO fiasco of 1999 and the Mardi Gras riots of 2001—that led voters to see Schell as out of touch with the average Seattle resident. In the primary election of 2001 he came in third.

To be fair to Schell, though, we need to acknowledge that he faced two problems that Rice did not have to cope with. First, the election in the late 1990s of a series of neighborhood-based councilmembers made it difficult for Schell to round up council support. Whereas Rice and Royer could generally muster five votes for projects related to advancing the economy, Schell faced a more fractured council that had less interest in economic matters (this was the council that tried to ban circus animals and Navy submarines from the city). Many of these councilmembers did not last long in office, and the council returned to a more business-friendly group by the mid-2000s, but they did cause major headaches for Schell.

We also need to remember that Rice had presided over an eight-year period mostly characterized by growth and the growing prominence of Seattle: it must have been a fun time to be mayor. Schell, on the other hand, presided over the city during a really tough four years as described in Chapter 3.

Next in the mayor's office came Greg Nickels, the anti-Schell. A college drop-out from West Seattle, considered the last bastion of old blue-collar Seattle, Nickels had spent his entire career in and around politics. He had served as a council aide to future mayor Norm Rice and held a seat on the King County Council from 1987 to his election in 2001. Nickels had strong backing in the neighborhoods but had also spent considerable time as a county councilmember working on regional issues, especially rail transit. But even as he narrowly defeated City Attorney Mark Sidran, no one was quite sure what he stood for as far as city priorities. As a county councilmember he participated in major regional issues but had never weighed in strongly on Seattle city matters.

At the beginning of his administration Nickels played small-ball, exemplified by his proposal to station tow trucks near congested areas at rush hour to make sure accidents got cleared. In his mayoral campaign he frequently discussed the death of a young man that had occurred during the Mardi Gras riots of that year and vowed to improve public safety. Once elected he gradually he took on the air of a tactician and pragmatist, generally open to initiatives that made sense, but not seeming to operate from any larger vision, as Schell had attempted, or major priorities, as Rice had. Nickels' time in office is mostly considered successful, although like Schell he did not survive a primary, and also like Schell, it was a basic public safety failure—snow removal in his case—that sealed his fate. And the departure of the Seattle Supersonics in 2008 did not help.

Nickels' political position is a curious and unusual case for Seattle. A native of Chicago, he openly expressed his admiration for the Daley dynasty, and, intentionally or not, cultivated an air of ruthlessness (abetted by his deputy mayor, Tim, "The Shark" Ceis) that scared off challengers. He had only nominal opposition for re-election in 2005. In his second term, especially after the snowstorm disaster of December,

2008, polls consistently showed him as quite unpopular, but when the primary of 2009 came along, he did not draw any A-list challengers. Potentially strong candidates did not want to risk losing to him, and as a result, two unknown newcomers to city politics emerged from the primary, with Nickels coming in third.

Nickels had never assembled a governing coalition that would support him when his position weakened, and although the usual establishment players did back his candidacy in his final primary, that support was thin. Nickels' failure to build a strong coalition stemmed in part from a governing approach in which he distanced himself from the city council and did not invite close partners, but also from his lack of a coherent agenda around which coalition partners might rally. What the Nickels administration did embrace, however, was commercial development, in South Lake Union in particular. Nickels pushed for required zoning changes, a city-financed streetcar, South Lake Union Park, and the rebuilding of Mercer Street and the downtown Seattle tunnel, all of which facilitated the rapid growth of this area just north of downtown. Most of the development was undertaken by Vulcan, wholly owned by Microsoft co-founder Paul Allen, who had acquired large land holdings as a result of his funding of the failed Seattle Commons project.

In our description of local governing structures, the Nickels administration begins to look like a "growth machine." With his heavy focus on South Lake Union development and light focus on anything else, and with a governing coalition that sometimes seemed to consist mostly of himself and Paul Allen's real estate arm, the description seems to fit. Having concluded that, though, I do need to emphasize that the development of South Lake Union has proved extremely successful and has engendered little sustained opposition. History will, I think, be kind to Nickels, as his legacy is substantial. Time will soften the impression that he accomplished it in a very un-Seattle-like way.

The 2009 mayoral election, in which Nickels was ousted, gave us the singular character of Mike McGinn. McGinn, a lawyer, was brand new to electoral politics, but not to controversial issues. As a leader in the Sierra Club he had fought a number of local battles, and he based his mayoral candidacy on opposition to the proposed tunnel through downtown that was to replace the aging and dangerous Alaskan Way Viaduct. Having no ties at all to any part of the city's establishment, and having thoroughly alienated himself from most of it over the tunnel issue, McGinn began his term of office with no semblance of a functioning governing coalition. His support from the Sierra Club and other environmental groups proved of limited usefulness as these groups have very narrow agendas and bring few resources.

As of this writing McGinn has still not assembled a recognizable governing coalition. This has given rise to a curious situation in which the answer to the question of "who governs" might not include the mayor. The city council repeatedly rebuffed McGinn's legislative efforts and gave him a series of defeats on matters related to the tunnel, which proceeded despite his opposition. To their credit, McGinn and his appointees have proved competent at running city government and he has had reasonable success with budget and police challenges. But when it comes to outlining the future direction of the city, the leadership vacuum in 2012 is large. However, with the weakened economy and several major projects underway, perhaps the city can afford to take a breather.

Regional politics

While Seattle's boundaries became fixed by the mid-1950s, suburban areas changed dramatically. Small market towns like Redmond and Kent became booming cities, and Bellevue, which consisted of one small commercial strip in the 1930s, grew forty-story buildings. Smaller communities with their own local governments have distinct attractions, but fragmentation of a metropolitan area inhibits action on important infrastructure and services that regional governments do the best job of providing.

The problem, as Barnes and Ledebur point out, is that economic regions and political boundaries almost never line up.[12] So when local governments that serve just a portion of an economic region need to make investments, they can never be sure they will reap the full benefits of those investments: why build a road so commuters can pass through your city on their way from their home in another city to a job in yet another jurisdiction? Hence the interest in creating some larger government, the boundaries of which more closely match those of the economic region, to look after the major infrastructure and service requirements of the economy.

In the 1950s, as the need for improved regional governance became apparent, counties just did not fit the bill. County governments existed originally as subdivisions of state government that allowed state business to take place close to where people lived. (Some states laid out very small counties such that an individual could travel to the county seat and back on a horse in one day.) Thus, the root responsibilities of counties consist of courts that enforce state law, assessors and treasurers that collect state property taxes, elections officials who run state elections, and so forth. County Sheriffs were not meant to serve as police departments, but rather to assist with the courts and jails.

Counties certainly evolved beyond these basic state functions, but still lacked, and lack today, the taxing authority to provide urban-level services in unincorporated areas. And as neighborhoods in the urban counties have, one-by-one, incorporated or annexed to existing cities, counties have been left with smaller tax bases and fewer constituents who receive direct services. This, in turn, leads to diminished political legitimacy among city-dwellers, many of whom supported those incorporation and annexation with the specific purpose of getting away from county government. So, as suburban residents looked for ways to get the big things done, counties simply fell short as vehicles for action.

The first major attempt in the Seattle area to undertake a true regional action came in the 1950s when it became obvious that the areas ringing Lake Washington needed a central sewage collection and treatment system. Leaking septic tanks, as well as outright sewage dumping, had turned the lake into a cesspool, and summer algae blooms led to regular beach closures. But no individual jurisdiction, including the county, had the financing capacity or political strength to build trunk sewer lines and major treatment plants. A group spearheaded by Jim Ellis convinced the state legislature to authorize creation of metropolitan municipal corporations (metros), independent regional governments with substantial bonding capacity. The original enabling legislation permitted these new entities to undertake five other functions in addition to sewage treatment: transit, water supply, regional planning, regional parks and solid waste disposal. Each of these functions would require additional legislation before a metro could take them on.[13]

Metros would be governed by a federated board made up of elected officials from the cities and counties covered by them. Like special purpose districts, metros did not need to be coterminous with counties, and could provide service across county boundaries. In 1958, voters representing most of King County's urbanized areas approved the creation of the Municipality of Metropolitan Seattle (known simply as Metro) and construction of a sewage treatment system. In 1972 voters expanded Metro to include the entire county and gave it power to create a countywide transit system out of existing public and private bus systems, as well as a countywide sales tax to fund it. The Metro sewer system and transit system are both considered major successes.

Although it gave disproportionate board seats to Seattle and provided more extensive bus service within the city, Metro did have the effect of tying the cities in the county more closely together. Finally, suburban officials had a seat at the table and had real voting power. The suburbs put this power to work vividly in 1989 when the board voted to expand the Metro treatment plant at West Point, in Seattle, over the strong opposition of Seattle's Mayor Royer.

Metro was never able to move beyond its two services into the other four the legislature had authorized. Then, in 1989 several citizens, backed by the American Civil Liberties Union, filed a lawsuit in federal court challenging the constitutionality of Metro's governing structure, claiming it violated the one-person-one-vote doctrine. Indeed, seats on the board did not reflect population, with Seattle over-represented and unincorporated areas under-represented. A federal judge ruled against Metro in 1990, but left the remedy up to local officials to decide. In the end, voters approved a measure dissolving Metro and merging its functions into King County, which operates the transit and sewage treatment facilities today.

The story of Metro is important because of its success in cleaning up Lake Washington and providing infrastructure and services to enable growth. But the story also illustrates one way to bridge the central city/suburban city political gap. Suburban cities enjoy their independence but lack the capacity to build regional infrastructure. At the same time they have historically distrusted both central city government and county government. Having a decision-making role at Metro allowed suburban cities to mature as regional players, and even now with Metro gone, its impact remains, as suburban cities confidently participate in regional growth planning and in Sound Transit.

Formal regional governance has made little progress since the dissolution of Metro in 1992. The state Growth Management Act (GMA), put in place in 1990, requires cooperation between cities and counties, but since local plans are presumed valid unless challenged at the state level, individual cities maintain their fundamental land use prerogatives. Under the GMA cities must conform to a negotiated set of countywide planning policies, but experience has shown very few instances where a city was actually compelled to accept planning elements against its will. There are no real regional plans, but rather a series of countywide patchwork quilts of individual city plans and county plans covering only unincorporated areas, as one would expect from a bottom-up, federated process.

The GMA requires an extra, multi-county planning layer for the four-county region, overseen by the Puget Sound Regional Council (PSRC). This layer looks at the region from an even higher elevation, forecasting growth and sketching out very broad planning concepts. The PSRC, also a federated body governed by representatives of counties, cities and ports, does have an important tool, however. It serves as the metropolitan planning organization under federal law, and has authority over distribution of federal transportation funding. But again, the federated governance structure means that it makes few bold decisions and that its plans generally conform to the desires of the individual cities and counties.

Sound Transit, authorized by voters in the three-county region in 1996, is governed by yet another federated body, made up of city and county councilmembers. In making route and station decisions for the agency's light rail system, Sound Transit has mostly deferred to the wishes of cities. For example, the highly controversial decisions in 2011 and 2012 about how to route a light rail line through Bellevue divided the Bellevue City Council and the community. In the end the route was negotiated among city councilmembers and a decision presented to Sound Transit. The Sound Transit board itself, although requiring Bellevue to stick within budget parameters and service requirements, did not force a decision, and let the process within the city take its course.

In his 1994 book, *CitiStates*, Neal Peirce was among the first to take a close look at the emerging phenomenon of the global metropolitan region.[14] Seeing the need to do more than just muddle through with regional decision-making, Peirce advocated strongly for formal regional governments. A few metro areas in North America have had true regional structures, such as Nashville's uni-government and Toronto's two-tier system, but these have always been isolated exceptions. During the debate that followed the invalidation of Metro's governance structure, some held out hope that the Seattle area could move toward the original vision of Metro: a two-tier government structure that left most services at the city level but elevated some functions to the regional level.

The problem with regional government, however, has always been the threat that it poses to city, county and state governments. Under a two tier system cities would have to give up some traditional functions, leaving them with fewer services to deliver to constituents but the same responsibilities for overall quality of life. Counties in urbanized areas have, as noted, struggled to remain relevant beyond their function as agents of the state, and a parallel regional government would make counties even less visible. For the state, a strong regional government centered on Seattle would exert pressure to push more investment into the Seattle area, presumably at the expense of other parts of the state.

With all this opposition to regional government, who would support it? Good question. The entire concept of regional government flies in the face of the Tiebout Hypothesis, which posits that residents of a region self-select into cities that meet their own preferences for service levels and taxation. A regional government, however, needs to apply uniform tax and service levels across all cities, giving residents fewer choices. The gains from scale and efficiency that a regional government would bring are not necessarily an easy sell beyond good-government groups.

In the late 1980s, during a period of optimism about the possibilities for regional government, a group called King County 2000 spent three years analyzing the options for regional government and developed a series of recommendations. Neil McReynolds, chairman during the third year, and I spent a great deal of time and energy trying to generate enthusiasm for these relatively modest and incremental ideas. Alas, we got a lot of earnestly nodding heads, but few pledges of real support.

In the end, voters seem to fall back on the old quip that "our founders promised us democracy, not efficiency." For better or worse, the federated service-specific approach to regionalism in the Greater Seattle area will likely persist for some time.

General purpose regional government with an independent elected governing body may be a pipe dream, but one set of institutions does have a regional economic role: port authorities. Not only do the ports of Seattle, Tacoma and Everett generate tens of thousands of jobs, they also serve as symbols of the globalization of the region and as focal points for international activities. Like Boeing, the marine ports concentrate almost entirely on global business, which contributes to the cosmopolitan atmosphere of the region. Ports are managed by elected five-member commissions, with commissioners running countywide.

From a leadership perspective, ports find themselves in a delicate position. Their focus on trade and transportation makes them natural economic leaders. Ports have a stake in a large share of the region's economic activity, from manufacturing to tourism to agriculture, and benefit from growth in the state. The stated purpose of ports is economic development, and since that purpose can be very broadly defined, and since ports have access to a substantial amount of money, they find themselves tapped for diverse leadership roles. This can lead to criticism, and in the case of the Port of Seattle in the early 2000s, a harsh report from the State Auditor. For now we can assume that ports will have their hands full staying competitive in the tough world of ocean shipping and air service and will not exert broader regional leadership.

In thinking about this problem of regional governance, it is important to keep in mind that the rationale for regionalism has gradually shifted. From the 1950s through the 1980s, regionalism was a response to the proliferation of small jurisdictions that could not fund large infrastructure projects. Regional approaches were needed for coherent planning and construction of sewers, roads, transit systems and other major public facilities which central cities or the state had taken care of in simpler times. But by the 1990s the focus of regionalism had shifted to the larger picture of economic competitiveness: it was no longer enough that a region function smoothly. Now, a metropolitan area needed to demonstrate to the world that it can serve as an excellent platform for globally competitive business. As we'll see later in this chapter, that requires a different style of leadership.

Business and civic leadership

Our review of leadership experiences of the past fifty years centered on mayoral administrations, but as regime theory notes, successful mayors rely not only on agreeable city councils but also on business and civic leaders to provide the resources needed to carry out the coalition's agenda. As we saw, the least successful mayors were the ones who failed to establish sufficient working relationships with key individuals and organizations around the city.

The trajectory of business and civic power in the region has followed a gradual curve downward. In the earliest days businesspeople ran the city, and only gradually did politicians gain real influence. Even as late as 1987, in a special report by *The Seattle Times*, titled "Who Runs Seattle," businesspeople filled all ten slots for the most powerful figures in the region.[15] But most of those individuals were relatively old at the time, and the next generation failed to emerge as strongly. As a result, the business and civic voice has become somewhat less influential.

Nonetheless, business and civic organizations do provide essential resources required for effective governance, and we will now look at those groups. Space, and your patience, dear reader, does not permit a description of every civic organization in the region, so I will focus on just few of those that have had a large impact on regional development during the past few decades.

Seattle Metropolitan Chamber of Commerce

The chamber (full disclosure—I worked there for ten years) underwent a significant change near the beginning of our era, when they hired George Duff as their president. Duff came from Detroit and knew first-hand what urban problems looked like. But when he arrived in 1967, Seattle was flying high—Boeing was booming, Forward Thrust bonds would pass and provide key infrastructure investments, Major League Baseball was sending a team to Seattle, City Hall was led by a business-friendly mayor and council, and the World's Fair glow had not entirely faded. Then, in 1969, all that changed. Boeing laid off 60,000 people within six months, the Pilots lasted just one season and a new young, liberal mayoral candidate easily defeated the chamber's hand-picked successor to businessman Dorm Braman. And shortly thereafter, the big urban renewal projects in Pioneer Square and at the Pike Place Market that the chamber had championed, got killed.

Organizations adapt, and the chamber did manage to reach accommodation with the new order in town. Duff established a working relationship with the Uhlman administration, as both tried to find a way out of the economic mess left in the wake of the Boeing Bust. The economy did recover, slowly, and the chamber generally supported the Uhlman Administration's city reforms. But then things took a turn for the worse. Charles Royer, who entered office in 1978, had few ties to business. And the economy got hit, again.

The national recession of the early 1980s was quite pronounced in the Puget Sound region, and the Chamber responded with two major initiatives. The completion of Interstate 90 from Bellevue to Seattle had been held up for ten years, and the Chamber saw this massive construction project as a way to use federal money to create jobs in the region. The chamber recognized that Seattle had no way to bring large conventions to town and led the charge in the state legislature to create the Washington State Convention Center Authority and to secure funding to build the center that now straddles Interstate 5 through downtown.

Both projects went forward after a struggle with the Royer Administration. The mayor successfully pushed for a very expensive and technically challenging tunnel beneath the Mount Baker neighborhood, instead of the massive cut in the original plans. But Royer's move to have the convention center built near the Seattle Center failed, and the freeway site was chosen. In the 1990s the chamber continued to promote infrastructure investments, especially the third runway at SeaTac airport and the program that would eventually become Sound Transit. Although it was not a chamber activity as such, Duff played a personal role in keeping the Mariners in Seattle and getting Safeco Field built.

Duff retired in 1996, and his successors, Bob Watt, Steve Leahy, Phil Bussey and Maude Daudon, presided over the organization during some challenging times that made it difficult to pursue major projects. Particularly troublesome was the decline of locally-owned and locally-focused large businesses. The "branch office town" trend discussed in Chapter 4 hit the chamber hard. As national companies acquired local banks, retailers and other place-bound businesses, the urgency of regional economic development diminished. Moreover, the executives in charge were no longer local girls and boys, but career corporate managers doing time in Seattle, but likely moving on at some point. The chamber saw its base of key volunteers drop as firms cut their public affairs staff and as mid-level managers saw less payoff in spending time participating in chamber activities.

Beginning in the 1980s the chamber did take on a key role that only it could: regional convener. In the old days the urban regime was a pretty simple thing: politicians and businesspeople from within the city limits. But by the 1980s it was clear that public policy success required a much larger tent with far more individuals and groups from throughout the region participating. Politicians need that tent but cannot erect it themselves. Enter the chamber of commerce, and its signature events—the Regional Leadership Conference and the Study Missions—described in more detail below.

Trade Development Alliance of Greater Seattle

TDA was the first of several efforts in the past 20 years to attempt to cut across traditional economic development boundaries. The brainchild of George Duff, at the Seattle Chamber and guided for its first 20 years by Bill Stafford, TDA has always had as its core mission to project the Seattle region across the world and foster the kinds of connectivity that this book argues is central to metropolitan economic success.

In 1991, the Seattle area had several groups working in the international arena, promoting trade-friendly public policies, conducting overseas missions, engaging sister cities and marketing products. The problem was that they lacked any coordinating body. Each group operating in its silo could satisfy the needs of its constituency but could not really promote the Seattle brand effectively. TDA aimed to cut across these efforts and bring together internationally minded leaders from business, local governments, ports and institutions and act, in effect, as a brand manager for "Greater Seattle." Over the course of twenty years TDA brought leadership groups to 17 regions of the world and hosted inbound missions from every corner of the planet.

TDA has become a model for other cities around the U.S. and abroad that want to increase their international presence. But those looking at TDA as a model need to understand that its effectiveness derives not from a large operation or an ultra-sophisticated program, but from its ability to keep a diverse regional leadership group together over a long period of time. TDA has been central to the process, described below, of creating cosmopolitan regional leadership, by making sure that the process of projecting the region outward is not just the province of some designated group of internationalists, but the responsibility of leaders from throughout the community.

Industry "ecosystem" alliances

Over the past 20 years several groups have arisen that, like TDA, try to cut across traditional organizational lines to promote a specific industry cluster. Cluster theory holds that industries form around an ecosystem of suppliers, service businesses, researchers, financiers and others who contribute to the supply chain or business process. These alliances have approached their sectors through a cross-cutting approach that differs from standard industry associations that typically treat service providers as adjunct members.

The first of these groups was the Technology Alliance, formed after the 1995 Intercity Visit to Silicon Valley. The hundred participants on that trip recognized that if the Seattle area hoped to compete with Silicon Valley as a center of information technologies and San Francisco as a center of life sciences, it needed a more concerted approach. Bill Gates Sr. served as the first chair of the Technology Alliance and brought together, for the first time, key leaders from the University of Washington, the newer technology businesses, local venture capitalists, traditional bankers and established technology firms like Boeing. Susannah Malarkey, my colleague from chamber days, has run the Tech Alliance from the beginning, and it continues to be a vital organization that keeps all these players in the room together.

More recently, the Washington Clean Technology Alliance came together around emerging industries in renewable energy, resource conservation, and other businesses forming around new environmental priorities. These groups might not naturally get together, since they employ different technologies and skill sets. But they do have one important thing in common: reliance on a policy environment that encourages new ways of using energy and conserving resources.

Another recent entrant to the field is the Washington Global Health Alliance. Seattle has become a major player in the field of global health, especially with the growth of the Gates Foundation. Like clean tech, the field is not well defined and involves diverse disciplines. But unlike clean tech, many of the players in global health are large, well established institutions that might not naturally seek out their colleagues in related disciplines. The Global Health Alliance performs that function.

Other alliances will likely spring up as industries realize that to grow they need to pay attention to the entire ecosystem within which they operate. Sophisticated global industries and institutions rely on a wide array of service providers, such as lawyers, accountants, financiers, consulting engineers and contract researchers that, together, form that ecosystem (recall Microsoft's massive B2B purchasing). But these elements of the ecosystem, although they may know each other individually, may not naturally come together often. The alliances help foster the kind of face-to-face contact that agglomeration economics points to as a vital source of progress. Silicon Valley may have sprung forth from the legendary Wagon Wheel restaurant, but twenty-first century Seattle requires a more focused approach.

The ecosystem alliances, like TDA, help manage and promote the Seattle brand. By calling attention to the strengths of each industry ecosystem, they remind the world that Seattle is about more than just airplanes and coffee.

Prosperity Partnership

The 2002 Regional Leadership Conference asked a fundamental question: are we organized as a broader region to pursue economic opportunity? Not surprisingly, the answer came back a resounding NO. The result of the conference was creation of a four-county economic development strategy group, the Prosperity Partnership, housed at the Puget Sound Regional Council. Its work is described below.

Economic development organizations.

Even with all of the big strategies and ecosystem maintenance, someone still needs to do the fundamental, bread and butter work of economic development. When a firm inquires about setting up operations, someone needs to respond, and that task falls to the economic development organizations in each county. This function has been relatively stable in two of the counties over time, but not so stable in King County.

King County's current organization came into being in the wake of the Boeing Bust, but underwent a strategic shift in the mid-1980s when it came under the spell of David Birch, who urged communities to emphasize home-grown businesses and not to go "smokestack chasing."[16] The Seattle-King County Economic Development Council began to resemble a chamber of commerce, concerning itself with basic public policy matters. By the 1990s this focus had died out and the EDC resumed an active business recruitment program, later renaming itself Enterprise Seattle.

The Snohomish County EDC combined with the Everett and South Snohomish County Chambers of Commerce in 2011 to form the Economic Alliance of Snohomish County. Pierce County is served by the Tacoma-Pierce County Economic Development Board.

Downtown Seattle Association

Formerly known as the Central Association, the Downtown Seattle Association (DSA) concerns itself with the health of the downtown business district. Twenty-four downtown property and business owners formed the Central Association in 1958 in response to the emergence of shopping malls. Northgate Mall, about six miles north of downtown Seattle was among the first integrated, auto-oriented malls in the country, and had opened in 1950, posing a threat to the traditional retail core. At the same time, federal urban renewal programs were injecting redevelopment money into downtowns across the country.

As would be expected of such an organization, DSA promoted the major redevelopment schemes that emerged in the 1960s, most notably the wholesale razing of Pioneer Square and the Pike Place Market, both of which were to become modern mixed use developments. DSA also supported construction of the R.H. Thompson Expressway through the eastern side of the city, and the Bay Freeway through South Lake Union. All of these developments were cancelled as a coalition of preservationists, civic organizations and neighborhood groups recast the idea of how the city should develop.

Since those bruising battles of the 1960s, DSA has continued to push for major development projects, but has also supported some historic redevelopment efforts and started its own low income housing agency. Since the late 1960s only two people have run DSA, John Gilmore and

Kate Joncas, and the organization has managed to keep focused on its core mission, resisting pressure to become involved in broader matters. That focus allowed it to deepen its involvement in downtown by forming the Metropolitan Improvement District (MID) in 1999. Downtown property owners pay an annual tax assessment that funds the MID's ambassador and cleaning activities. The MID represents the kinds of public-private partnerships that downtowns need to compete with suburban malls.

Leadership Tomorrow

A healthy region requires a large and continuously refilling pool of individuals who can take on civic leadership roles across the entire spectrum of local institutions. Hundreds of non-profits, boards, commissions and community organizations need leaders, and the quality and skills of those leaders will have a lot to do with organizational success. Leadership comes naturally to some people, but not to most, giving rise to organizations like Leadership Tomorrow. LT, and its suburban counterparts, put individuals through a rigorous training program designed to help them understand how civic life works and how they can be most effective within it. Graduates then become part of a remarkably cohesive and enduring network of 1,500 alumni around the region.

Municipal League

The Municipal League, a classic good-government group, was launched in the Progressive Era as a vehicle to promote reforms in local government and to oppose the "open city" policies of the mayor at the time. Its fortunes have waxed and waned over the past few decades, but it has played important roles in some key debates, especially those relating to regional governance. The League was a major supporter of the effort to create Metro in the 1950s and later took over the reformist mantle from CHECC. But although the League has always advocated for regionalism, it has had a difficult time expanding out of its traditional Seattle base.

Building cosmopolitan regional leadership

Clarence Stone and his fellow urban regime theorists paint a compelling picture of effective local leadership: elected officials working hand-in-hand with the private and non-profit sectors. The frustration with regime theory, though, is that it stops at the city limits of the central city and has had little to say about regional leadership. This conceptual gap is important, especially in the Seattle area where, you will recall, the *Fortune* Magazine cover featured three business leaders based outside Seattle.

The question is, can we identify a coalition that operates at the regional level and captures the "power to" promote regional economic progress? As noted above, we do have a set of regional institutions— ports, the Prosperity Partnership, the Trade Development Alliance— that cross jurisdictional and sectoral lines to advance an economic agenda. But do they, in turn, operate under the larger tent of a coalition that shares a common regional agenda and outlook? The answer, I think, is yes. The Greater Seattle area does have a regional leadership regime that maintains a cosmopolitan outlook and influences decision-making. But like the urban regimes described above, its members probably don't know it exists.

This is a "leadership" regime rather than a "governing" regime, for the simple reason that it the lacks the direct implementation power that a city-based regime has in the form of a mayor and council. But otherwise it functions in a similar way, having the same two basic criteria for membership as a city-centered governing coalition: adherence to a common agenda and contribution of resources for use in pursuit of that agenda. Let's look at those two pieces more closely.

The regional leadership agenda in central Puget Sound centers on global economic competitiveness and a high quality of life within the constraints of the region's unique environmental concerns. The leadership of the Seattle area certainly likes growth, but has little interest in the kind of hyper aggressive expansion that has characterized the big Sunbelt metro areas. Many Puget Sound leaders believe those regions, successful as they are, encourage a non-union workforce through right-to-work laws and have lower environmental standards. Obviously business and labor in the Puget Sound area do not always get along, and environmental groups remain problematic, but the sides have generally worked toward some accommodation.

Coalition members contribute mostly intangible resources, especially political support for major investments and initiatives. When a big regionally important project is on the line, groups that form the regional leadership coalition are expected to step up and endorse it. Project proponents will require help not just from business groups, but will count on labor support, as well as endorsements from the non-profit sector and community groups. As noted, the region leans toward a cosmopolitan orientation, so it is generally possible to mobilize enough support from the cosmopolitan side to tip the political balance.

When it comes to getting actual legislation enacted to move a project forward, individuals from within the leadership coalition often form ad hoc groups to fund and conduct the public relations campaign, line up formal support and, if required, hire lobbyists or launch a formal political campaign. Once decisions are finalized these ad hoc groups generally disappear, although the individuals involved tend to reappear for future efforts. The key point is that the ad hoc campaign grows out of a network of ongoing personal and institutional relationships that define the leadership coalition. These relationships cross public, private and non-profit lines, and extend across industry sectors and throughout the broader region. They also operate across a range of issues and persist over many years; people gradually come and go from the leadership coalition, but a core always remains.

Community leaders anywhere, when faced with a large opportunity or threat, will find a way to come together to address that particular situation. But keeping a diverse regional leadership coalition in place, and allowing mutual trust to develop such that the coalition can operate over time and across issues, does not happen by accident. Seattle's regional leadership coalition has evolved through a series of programs designed for exactly that purpose. We turn now to the mechanisms that help develop and maintain a cosmopolitan regional leadership regime.

Annual Regional Leadership Conference

This event grew out of an expanded Seattle Chamber Board retreat, with the first official Leadership Conference held in 1985 at the Alderbrook resort on Hood Canal. Within two years the event had moved to the brand new Semiahmoo resort near the Canadian border, and had over 200 attendees. Since then the conference has been held multiple times in Vancouver, BC, as well as in Spokane, Portland, Coeur d'Alene and, most recently, at the Suncadia Resort in Central Washington.

Attendees comprise a mix of local government, business, non-profit and education leaders from throughout the region. Agendas have varied widely, from broad issues like climate change or demographics to more specific issues like housing or transportation. In several cases the conference has taken a "meta" approach: a leadership conference about leadership. But whatever the agenda, a core group of participants always attends, supplemented by individuals associated with the main topics. Although the schedule is full, the agenda does provide time for networking and individual conversations.

At its best, the Regional Leadership Conference accomplishes two critical things. First, it solidifies the regional leadership coalition and provides a venue to introduce new people to that coalition. Individuals new to leadership positions are encouraged to attend and meet their counterparts from other organizations and businesses. Second, it brings leaders from a wide range of institutions up to speed on important issues that they might not otherwise have a chance to learn about. The regional leadership coalition is greatly strengthened when politicians understand business issues, when business leaders understand environmental or human service issues, when educators understand infrastructure, and so on. That cross-knowledge is a defining feature of a regional leadership coalition, and this annual event promotes it.

North American Study Missions

The program of North American Study Missions originally known as Intercity Visits, began under the Royer Administration with 25 people on a trip to Baltimore in 1983. Since then the program has included 28 trips to North American regions, with several being visited twice.[17]

The composition of the groups on domestic missions—usually between seventy-five and one hundred participants— resembles the attendees at a Regional Leadership Conference, and the events have substantial overlap in attendance. The agendas typically run two to three full days with little time on the official agenda for independent activity. Trip planners take care to ensure that no one gets the impression that these missions are all about golf and sunning around the pool. In nearly thirty years this program has generated very little negative press, even though a large number of public officials participate at taxpayer expense.

The difference from the Regional Leadership Conference, of course, is that study missions focus on how the host region has tackled the same issues that the Seattle area faces. Agendas typically include sessions with host region leaders on education, transportation, and economic development. In addition, sessions will cover issues that are unique to that region, such as high tech development in Silicon Valley, aerospace in Montreal, advanced manufacturing in Cleveland and regional government in Toronto. The agendas take full advantage of locations, moving sessions around town to interesting venues, riding rail transit systems, walking through parks and generally getting participants out of hotels and conference rooms. During my time at the Seattle Chamber I staffed seven of these trips, and my all-time favorite venue was a lunch program on infrastructure investment held in an abandoned subway station in Cleveland.

Like the Regional Leadership Conferences, the missions provide an excellent way for new leaders in the community to get introduced to the larger leadership coalition and its agenda. The conference program may be full, but participants have plenty of time on airplanes, in buses, at meals and late in the evening to share perspectives and build valuable relationships.

International Study Missions

In 1991, the Intercity Visit program had matured to the point where the chamber leadership felt it was time to go overseas. The Trade Development Alliance had recently been formed, and its Executive Director, Bill Stafford, had founded the Intercity Visit program while working for Mayor Royer. So although an overseas trip would add to the complexity of the program, the staff expertise was in place.

As to the first destination, the Port of Seattle had recently hired a Dutch Executive Director who had previously worked at the Port of Rotterdam, and Dutch institutions had been the inspiration for TDA, so Amsterdam and Rotterdam seemed natural destinations. Stuttgart, a region similarly positioned to Seattle, with a strong manufacturing base, was added to the week-long agenda, the closing dinner of which was described in the introduction. 75 participants made that first trip, and it was successful enough that plans were made for a 1994 trip to the Kansai region of Japan.

Since 1992 TDA and the Seattle chamber have co-sponsored 16 International Study Missions, touching four continents.[18] The trips typically last one week, with about 75 participants. As might be expected, participation leans somewhat away from local government officials and more toward individuals with a particular focus on international business. But the agendas do have a heavy public policy component, recognizing that local governments everywhere have things in common and can learn from each other. Even more so than the North American missions, the International Study Missions have packed agendas, and no one familiar with one of these trips will use the J-word (junket). Rather, one first-time participant called the agenda a "forced march."

Regional leaders around the world engage in trade missions on a regularly basis, but the International Study Missions have been different from the beginning. Their main purpose is not to connect business people with sales opportunities (although that could happen). Like the North American trips, participants will get exposure to new ways to address local issues, and with different political cultures and political systems these solutions can be real eye-openers. Regional leaders also gain in their own personal outlook and, as a result, the sophistication and cosmopolitan nature of the region's leadership strengthens. And Seattle gets a chance to raise its profile: a study mission will make it into the local papers where a trade mission would not.

Prosperity Partnership

Organizers of the Regional Leadership Conferences and the study missions never intended these events to drive the civic agenda to completion. Although some participants, especially first-time attendees, expect direct outcomes, that has never been their purpose. Each is a one-time event with a particular self-selected group that has no authority to do anything other than build awareness, knowledge and relationships. But it did gradually become clear that the region needed some organization to manage its economic agenda on an ongoing basis.

The 2002 Regional Leadership Conference, coming on the heels of the national recession that hit the Puget Sound area very hard, explored this gap in our ability to build and sustain a long-term economic strategy. Out of these discussions came the Prosperity Partnership, a four-county, public-private economic strategy effort managed through the Puget Sound Regional Council (PSRC). Since the PSRC also manages the Puget Sound Economic Development District, which dispenses federal funds from the Economic Development Administration, it had a pipeline to funding for regional strategy activities. Bob Drewel, the PSRC's Executive Director, had a long history on economic development issues, having served two terms as Snohomish County Executive.

A basic model for the Prosperity Partnership had been discovered during the planning stages for the 2003 International Study Mission to Barcelona. In transforming itself from a gritty port and manufacturing center to a major European cultural capital, leaders in Barcelona from all sectors and political persuasions had come together, recognizing that they could accomplish far more working together than trying to work separately.

The Prosperity Partnership immediately began constructing a regional economic strategy, focusing both on basic economic factors (e.g. education and transportation) and on the region's major industry clusters. But what has made the process most effective is that each year a set of discrete action items is pulled out of the strategy and addressed by the Prosperity Partnership and its affiliated organizations. Some action items are far reaching and ambitious, such as business tax reform or higher education funding, while others are relatively narrow, such as enabling truck drivers who leave military service to obtain a state commercial license with minimal further training.

Prior to the creation of the Prosperity Partnership the region had no organized economic agenda. Public and private sector leaders understood basic priorities, but did not have the capacity to manage those priorities in a systematic way. Ad hoc efforts would spring up around a priority, but then vanish, and if a perceived need did not attract a champion from among the many sub-regional organizations, it would languish. I do not mean to suggest that the Prosperity Partnership wins on every issue—far from it. But it does provide a place where concerns can stay alive until the window of opportunity for action opens.

These four programs, taken together, provide the mechanisms to build and maintain the regional leadership regime. Only a small handful of individuals have an explicit regional leadership portfolio, and the rest of the leadership coalition must be created. Leadership Conferences and study missions foster relationships and provide the knowledge and cosmopolitan outlook that gives an individual who leads a business, agency or local government the confidence to participate in the larger leadership process. That process, though, is defined not by the people who make up the coalition, but by the agenda they share. That agenda, in turn, needs definition and ongoing maintenance, which the Prosperity Partnership provides.

Now do not get the impression that I have described some smooth running machine. This book has described the region's many unresolved problems and missed opportunities. But having a strong regional leadership coalition that renews and strengthens itself on a regular basis does help get things done. Moreover, intentional efforts to maintain the coalition are necessary to keep individuals and groups that otherwise might not naturally mingle (e.g. labor and business), working together on an ongoing basis. As discussed in the next chapter, regional leadership is largely synthetic—these institutions and programs do not exist in nature.

This effort at intentional creation of a regional leadership coalition began about thirty years ago. Recall that a decade prior to that, in the late 1960s, the long-standing arrangement of business-backed local government gave way to a new generation of leadership that did not naturally grow out of the business community. It took a decade to figure out how to rebuild the kind of leadership that brought us the World's Fair and Forward Thrust, but the new regional coalition seems as effective as the old model, considering the far more complex economic, social and political environment.

Dealing with concerns (panic, actually) about the future of Boeing's manufacturing presence in the region provides a recent example of the effectiveness of the regional leadership coalition. The effort in 2011 to help ensure that Boeing chose its Renton site for assembly of the 737MAX came together very quickly because relationships existed within the broad range of people whose cooperation was needed. Furthermore, those people knew very well what was at stake, since for several years the Prosperity Partnership and other groups had made aerospace a priority. The 737MAX program had grown out of the successful Air Force refueling tanker campaign. Furthermore, many of the participants in that effort, including its leader, Tayloe Washburn, had also worked to support the Downtown Seattle tunnel project, demonstrating that regional leadership is not issue-specific but looks out for the larger picture of economic progress.

Leadership matters

After this slog through local and regional leadership, what can we conclude about the state of governance and leadership in the Seattle area and the roles that they have played in the recent economic history of the region?

To start with, we can pretty much conclude that the formal government structures we have today are here to stay. The region is as far as it has ever been from any kind of formal regional government beyond counties, and I cannot imagine counties themselves gaining any more responsibilities than they have now. We will make do for the foreseeable future with the combination of cities, counties, special purpose districts and federated bodies now in place: a lot of people have a stake in the status quo and although we might see some theoretical benefits from further regionalization of services, I doubt anyone will spend the political capital to make that happen.

At the informal level, however, regionalization has taken hold. Because governments remain highly fragmented we can have difficulty recognizing it, however. A regional leadership coalition clearly operates throughout the Greater Seattle area, whether it knows it or not, and that coalition can drive decisions at both the state level and the local level, where actual policy is made. From what I know of other regions in the country and around the world, this is no small accomplishment, and is one of the reasons I remain optimistic about our future economic competitiveness.

Chapter 8

What We Have Learned in Fifty Years

C ities form and grow because they have an economic base, as described in Chapter 6. Small cities mostly formed as trading centers around transportation hubs and to support farms that exported their products to distant markets. Small cities grew into large cities to process local raw materials, to manufacture things destined for distant customers, and to serve as commercial centers for larger regions. We cannot understand the evolution of a city outside of its economic context, whether that be in trading, processing, manufacturing or providing services. But no city follows a totally linear evolution: the economic base that has enabled a city to grow changes over time, and the city with it.

Economists celebrate the idea of creative destruction. Articulated most clearly by the economist Joseph Schumpeter in 1942, this principle describes the process by which new technologies and preferences rise up and make existing ones obsolete.[1] Those who benefitted from the old ways may lose out, but society as a whole gains, since creative destruction is a primary source of growth. In their 2012 book *Why Nations Fail*, economists Daron Acemoglu and James Robinson demonstrate that the most common path to failure begins when elites, who prosper under existing economic conditions, resist creative destruction and thereby consign their societies first to stagnation and eventually to decline.[2]

We need to think about how metropolitan areas fit into this process.

Cities form around technologies and ideas, and provide the physical space where skilled people make them blossom and produce the goods and services that we all use. Cities and their surrounding metropolitan areas usually specialize in a handful of technologies and sectors, taking advantage of agglomeration economics: an increase in the density of an activity leads to more productivity in that activity.

But what happens to a city as the technologies and markets that underpin its economy change; that is, how do cities respond to creative destruction? And how do their citizens, cope with that change?

One thing is for sure: we cannot treat cities the same way we treat the makers of typewriters or instant cameras, thanking them for their noble service, and watching them fade away. Cities may start with an economic rationale, but they rapidly become defined by the people who live in them. It turns out that cities themselves—people, neighborhoods, schools, homes, local businesses—are far more durable than the industries that gave rise to them. The great challenge for cities across the Western world has been to deal with the process of creative destruction within their economic base as it not only alters industries but threatens the communities in which those industries operate.

There is a very lively debate around this problem, and it mostly boils down to the question of whether we aim our efforts at people or at places. Policies aimed at people would focus on retraining and possible relocation to more promising cities. Policies aimed at places attempt to reinvigorate the economies of cities so people can stay in them. Neither is very satisfying: people-based policies seem harsh and manipulative, while place-based policies have a poor record of success.[3]

This book has traced the history of one city and its surrounding region as its economic base has grown and changed over the past fifty years. I have presented data suggesting that Seattle has evolved successfully and has the opportunity to sustain that success. This chapter attempts to draw some conclusions about what has happened in Seattle. First I will take a stab at summarizing why Seattle has succeeded. Next I will talk about things we thought might lead to failure and why they have not. Third we will look at some additional lessons that can provide guidance as we try to keep the economic bicycle moving forward. Finally, I have identified four interesting threads that run through the story of Seattle and the Puget Sound region that I think will be of interest to readers focused on more general questions of metropolitan development.

Why Seattle has succeeded

First, we need to define success. Summing up the pluses and minuses of Chapter 2, I would suggest the following two elements for a definition of success for a metropolitan region in the twenty-first century:

> An economic base with a heavy representation of knowledge-intensive industries that have a strong potential for future growth as well as industries that support substantial numbers of high skill blue collar jobs.

> A strong position as a node in the global web of regions, with a sense of connectivity and a high comfort level with globalization of business and community.

A region needs to be smart and connected, just as the World's Fair organizers knew. But it also needs to avoid the hourglass shaped economy which concentrates high productivity activities at the top and low-paid service jobs at the bottom while offering scant opportunities in the middle. "Smart" needs to include the highly skilled people on the factory floor and on the waterfront who are well paid because of the unique knowledge and skills they have accumulated.

Seattle has enjoyed a degree of success by this definition, and has plenty of room for further advancement. To what can we attribute that success? I would suggest three basic elements. The first two, geography and talent are pretty straightforward. The third, the local culture, is a bit more speculative, but worth thinking about.

Geography

All cities exist on a certain spot on the planet for a reason, and that spot has a large influence on what can and cannot happen in that city. As noted through this book, Seattle's position in the far corner of the country has cut several ways.

The city has its origins in access to a highly valuable resource: Douglas fir trees. The Douglas fir grows straight, tall and abundantly, but only in the coastal regions of the Northwest. Of all commercially harvested trees it offers an optimum combination of structural properties and has, as a result, become a standard building material used throughout the country and overseas. This put Seattle in a very nice position in the early days. Being surrounded by a large region that had lots of these trees, and the waterways to float them out, Seattle could grow into the commercial center for scores of timber communities: one hundred years ago, steamers of Seattle's Mosquito Fleet served 350 docks around Puget Sound, most of which had something to do with timber.

Seattle also had access to another valuable resource: fish. Although diminished from its earlier days, the fisheries and boatbuilding industries formed a second main pillar for the Seattle economy, both from activities on local waters and as a base for the Alaska fishing industry.

Seattle also had the steamship and rail terminals from which to transport products made from those trees and fish. The ports of Puget Sound provide the closest U.S. gateways to both Alaska and East Asia. While timber and fishing are no longer major parts of the economy, ports still generate large numbers of jobs and play and an important role in promoting that all-important connectivity.

The sawmills, towns, trains and steamships were all powered by another local resource: coal. Mines in the east and south part of King County supplied coal to homes and industries, railroads and ships, and still had some left over to export to California.

But, critically, the region's relatively remote location confined its manufacturing activities mostly to timber, ships, fish and farm products. It would never make sense to manufacture most consumer and capital goods in a place so far from the bulk of the nation's population and industrial base. From the 1850s to the 1950s, as America turned itself into an industrial powerhouse, the Puget Sound region participated only at the margins. In 1850 most Americans lived in shacks on farms, and by 1960 most Americans lived in nicely appointed homes in cities and towns, and all those nice appointments got made somewhere else.

But this lack of a conventional Fordist industrial structure would prove to be the region's key to success. With no large incumbent base of manufacturing, Seattle never experienced the trauma that other cities went through as their industries faced technological changes and challenges from foreign producers. That is, Seattle simply never had to deal with creative destruction on a large scale.

As noted in Chapter 4, Seattle made the leap directly from a re-source-based economy to a technology-based economy, neither of which ever had to contend with much import competition. And at the same time, the region developed industries like fashion and outdoor apparel that depended on overseas producers. So, when globalization became an inevitability, starting in the 1970s, the region found itself uniquely re-ceptive to that new economic order. It had lots of winners and not many losers: strong exporters and importers, ports to handle cargo going both ways, and, most important, few legacy industries seeking protection.

We can be pretty smug in this region, and many of us probably think that Seattle residents possess inherently forward thinking and prescient virtues that have given us that superior global outlook. Nonsense. Like anywhere else, business and civic leaders in Seattle have looked out for their self-interest, and it has just so happened that that self-interest has involved embracing globalization while equally self-interested leaders in other communities have seen globalization as presenting a threat. We have found ourselves on the right side of history, but I see little evidence that anyone planned it that way.

We can also be pretty smug about our success and assume that it will continue indefinitely. But if Seattle's lack of incumbent industries meant it did not have to deal with creative destruction fifty years ago, it cer-tainly has incumbent industries today that face that threat. Just look at how Microsoft has scrambled to gain its footing in mobile and tablet technologies that threaten its established position in desktops and lap-tops.

Talent

Chapter 1 states that "smart cities win." Seattle and its surrounding region have become smart, at least as measured by the educational attainment of the resident population. This is very obviously not because of the wonderfulness of our education system. In fact, on-time high school graduation rates in the state of Washington are far below the national average, and have worsened while the rest of the country has improved significantly. It appears that the state's families, on average, place less emphasis on education than families in most of the country. And with an underfunded K-12 system and a dramatically undersized higher education system, it appears that leaders in the state do not place too much emphasis on education either. We are smarter than average because smart people have chosen to move here and stay here.

The trend toward well-educated people moving to the region began mostly in the 1930s, as Boeing grew from a small shop to a bigger company. But it really accelerated during World War II as the aerospace sector expanded dramatically. Designing and manufacturing airplanes takes a lot of really knowledgeable people, and talent flowed in from around the country. Then, when the war effort ended, and Boeing fell into a manufacturing lull, many of those newly-arrived engineers and machinists stuck around, so as the company ramped back up with military jet programs, the necessary talent had stayed in the region. The talent ramp-up continued in the 1950s and went seriously upward in the mid-1960s as the company grew rapidly on the commercial side. Remarkably, after the Boeing Bust of 1969, the smart people again stayed around.

The next big magnet for technical skill, software, began to test principle that regions have become the aggregators of talent. As Microsoft began to break out of the pack in the 1980s, it could recruit engineers and computer scientists from around the country and around the world. But would they remain in the area and help the talent cluster self-perpetuate? The evidence seems to say yes. After all, why would firms like Adobe, Google, Facebook, Yahoo and Zynga establish engineering offices in the region if they could simply drag the people they want back to Silicon Valley and San Francisco? I suspect they found out that the people they want to work for them don't want to leave the Seattle area.

In her book *World Class*, Harvard Business School Professor Rosabeth Moss Kanter talks about the need for magnets and glue.[4] Magnets draw people to a region, and glue helps them to stick around. Given the demonstrated ability of Seattle to become one of Richard Florida's talent aggregators, the region would seem to have both magnets and glue. I will argue, however, that we really have no coherent strategy for keeping the magnets charged and the glue fresh.

But, you might object, all that talent needs to work somewhere, and how can we account for the presence of the employers who recruit those people and pay them well. Companies like Boeing, Microsoft and Amazon do not just hop out of an empty boxcar in the freight yard. And you would be right to raise that objection. In the case of Microsoft, the founders grew up in Seattle and decided to pursue their business in their home town (Microsoft started in New Mexico, but moved to Bellevue shortly after). Bill Boeing was attracted to the region's supply of spruce lumber and boatbuilding skills that translated well to aircraft. Jeff Bezos liked being near the California market but exempt from its sales tax. And why these firms, as opposed to their competitors, came to dominate their industries is another set of stories entirely.

The more pertinent question, though, is why these firms stayed in Seattle. After all, a number of other major companies—United Parcel Service and United Airlines, to name two—started in Seattle but moved elsewhere. Boeing could have joined the larger airplane industry in Southern California and taken advantage of its deep talent pool, especially after it stopped relying on wood components. Microsoft could have set up shop in Silicon Valley. Amazon might have done better in Arizona, with its low cost of doing business. But they all stayed and grew in the Seattle area. I can only conclude that the founders of these companies had a high degree of confidence that they would be able to assemble the right people in Seattle and get them to stay put.

Yes, Seattle has benefitted from some remarkably good fortune in having so many signature companies started in the region. Louis Pasteur noted that "chance favors the prepared mind." Well, chance also favors the prepared region. Good ideas pop out of fertile brains all over the world, but those ideas and the businesses they generate do not always settle where they started. A number of very successful firms have been born in Seattle and grown into international prominence while remaining here. At the same time, I cannot think of a major firm in recent years that was born in Seattle and grew into international prominence somewhere else. So, I suppose the magnets and glue that work on people also work on the places they are employed.

Die Weltanschauung

The Germans have such useful words. This one translates as "worldview" and encompasses an entire point of view about life. That may be a bit of a stretch here, but, as I suggested in Chapter 5, cities do have distinct cultures, tied to their history and experiences. I would argue that the Weltanschauung of the Seattle area is well suited to the global economy as it has emerged in the past fifty years. We have talked a lot about "smart" and "globally connected." But as you have read this story, I hope you have sensed two other pieces of Seattle's Weltanschauung.

Resilience. The ups and downs of the Seattle area economy over the past fifty years, as reviewed in stomach-churning detail in Chapter 3, have left the region bruised, but generally optimistic. The lows drop lower, but the highs get higher. We've recovered before, and we'll recover again. Not every region could come back as fast as Seattle did after the Boeing Bust, the 12 percent unemployment of 1982 or the series of pummelings of 1998 to 2002. But Seattle dragged itself off the mat each time, and that counts for a lot. Most important, the best talent does not always leave for a safer place; people stick around to form the skill backbone for the next wave of growth.

Entrepreneurism. The appetite for risk that I have described has resulted in very high levels of business formation in the region. Most new companies will not survive, and their founders and funders know that. But they also know that wealth comes from the creation and expansion of new business, and more than an average number of people in the region are willing to take a shot at it. Moreover, entrepreneurism is not just a feature of business. The University of Washington consistently wins more competitive federal research grants than any other university in the country in large part because the internal culture at the UW drives researchers to compete for them.

None of this is new. *Seattle Spirit*, a charmingly dreadful piece of doggerel written by Philip Carlow for the Alaska Yukon-Pacific Exposition in 1909, begins:

> *Howdy! Old Skookum Friend, How do you do?*
> *Perhaps you are starting life anew.*
> *Then try Seattle, the Queen of the West,*
> *The Place that's setting the pace for the rest.*
> *It's a swift new burg, full of life and mirth.*
> *Growing faster than any place on earth.* [5]

Ah, Seattle. Washed clean by the rains, far from the hide-bound East, the starchy Midwest and the lurid degeneracy of California. A place for a fresh start. A place where an ambitious woman or man can make a real mark. . .

> *There is no equal to Seattle's worth.*
> *Nor was there ever one on all the earth.*
> *It's the best Town, bar none, in any State.*
> *It's mushing along ahead of the date,*
> *With its onward rush, with its ceaseless grind,*
> *Fast leaving old precedent far behind.*

That whole idea of finding second chances and new thinking out on the edge of the world has an irresistible appeal. And doesn't this sound like the argument James Lyons makes in his book about Seattle's cultural rise: the clean city untouched by the urban turmoil of the 1980s? And what about the Hugo Montenegro song made famous by Perry Como:

> *Like a beautiful child, growing up, free and wild*
> *Full of hopes and full of fears, full of laughter, full of tears*
> *Full of dreams to last the years, in Seattle*

Seattle has had its mythmakers from the beginning, and they continue to spin out stories today. Whether we find these stories deeply true or deeply silly, the myths, the Seattle Spirit, the whole Weltanschauung itself, draw people here. And the ability to lure people to our funky little corner—from Arthur Denny to Bill Boeing to Jeff Bezos—is at the heart of Seattle's success.

Throughout this book I have tried to back up my story with data. I can't do that here. I realize I am about to suggest that "there's something in the water." And I know I romanticize more than a bit. But I just cannot believe that the extent and quality of industrial and cultural leadership that Seattle has conjured up out of its *Here Come the Brides* past is mere coincidence.

> *With energy turning it inside out,*
> *Doing things that never were dreamed about;*
> *In this Wonder Town, great, bright Seattle,*
> *Of hustle, bustle, rustle and rattle.*

Why hasn't Seattle failed?

Let's go back one more time to the "Region on Trial" story, in which attendees at the 1991 Regional Leadership Conference tried and convicted the business and political elite on charges of failing to meet the pressing needs of the Puget Sound region. The same theme—the threat to prosperity from failure to address economic fundamentals—gets repeated continually anywhere leaders gather to address civic concerns. Consider some of the factors that presume to determine economic success or failure.

Begin with the tax and regulatory environment. Every magazine ranking that lists Seattle or Washington as good for business causes some degree of discomfort. By conventional measures of the business climate, Washington and the Seattle area do not look good. The region has high business taxes and burdensome levels of regulation and it takes too long to get things built. Moreover, political leaders often do not put business and economic success at the top of their list of priorities. As such, business leaders have gone so far as to take magazine editors to task for these high rankings, feeling that such praise undercuts efforts to remedy deficiencies.

Next, consider education. We are often told that our substandard education system damages our competitiveness, with dire consequences for our economic future. Indeed, Washington's K-12 education system does not stack up very well against other states, with poor funding and poor outcomes. One might even make the case that we should not bother expanding our higher education system until we figure out how to send better students to that system from our high schools.

The other hardy perennial is transportation. The Puget Sound region consistently gets poor marks for transportation infrastructure. Roads and bridges are crumbling, and measures of traffic congestion rank us high in terms of wasted time and fuel. We are told that the ports will suffer as trucks get stuck in traffic going to and from the terminals.

Once a group of civic leaders gets together they can work up a pretty good lather about these and a host of other failings of the region. Yet . . . the region has not failed. It has, in fact, succeeded quite nicely and has grown about as fast as our nerves can take. Wages and incomes are among the highest in the country and job growth has outperformed other high income areas. The region has far more than its share of world-leading firms and has strong industry and talent clusters in several key fields. Clearly, many firms do not find the tax and regulatory environment of the state and region onerous and do not suffer from poorly educated workers and traffic jams. On the contrary, firms must find the region conducive to business growth or they would, presumably, move somewhere else with more favorable conditions. And given the steady growth in the region, the firms that find Seattle a good place to do business must be part of growing sectors.

How can we reconcile measurable business climate failings and measurable economic success? If the region wants to have a coherent economic development strategy it needs to address this contradiction, which, for want of a better term, we'll call the "business climate paradox." To wrap our brains around this problem I would suggest focusing on some things that have come up earlier in the book. Following are three slightly different angles from which to look at the paradox.

Angle number one asserts that the factors most often cited as business climate problems, while important to many businesses, simply do not rise very high on the priority lists of a large number of the businesses that make up the economic base.

The knowledge-intensive businesses that have provided nearly all the growth in the economic base in the past 20 years do not have a high level of sensitivity to basic business climate factors. Many of them operate with high margins, so business costs do not pinch them very much, and they work from office buildings, so development and environmental regulations have little effect on them. Because they typically recruit their most important talent nationally and internationally, the students from local schools do not affect their human resource plans. Traffic congestion does not harm them since they don't have elaborate supply chains and their highly paid employees have incomes that allow them to choose homes close to work. These firms mostly concern themselves with attracting and keeping talented people (who benefit from the absence of an income tax!), and view these other issues as irritants but not fatal flaws. We'll talk below about the weakness of this particular viewpoint when it comes to other, lower-tech parts of the economic base.

For another angle from which to view the business climate paradox we can turn to some advice from Peter Drucker, the legendary management expert, who warned against a common failing in organizations: feeding problems and starving opportunities. "All one can get by 'problem-solving' is damage-containment. Only opportunities produce results and growth," Drucker wrote.[6] The same principle applies to entire metropolitan areas. We can keep trying to solve problems—fixing roads and schools, untangling regulations, lowering taxes—and yet these actions by themselves will not produce a dynamic, growing economy.

The temptation to focus on problems is strong. After all, they stare us in the face, and they tend to be of interest to leaders of established, mature industries, who influence the civic agenda. It is hard to argue with the proposition that a community should take care of the businesses and institutions it already has. Opportunity, in contrast, will have a weak political voice since, by definition, it involves economic activity that does not yet exist. But at the end of the day, regions that prosper over the long term do so through new, high growth industries that were once just speculative blips on the regional screen.

And that has been the case in the Seattle area: growth from new business opportunities. Although little civic action went into it, local entrepreneurs did capture opportunity in the software sector, providing a large share of the region's recent growth. As an example of proactive efforts to seize an opportunity, one could argue that the zoning changes and investments the City of Seattle made in South Lake Union have contributed to the growth of the life sciences industry in that neighborhood. In the same way, construction of cruise ship terminals allowed the Port of Seattle to capture the opportunity presented by expansion of the Alaska cruise industry and the introduction of faster ships.

In other words, this argument says that the economy grew over the past 20 years because good things happened, and not because we did anything to stop bad things from happening. No doubt, to the extent we failed to stop bad things we probably experienced some deterioration in the economic base, but the good things more than made up for it.

A third angle is found in the World Economic Forum's 2011-2012 Global Competitiveness Report.[7] That analysis of global competitiveness, by the mandarins of Davos, suggests that improvements in basic factors such as infrastructure, primary education and basic healthcare have the most benefit for the least developed economies, and that these benefits diminish as economies become more advanced. Paving a dirt path brings a large return, while widening an existing roadway brings less return. Similarly, basic literacy has a major payoff in terms of productivity, whereas incremental improvements in test scores do not lead to great economic leaps. When compared to the challenges faced by developing countries with respect to these factors, our complaints seem petty. In developed countries these systems and services may have flaws, but they work well enough to support business activity.

In reality, the WEF would assert, the tax and regulatory environment, local transportation and K-12 education make up only the bare framework for success. To compete at the highest level of the world economy requires far more. The U.S. and other advanced countries build their economies around innovation, in products, services and processes. Innovation, in turn, requires strong higher education systems, deep talent pools, a highly flexible and mobile workforce, advanced capital formation mechanisms, an entrepreneurial culture with sophisticated first-adopter markets and all the other features of innovation ecosystems. In a region with excellent conditions for innovation, lousy traffic or long waits for a building permit will not bring the economy to a halt.

The three angles all point to the same place: Seattle did not fail because, well, it succeeded. The region was too busy building up new industries to get too worked up about the flaws in its business climate. Maybe we're a bit like Wile E. Coyote, running off the edge of a cliff and defying gravity while we're chasing the Roadrunner. If we look down—if we get too obsessed with basic business climate factors—we might plunge to the bottom of the canyon.

This realization has been a bit hard for me to swallow, having spent many years advocating for infrastructure improvements as a way to strengthen the economy. But thinking about it, I realize that many places succeed despite their failings. I cannot imagine that New York, San Francisco or Chicago have anything to brag about when it comes to the basic business climate, and yet their economies continue to roar along.

These factors still matter because, as we will discuss, they affect some parts of the economic base and have a large impact on the success of local service industries. We need to address them. But at the same time, we cannot have any illusions that doing so will provide us with long term growth.

What else have we learned in fifty years?

Getting a little finer grained, we can find some important lessons from Seattle's story that should inform the kinds of forward-looking notions we will get into in the final chapter.

A cosmopolitan, global outlook takes effort

In Chapter 7 we discussed the idea of the regional leadership coalition, the informal regime that worries about regional competitiveness and connectivity. From what I can gather about other regions in the nation and in the world, the existence of this layer of leadership sets Seattle apart from a large number of its peers. Many regions, some quite sophisticated, cannot keep suburban leaders talking to urban leaders, business talking to labor, academics talking to bureaucrats, and so forth. Seattle's regional leadership coalition manages not just to keep these groups talking to one another, but allows trust to develop such that they can work together on important efforts. This is a singular accomplishment that has paid off in many ways.

I cannot emphasize enough that the relationships that underlie the regional leadership coalition do not happen naturally. Not only do the necessary individuals inhabit different, and sometimes hostile, worlds, most of them do their leadership work on a volunteer basis. These women and men spend their time thinking about their day jobs, not how to improve the economy.

Moreover, they come and go from their institutional positions. New people arrive in business, government, labor and other institutional leadership positions regularly and need to get "inducted" into their new regional roles. George Duff, longtime Seattle Chamber president and one of the key figures in the creation of the regional leadership coalition, had a framed anonymous quote on his office wall that read:

> *Remember, you are talking not to a crowd, but to a parade that is changing all the time. You must communicate with all the marchers—young people are growing up, new people are assuming the burdens of the old, different people are moving into your area, even the same people are changing their thinking.*

We can never take for granted that a cosmopolitan, global outlook persists among all the region's leaders, since the cast of characters evolves continually. The WTO fiasco of 1999 revealed the degree to which the pro-globalization, pro-trade outlook that had seemed so permanent among leaders in the 1980s had deteriorated.

Hence the importance of the formal and informal programs and events, described in Chapter 7, that create relationships and massage the regional agenda. These programs take resources and must occur consistently over time. A functioning regional leadership coalition does not pop up over night and does not maintain itself. Unless dedicated organizations and staff wake up every day thinking about managing that coalition, it will not function over the long run. Seattle has been fortunate to have some very talented people to "lead the leaders," and they have had the luxury of time.

The regional economy has an Achilles heel

In the discussion about why Seattle has not failed in spite of weaknesses in the business climate, I assert that those weakness just do not matter a great deal to the firms that have driven growth. We have created what I have characterized as a boutique economy: specialized, imported talent, high margins, high overhead, clean fingernails. This works well for software and life sciences, and adequately for aerospace and medical devices. But it does not necessarily work for other businesses that make up the economic base. Consider two types of enterprises.

The Seattle area has some excellent businesses that export value but have no compelling reason to operate in the region. My favorite example, of course, is the Kenworth Truck Company and its plant in Renton. (During college I spent a very educational summer at the original Kenworth plant on East Marginal Way). Kenworth's parent company, Paccar, has its headquarters in Bellevue, but it has plants on four continents. It sources few components locally and sells its output all over the country. How much sense does it really make to bring engines, transmissions, frame rails, electronics, suspensions, axels, seats and all the other component from factories in the Midwest, assemble them in Seattle, and ship them again out of the region? Kenworth could easily move its Renton operations to a lower cost area. (But please, Mr. Piggott, don't!)

Another group of enterprises consists of place-bound elements of the economic base, such as ports and tourism. They may not get up and move, but they may draw fewer national and international customers if the skill base and infrastructure supporting them is poor. Ports compete, in part, on total transit time, so if cargo cannot make it to and from the docks easily, the competitiveness of the ports could suffer. Both ports must contend with inadequate links to the waterfront from the region's freeway system.

Employers like Kenworth, and the ports, that provide good jobs at favorable multipliers, are the Achilles heel of the region. The boutique economy works against them. They hire from the local workforce, rely on good freight mobility and operate at margins that cannot absorb high taxes and regulatory costs. Remember, at last count, the ports support 34,000 direct jobs, and 92,000 direct jobs fall under the "diversified manufacturing" rubric. It would behoove us to understand how the boutique economy affects these operations and adjust accordingly. Drucker's admonition notwithstanding, the problems that affect these industries are definitely worth fixing.

The boutique economy comes with a high cost of living

Local service industries in the non-traded sector (the other 70 percent of the economy), do not operate comfortably in the boutique economy either. Since they tend to compete on price, local service firms will feel the burden of taxes and regulation. They mostly hire out of the regional labor force, so the quality of that labor pool will affect training costs and productivity. And local service businesses rely on customer access, deliveries and movement of service vehicles, all of which feel the affect of traffic congestion: every time I see a service technician's van stuck in traffic I think, there is someone not making any money.

Local service firms differ from firms in the economic base in one very important respect, however: they will not go anywhere in response to high costs or inefficiencies. All service firms operating in the region face the same conditions, so the position of each firm relative to its competitors will not change as costs increase. Businesses will eat some costs and pass others along to their customers. If you have ever looked at your lunch tab in New York City, you know what happens to service businesses in a high cost environment.

High costs will generally not result in the reduced availability of services—entrepreneurs will usually find a way to meet demand for local services—but in a higher cost of living. Remember that the **C** in the spatial equilibrium formula in Chapter 1 stands for the cost of living. Well, that includes not just housing costs but the cost of locally produced services.

We do not need to accept this. At the risk of sounding like a corny motivational speech, I'd suggest we look at opportunities as the flip side of problems. By lowering the cost of doing business, we lower prices in the local service industry and thereby increase our living standards. The result is the same as increasing wages. We should look at improved living standards through greater productivity in the non-traded sector as an opportunity for growth.

Looked at this way, advocacy for improved transportation and schools and for more reasonable taxes and regulations should change. The message should shift from promoting a more competitive economy to promoting lower prices in local service industries and a higher standard of living for everyone.

The hourglass economy looms in the background

We talked earlier about "superstar cities," those places where industries with high value employment concentrate.[8] This pattern has tended to result in high housing prices. The prevailing attitudes among residents in these regions discourage development, and high wage employees can afford to bid up prices of scarce housing. But for firms outside the high wage sectors, such as most manufacturers, high housing prices become a big problem. Firms that compete in national and international markets will struggle to pay their employees enough to live in the region. As these firms leave for lower cost areas, superstar cities can end up with the hourglass economy: a lot of highly paid people at the top, and a lot of low skilled service employees at the bottom living in multi-family housing or commuting long distances.

Seattle sits on the cusp of superstardom. It has the high wage industries, but so far has avoided the hourglass economy. Thanks to Boeing, the ports, the maritime and fishing industries and manufacturers like Kenworth, the region still has a thick layer of highly paid blue collar employment. As noted earlier in the chapter, some of this layer may be at risk due to the higher costs of doing business in the region's boutique economy and the lack of infrastructure investment.

The long term sustainability of this layer of employment, and its ability to keep the region from becoming an hourglass, cuts different ways. These jobs can only be sustained over time if they have a large knowledge and skill component, such that employees bring high value added to their jobs. No longer can unions win high wages for low skill work. Boeing machinists get paid well because they carry with them tacit knowledge and experience that Boeing finds valuable and hard to replace. But the rub comes from the fact that high value blue collar jobs tend to follow from automation, and, automation results in fewer jobs.

Therefore, we need to assume that the current base of high wage blue collar employment will shrink over time. We need a strategy to backfill, growing existing manufacturing and transportation industries or bringing in new ones. Fortunately, Boeing employment appears stable for some time, but we need to attend to the ports and the "diversified manufacturing" category in order to minimize the hourglass effect.

Maintaining moderate housing prices is the other key to avoiding full "superstar" status. Housing prices in the region shot up to unsustainable levels well before the 2007 bubble hit, and did not returned to earth as they did in other cities. By 2012, low interest rates had made homes more affordable, but as we have seen over the past decades, prices can resume their upward climb when the economy becomes more robust.

We don't understand the role of amenities

We know that quality of life and amenities play a central role in attracting and retaining talented people: come for the job, stay for the lifestyle. We don't know much beyond that general thought, however, and just about any feature of the community can get lumped into the broad category of amenities. Since we have limited resources with which to develop and enhance those amenities, we need a more sophisticated understanding of what features will make the most difference.

The challenge comes from the diversity of the people we wish to attract and keep. Richard Florida built most of his widely-read books around this question of urban amenities, but focused on a relatively narrow segment of the "creative class."[9] Yes, some young hipsters want to immerse themselves in the bohemian lifestyles that they can find in certain urban areas. Yes, they seek authenticity and unique experiences and have a taste for exotic music and ethnic food. But many, many other very talented people do not fit that mold and will have their own version of what constitutes a high quality of life. A broadened amenity discussion will confront two demographic factors, in particular.

To begin with, we need to remember that needs and preferences change as people age, and since the strategic imperative is to keep talented people in the area for their working lives, we need to understand how amenity values evolve during different stages of life. The hipsters will likely get married and have children, and that means schools, playgrounds, sports and other activities. As they form families, their concept of a good neighborhood may change, and they will start thinking more about safety and less about street life. As they get even older and become empty nesters, they shift into the "active adult" lifestyle, returning to a version of their hipster youth that's easier on their knees, livers and waistlines. So, if we want talented people to move here (or stay here, if they are homegrown products) we need to offer a place that will meet their desires over a lifetime.

Then, since many of the in-migrants to the area come from other countries, we need to consider whole new sets of needs. Now, these immigrants have freely chosen to come to the U.S., and media images will have given them a pretty good idea of what to expect about life in America, but we still need to be sensitive to the diverse needs and preferences of our foreign-born residents. For example, many immigrants groups make much more use of public spaces, like parks, and libraries than do locals. And many spend time with extended families and live in multi-generational households. Communities must find ways to make themselves comfortable places for immigrants to settle into.

The whole point, again, though, is that WE DON'T KNOW. Lots of self-serving speculation and conventional wisdom floats around about amenities and quality of life, but I have not seen any good social science that identifies priorities and hierarchies of preferences and needs with respect to different demographic groups. Complicated? Yes. But as I have suggested throughout this book, attracting and keeping talent is by far the most important economic development task before us, so we need to put some effort into a better understanding of the role of amenities—the magnets and glue—in talent attraction so we can direct resources intelligently.

Governments and businesses spent about a half million dollars in 2011 to understand the needs of the Boeing Company as it made its siting decision about the 737MAX. It was money very well and appropriately spent and we got the result we needed. But if we can spend that kind of money keeping physical capital in the region, we should spend even more figuring out how to get intellectual capital to stick around.

Multipliers create opportunity

Throughout this book I have used the principle of jobs multipliers to discuss the relationship between the economic base and the local service economy. Economic strategies need to concentrate on building the economic base, but as we have seen, not all elements of the economic base have the same impact on the rest of the economy. Multipliers vary widely, indicating that some industries throw off more impact than others.

The startlingly high multiplier reported for Microsoft gives it an outsized role in driving the local service sector. Boeing also has an attractive multiplier and continues to support a large share of the economy. The impact of the two companies seems to differ in two important ways, though. To begin with, Boeing purchases relatively little in the regional economy. Some suppliers have facilities in the Puget Sound region, but compared to the size of Boeing's global purchasing, the Washington supplier footprint is relatively small. Thus, the "indirect" impacts are not very high. In contrast, Microsoft spends a large amount of money in the state, mostly for services, and these services tend to keep the dollars circulating more times. Thus, Microsoft has a substantial indirect impact.

The "induced" impact, the second component of the multiplier effect, comes from household spending by employees of the firm itself, and by the employees of its suppliers. And here, Microsoft's high wages come into play. As households get more affluent, they tend to spend more of their earnings on services, and a smaller proportion on physical goods.

Since we know that the region produces very few consumer products, we can assume that when households spend money on such products, most of that money leaks out of the area immediately, since the goods came from somewhere else (retailers keep less than half the sales price of merchandise, sometimes as little as ten percent). With services, though, the money goes back into someone else's local paycheck and gets circulated again. Money spend on services will eventually find its way out of the area, but it gets more of a chance to circulate, thereby increasing the multiplier.

I raise all this because, to the extent that we can target industries for development, going after ones with strong multipliers makes sense. This is not to suggest we ignore opportunities across the spectrum of industries that make up the economic base, but simply to acknowledge that when we can make choices, high multiplier industries, like software and manufacturing, have the bigger payoff.

These strong multipliers also address a concern that I have always had: why do we go to all the trouble of promoting job creation when the good jobs just go to elite recruits from out of the area? What about our own kids and neighbors? Are they getting squeezed out and forced to scramble for the leftovers? Not really. True, competing for high paying jobs in the software or engineering world means going up against some of the best talent in the world, and many people who grow up here won't make the grade. But the multiplier effect means that those hotshots who do get the high end jobs generate a lot more good jobs in the economy. The indirect and induced jobs cover the landscape of skills and income categories.

We certainly do need to do a better job of providing the engineering and scientific educations necessary for our own kids to compete for jobs at the region's high tech employers. But for those who will not find themselves in one of those environments, the multiplier effect does create many other attractive high skill opportunities.

The best laid plans . . .

In the Seattle area we love to plan. And before we plan, we have a scoping exercise, which is a plan for a plan. And I seem to recall being in a session that was planning the scoping process, raising the prospect of an infinite regress of meta-planning. I have also been around long enough now to see how well some of these plans have worked out, and in this book I have taken a few pokes at plans and projections that have not proved very helpful or accurate. In some sense that is not fair at all, since no one can predict the future with any degree of accuracy. But at the same time, planning does have consequences, and although we sometimes treat it as a harmless exercise, decisions that get based on faulty projections and planning can come back to haunt us.

Two examples. In the 1970s the City of Seattle decided to start planning for fewer cars, and cut back on the parking allowed in office buildings. Several large buildings went up while that ordinance was in effect, and they ended up with inadequate parking. This affected their long term value, since tenants would not pay as much rent if they had to park somewhere else. Similarly, the Washington State Convention Center was designed with a relatively small exhibit floor, under the assumption that in the future age of electronic communications big trade shows would become obsolete. Exactly the opposite happened. Trade shows grew dramatically as industries found them an excellent way to communicate with customers in specialized fields. After losing too many conventions to cities with bigger exhibit halls, the convention center had to undertake a technically challenging expansion across Pike Street.

Again, to be fair, we cannot anticipate things like the emergence of the software sector. The industry that has driven regional growth did not appear at all in a major economic development strategy as late as 1988. We could not have predicted that the commercial biotechnology industry, which showed such promise in the 1990s, would never get much past the R&D stage in the region. And no one predicted that the region would become a major center for global health.

But planning still must be done in a responsible way, and the dilemma is that we have no feedback loops, no ways to hold planning processes accountable for outcomes. Frequently, when misguided plans result in unfortunate consequences, nothing happens. Seattle's recent history suggests two ways NOT to think about planning, and one way to think about it.

First, we should not create plans based on some change in behavior unless we have really good levers to make that change happen. Broad societal changes, like everyone driving less or eating more vegetables, require either large economic incentives and disincentives, or some big disruptive force that changes people's preferences. But heavy duty social engineering went out of fashion about the time the Berlin Wall came down, so plans that require big behavioral shifts usually don't get much traction. For example, recall that there has been no change in the desire of people in the region to live in single family detached housing.

Second, we need to take great care in predicting the emergence and influence of new technologies. For example, at the dawn of the micro-computer age, way back in the 1980s, it was widely accepted that people would use these new tools to work from remote locations, staying away from the city and avoiding commutes. But that never really happened. Innovations like telecommuting centers never caught on. We learned, in fact, that people actually like working around other people and benefit greatly from doing so—the agglomeration effects.

So how do we think about planning, given our weak ability to compel or predict outcomes? Military strategists often invoke a famous dictum from the Prussian general Helmuth von Moltke: "battle plans never survive contact with the enemy." In the same way, plans that involve economic decision-making never survive contact with the marketplace. But, military leaders still make elaborate plans, not because they necessarily expect to follow them very far into combat, but because planning compels them to consider all the variables in play and all the contingencies they must confront. This leads to Moltke's other famous dictum: "strategy is a system of expedients."[10]

So, we must draw up plans to force ourselves to think about the opportunities in front of us and the variables we will confront as we pursue them. But as the battle unfolds we need to remain flexible and adjust our plans as evolving circumstances dictate. In an influential 1959 article, economist Charles Lindblom referred to this as the "science of muddling through." Lindblom states that although we may claim to plan comprehensively and objectively, in reality,

> *Policy is not made once and for all; it is made and re-made endlessly. Policy-making is a process of successive approximation to some desired objectives in which what is desired itself continues to change under reconsideration.*[11]

One school of thought has always maintained that World War I came about because of inflexible plans that, once set in motion, could not adjust to changing circumstances. Local economic outcomes will not get quite so dramatic, but the lesson is clear. Planning should not be about predicting or forcing the future, but about keeping prepared to make the best of a variety of possible futures. Back to the paraphrasing of Pasteur: chance favors the prepared region.

Four final thoughts

In the introduction I noted that Seattle's story can perhaps be instructive to leaders in other cities who are working to improve regional economies, and I hope that useful lessons bubbled up out of this and other chapters. Stepping back from the story, though, I see four threads running through this narrative that would seem to have broad applicability.

The first two address the notion of path dependency, and how the past shapes the future. As noted several places in this book, Seattle has been fortunate in this respect. The emergence of the aerospace industry as a major economic force during World War II provided a way to begin to break from reliance on natural resource-based industries. Regions around the world continue to struggle with this problem, as established industries diminish in their employment capacity but continue to dominate the economic and political environment.

Geography is destiny

The further I got into Seattle's story, the more I realized how problematic the whole flat world/death of distance argument really is. Geography has been at the heart of Seattle's story from the beginning and still drives its development. The world has, of course, shrunk and leveled, but there is still a physicality to Earth and the human race that just stubbornly resists digitization.

Communications and transportation technologies have indeed changed, but the fundamental shape of the planet and the continents have not: Cincinnati and St. Louis are still far closer to the heart of the U.S. consumer market than Seattle or either of the Portlands, just the same as one hundred years ago. We still use raw materials to make physical products, and the source of materials and the location of consumers continue to shape the economic bases of cities.

This book has celebrated globalization and the opportunities it brings, but we cannot forget that national boundaries still count for a lot: the "borderless world" of Kenichi Ohmae does not exist.[12] As Acemoglu and Robinson convincingly point out, the quality of political institutions will heavily influence economic outcomes. Those institutions are created mostly at the national level and, as the persistence of truly awful governments around the world demonstrates, there are few natural mechanisms to improve institutions where they function poorly. Thus, for example, two entrepreneurs with the same idea but separated by a national border will have very different experiences under different standards of intellectual property protection. Seattle may consider itself a global city, but it nonetheless enjoys the many advantages of operating within the U.S. economic and legal system.

And within countries, Zipf's law still holds. The hierarchy of metropolitan regions means that no city has a hope of challenging the largest cities, and the mid-sized regions like Seattle must become comfortable with an intermediate role.

The weather has not changed much either, the impact of greenhouse gasses notwithstanding. Cities that were pleasant places to live a century ago are still nice places to live. Granted, air conditioning has made some otherwise uninhabitable places livable, but no one has come up with a technological cure for the gloom of Seattle, the bitter cold of Minneapolis and the snows that bury Buffalo.

But the most important way that geography continues to matter is found in the pattern of industrial agglomeration: similar businesses and people with similar skills benefit by sticking together physically. Silicon Valley is not just an idea, it is a distinct place. It has lovely weather, pleasant surrounding countryside, undistinguished architecture, horrible traffic and outrageous housing prices . . . and many of the most brilliant technologists and entrepreneurs in the world flock there.

Perhaps the greatest irony of our time: companies which developed the technologies that allow us to live and work anywhere have confined themselves and their employees to the narrowest of places.

Seattle has had some success working within the confines of its geography. It is a difficult place for a domestic business hub, but a very good one for a hub for Pacific Rim trade. The weather will not attract people, but the abundant recreation opportunities will. Hills and water make infrastructure a nightmare, but provide nice views.

Regions ignore geography at their peril. A smart region learns to work with the advantages and to mitigate limitations of its location, while not pretending that the world has become an undifferentiated tangle of fiber optic wires and office parks. Denying the deep impacts of geography does not provide a way to break the cycle of path dependency.

Demography is *not* destiny

Yes, I am turning one of the clichés of the social sciences on its head. At a global level, demographics certainly is destiny: the children born today will be the new adults of 2030 and the senior citizens of 2077. But the narrower the geographic confines, the less any demographic snapshot matters (provided of course, that people are free to live and work where they choose).

Labor mobility is one of the greatest strengths of the American economy, as it allows people the maximum opportunity to find the place their skills will be best used. This makes people more productive and allows agglomeration effects to take hold. In contrast, a lack of mobility, driven by cultural and language factors, has kept the European Union from reaching its true potential.

For individual cities and regions, this mobility presents both an opportunity and a threat. Seattle has benefitted enormously over the past 20 years from labor mobility, as hundreds of thousands of smart, ambitious people have come to the region to work in software, gaming, life sciences, aerospace and other technology-based industries. But we need to be honest: Seattle's gain has been a loss for other regions, as they have seen their own smart people leave. As I've said repeatedly, those regions that grow, attract and, most importantly, keep, high level talent will be the winners.

When thinking about migration we usually focus on the *net* change in population, since that serves as an indicator of success or failure. But we really should pay more attention to the total flows in and out of a place. For example, while we know that Detroit has been losing people and

Seattle has been gaining population, in 2010, 13,000 people moved *into* Wayne County from other states and 35,000 people moved out of King County to other states.[13] There is a big flow swirling around underneath the net gain or loss, and that total flow—all those individual people moving around the country with their skills, or lack thereof—is what shapes the character of metropolitan regions.

One of the most disconcerting pieces of research I found while writing this book was the paper that demonstrated the disconnect between the output of a state's higher education system and the educational attainment of that state's workforce at any point in time. All over the country, taxpayers and parents are funding college educations for young people who promptly leave their state. Seattle has, of course, been a beneficiary of this trend, and I think our heavy reliance on other states to educate our workforce reflects poorly on us.

Observers of America, from de Tocqueville onward, have noted the country's remarkable mobility. Horace Greeley famously declared "go West, young man," and real and literary characters have been flowing back and forth, up and down and all around since the first colonists crossed the Cumberland Gap. Today's migrants almost always head to urban areas, changing the demography of cities by the hour. In that sense each region's destiny remains wide open.

Mobility and migration do provide a way to break the cycle of path dependency.

Growth and quality of life come from different places

I hope that by now you have internalized the idea that the economy consists of two broad categories of activity: the traded sector with customers outside the region, and the non-traded sector with most of its customers inside the region. It is important to understand that each of these categories of activity produce different effects on a region.

The traded sector, also referred to as the economic base, is responsible for most growth. Autarky does not exist outside the most primitive societies, so we need to trade with others to get the things we do not provide for ourselves. The more people are employed making stuff to sell outside the region, the more people can provide locally-produced goods and services. In other words, the growth of the traded sector determines the growth—or shrinkage in the case of places where the traded sector has diminished—of the region. It's those multipliers again.

And as I hope I have made clear, the traded sector grows primarily through the capture of opportunity, not by fixing the business climate. In the current environment in which growth is occurring primarily in knowledge-based sectors, great transportation and education systems and advantageous tax and regulatory climates will not, by themselves, result in growth.

But the traded sector, important as it is, does not give us much of what we need on a daily basis: few of us need a jet or an ultrasound machine. The non-traded sector provides locally-generated goods and services, and the quality, price and availability of those goods and services has a large impact on our quality of life and the cost of living—two of the three components of the spatial equilibrium formula.

We need to remember that a highly productive traded sector does not necessarily lead to a high quality of life and an affordable community. To take an extreme example, back in the 1970s we all heard stories about how much money workers were making in the oil fields of Prudhoe Bay, Alaska, yet how lousy and expensive the life was up there: productive traded sector, inadequate non-traded sector.

To repeat: the traded sector provides growth, and the non-traded sector provides quality of life.

In thinking about how their regional economy should develop, leaders need to keep both the traded and non-traded sectors in mind, and to keep their respective needs and roles straight. I have argued that we seem to confuse the two when we think about public policy. As discussed earlier in this chapter, improvements in many of the basic business climate factors do not help much with the traded sector, but make the non-traded sector more productive and allow for lower prices.

Remember, too, that multipliers are based on the assumption that there will be workers available to fill jobs in the non-traded sector. If high housing and transportation costs make it difficult to recruit employees to work in local businesses, service quality will suffer. Think of the frustration felt by those living in affluent communities who have to wait two hours to get their pizza delivered!

Regional economic leadership involves parallel efforts to work on behalf of the traded sector, ensuring growth, or at least stability, and on the non-traded sector, ensuring affordability and quality of life. It does not do any good to help the non-traded sector if the traded sector is shrinking, and, conversely, it does not do much good to expand the economic base if people cannot afford housing and services and enjoy their surroundings.

Regionalism: economic necessity, political impossibility

From a business and economic perspective, the fragmentation of metropolitan areas makes little sense. A business operating in multiple cities in the Seattle area might pay ten separate local bills for water that started out in the same reservoir. That same business will have purchased ten separate business licenses and will pay business taxes according to ten separate formulas. It's nuts.

Want to do something about it? Good luck! Regionalizing government is as politically impossible as it is economically desirable. The idea of regional government first arose among the "good government" progressives of a century ago, and has remained a pet project of civic leagues ever since. But you can count the number of true regional governments in the country on one hand, and I am not aware of any that have been instituted in the past few decades.

Local government structure is a clear case of the divergence of the interests of businesses and residents: businesses like their governments big and residents like them small.

As residents, we identify with our small towns, and those who live in central cities tend to identify with their neighborhoods, rather than the whole city. Social scientists from Tiebout onward have discovered that residents self-select into these small communities to be near people like themselves. Diversity is a wonderful idea, but few people go out of their way to live among neighbors who are totally different from themselves. Residents of small, homogenous cities can elect leaders who reflect their values and who will preserve the status quo, which was the reason people moved there in the first place.

For residents, this is a very nice system. I live in a small city of about 3,000 people, and along with three adjacent small cities we provide our citizens with a friendly bulwark against Seattle on one side and Bellevue on the other. Our residents have no intention of giving up that autonomy, and while our towns are relatively affluent, I assure you that the residents of Algona and Fife feel exactly the same way. Small cities can have the best of both worlds, controlling important things, like zoning and development regulations, and contracting with larger jurisdictions for complicated services like utilities and fire protection.

We need to remember that regionalism is an economic construct, not a political one. So while regional government makes a great deal of sense from a government efficiency and economic development point of view, it has no constituency among the voters who would need to approve such a beast. Voters have willingly created narrow, special purpose governments to provide services that clearly operate regionally, such as transit and wastewater. The authorities of those entities will, however, be carefully circumscribed and their governing boards controlled by cities and counties.

But while any region can jury rig its way to some limited range of regional services, metropolitan economic leadership is much more complex. Leadership at the local level usually emphasizes stewardship and preservation of the status quo, while leadership at the regional level involves adjusting to change and seizing opportunities for economic growth. These are two very different kinds of leadership, and as Barnes and Ledebur point out, it is not obvious who takes on the larger regional role and assumes responsibility for a regional economy that transcends political boundaries.[14]

Counties have a limited ability to rise above their rural origins. Central city leaders, while having the largest constituencies of a region, must deal with the fact that suburban residents have explicitly rejected the central city. Governors can occasionally play a role in metro areas, but they have their hands full with state government.

So, who is in charge at the metropolitan level? In most places no one has a defined leadership role for the entire region. Whatever leadership structures take hold will be contrived and artificial since they will not grow out of any democratically elected government. They will not self-maintain and will need constant tending. They will have no, or very limited authority, and therefore will need to push their agenda and point of view toward the governments that do have authority.

Chapter 7 describes how this process works in the Seattle area. Although regional leadership in Seattle is far from neat and tidy, it has accomplished some important things to advance the metropolitan economy. Every region will need to develop its own version that fits with its own unique pattern of governance, and I would guess that most efforts at economic regionalism will end up as untidy as Seattle's.

Such arrangements are far from ideal, but until economic considerations outweigh the enormous pressures for local control, informal structures may be the best we can get. In a world where economic progress happens at the metropolitan level, regions need to create leadership of some kind that reflects more than just the sum of the aspirations of a collection of cities, towns and neighborhoods.

Chapter 9

Seattle in the Global Economy— the Decades Ahead

eattle's integration into the global economy, which has grown
steadily since its founding as the commercial and trading center
of a resource-based economy, has accelerated in recent years,
along with the nation's expanding global footprint. A 1987 study found
that, at that time, one out of every six jobs in the state depended on
exports, up from one out of nine in 1963. The study was updated in 1997,
raising that figure to one out of four jobs. But as we discussed several
times, the region has quite a number of businesses that rely on imports,
and a 1999 study looked at jobs in those industries. By this time we
could say that one out of every three jobs in the state depended on two-
way trade.[1]

The Washington Council on International Trade and the Trade Development Alliance updated the study again in 2012, this time pulling in
services exports and the impact of foreign direct investment. This study
indicates that one out of every 2.5 jobs depend on trade and other international activities.[2] If you doubt this, go back to Chapter 6 and do a back
of the envelope summing up of the impacts of the various globalized
industries. They add up very quickly, and do not include the huge exports of the state's agricultural producers.

These studies have shown that the Seattle area has become as globally integrated as any region in the U.S. And if we take Drucker's advice
and focus our attentions on opportunities, we will find most of those

through further expansion of global ties. I hope you have become convinced that Seattle's role as a supplier to purely domestic markets will be limited by its location, so the region must look to global markets for its primary growth prospects.

As anyone who has ever tried to do business internationally knows, however, it's tough out there. Every step away from the comforts of home markets introduces new opportunities, but also new variables and risks. In this final chapter we'll look at some big trends and forces and try to see how they might affect Seattle's future prospects, for better or worse. This is the fun part, where we get to pretend we are in one of those shadowy think tanks that assess geopolitical risk and cook up doomsday scenarios. But, in the spirit of this book, we'll focus mostly on the business opportunities and leave asymmetric terrorist threats and nuclear Armageddon to others.

Global growth and stability

We could definitely have a better year than 2012 to be talking about global growth and stability: growth is uneven and few places seem very stable. But the weaknesses around the world have stripped away the fluff and given us a good look at the underlying fundamentals of national and regional economies to see where the near-term and mid-term opportunities lie. Let's begin by thinking about the two terms in the subhead.

We need global growth in order to find new and expanded markets for the products we export. But global growth has a more significant role for the Seattle area economy, given the large role that aerospace plays in it. We need to consider the relationship of economic growth to demand for air travel, and, therefore, demand for commercial airplanes. As economies around the world grow, people have more money with which to travel. Demand for travel picks up very quickly as countries move from underdeveloped status to more advanced status, which is why China's travel market has expanded so rapidly. Boeing estimates that in China and India alone, one billion people have never set foot on an airplane. Since air travel is mostly a discretionary expense and the cost can only fall so far, economic growth alone can increase travel demand and increase plane sales.

We need stability in order to lower the risk and complexity of entering new markets and to protect the investments that businesses and institutions make overseas. In domestic markets and most developed country markets, businesses do not have to worry about arbitrary political maneuverings that interrupt trade and capital flows, or about expropriation of assets. But in global markets the possibility of disruptive events puts a chill on expanded global ties, especially for smaller, less sophisticated businesses. Moreover, political stability raises the likelihood of improved intellectual property protection that software and biomedical firms rely on. And, more pervasively, unstable countries tend to have higher levels of corruption, leading to more greasing of palms, or what economists quaintly call "facilitating payments."

These variables suggest four ways to categorize world markets. Let's have a quick look at the major regions of the world, how they fit into those four categories and what that indicates about opportunities for Seattle area businesses.

Low growth, high stability

This characterizes most of the large, mature markets. In 2012, much of Europe is a mess. Governments there must wrestle with some incredibly intransigent problems. Growth has slowed to a crawl and unemployment in most European countries remains high. National governments are under great political pressure to rein in deficits, even if doing so further slows growth. And in the midst of this weakness, the "Europe project" has come under severe strain. As of this writing, no one can say for certain that the Euro will still be around in a few years. So, while European countries remain politically very stable, and no one worries about expropriation or open piracy, economic uncertainties seem likely to persist for many years. European countries are among the region's largest trading partners, but growth prospects seem minimal in the near and mid-term.

Despite having the third largest economy in the world, Japan is in a terrible rut. When I first started working in the field of international trade policy in the mid-1980s, Japan struck fear into the hearts of American businesses and communities. The Japanese could seem to do no wrong, as their products and brands began to dominate U.S. markets. Many Americans assumed it was only a matter of time before "Japan Incorporated" took over the planet. Well, not long after that high point, the Japanese economy went into a deep swoon, from which it has still not entirely recovered. Japanese businesses developed extremely good manufacturing capabilities and came up with some excellent products, but could never get into innovation game as it was played in Silicon Valley. Japan largely missed out on the technology boom of the 1990s, and still has not established leadership in fast growing industries as it did in cars, machinery and electronics in the 1980s.

Europe and Japan share a significant long term demographic trend: extremely low or no population growth. Very low birth rates in Japan and most European countries have brought these countries to near zero population growth, and most will move into negative growth in the next decade.

The International Monetary Fund (IMF) projects that Japan will grow by 1.7 percent in 2013, and that Europe will grow less than one percent.[3] But despite the slow growth in these countries and their current economic problems, they remain quite wealthy and productive. They have excellent potential for partnerships in the life sciences, which operate at quite advanced levels in them. But perhaps the most important potential for the Seattle area in these markets lies in tourism. As noted, wealthy people tend to travel more, and these countries have the wealth to undertake international travel and the traditions of doing so. But Seattle does not appear prominently on travel agendas, except perhaps for Japanese visitors lured by baseball. Product markets may not have a lot of room for growth in these countries, but for Seattle, tourism markets do have good growth potential.

Low stability, high growth

Over the past two decades the world has become more stable overall, but many areas outside of the developed Western economies still lack the kinds of safeguards for business that we take for granted in Europe and Japan. Many of the fastest growing markets in the world can still be characterized as relatively unstable from a commercial perspective.

Does it make sense to put China in this category? The growth part is a non-issue. Even if China's blistering pace of growth slows, it will still offer huge opportunities, especially as the broad base of Chinese consumers gain enough income to shift into branded consumer products. The stability side suggests some room for concern. In *Why Nations Fail*,

Acemoglu and Robinson argue that countries with authoritarian governments cannot sustain long term growth due to internal resistance to change. Indeed, we have begun to see cracks in the state capitalist model, and no one really has any idea where those cracks might lead. So although China will likely grow quite well over the coming years, enough unpredictability enters the picture to give pause.

India is even more complicated. Seattle area firms have extensive ties to India, and the region's Indian population has increased substantially in the past 25 years. India has even become an important and growing market for Washington apples. But it is far from a completely stable place, with a relatively high corruption rating from Transparency International (TI).[4] Nonetheless, the size and growth potential of the market and the rise of the middle class make India a prime target for globalized businesses. The IMF expects India to grow at about a seven percent annual rate. Seattle can boost its success with Indian markets by further exploiting the personal and family ties in the region.

The ASEAN countries, Thailand, Malaysia, Indonesia, Philippines and Vietnam, show good growth potential, with the IMF projecting an average of about six percent annual growth in the years ahead. These countries remain relatively poor in many parts, and TI indicates high levels of corruption. Nonetheless, like other Asian countries they are large nations with emerging middle classes.

Latin America has experienced improvements in political and economic stability in recent decades, although TI still indicates that all but Chile and Uruguay have above average levels of corruption. Democracies have taken root where dictatorships once dominated, and economies have become more productive as a result. Brazil appears to be on the cusp of a major move onto the global stage. The IMF expects all countries in Central and South America, except Venezuela, to grow between four and six percent in coming years.

Seattle firms will struggle to get traction in Latin America because of the physical distance and lack of close ties. Business with Latin America remains captive of Miami and Houston, and the lack of direct air service will make it difficult for Seattle area businesses to break into those markets. But if you grab that globe and string you used while reading Chapter 6 and trace a great circle route from Seattle to Santiago, Chile, you will see that it is about the same distance as Seattle to Hong Kong.

In the Northern Hemisphere we tend to think about east-west, but perhaps we should be looking at opportunities oriented in a north-south direction.

Sub-Saharan Africa has experienced remarkable growth in recent years. But since most of these countries start from such a low base, exporters tend not to notice that they may present business opportunities. Because so much of the international activity around Africa involves relief, aid, philanthropy and basic development, it is easy to forget that the continent is full of consumers and businesses. According to TI, however, only Botswana has relatively low levels of corruption.

High stability high growth

Unfortunately, as you might imagine, this list is not long. In the World Economic Forum's stages of development model, growth in the most mature and stable of countries comes primarily through innovation. Europe and Japan have struggled to become more innovative, in spite of ongoing programs and policy initiatives designed to shake up their industries and research establishments. That leaves just the stable, newly industrialized countries of Asia, such as Korea, Taiwan and Singapore, as well as Australia and New Zealand as the only places that have combined a high level of political and economic stability with reasonably high levels of growth. Fortunately, Seattle area businesses and civic leaders have strong ties to these countries, leaving the door open for new export and service opportunities.

Low growth low stability

This list, thankfully, is fairly short, consisting largely of countries formerly in the Soviet Union. Many of these places are large and have substantial income from petroleum, so they do present market opportunities. Doing business in them can be a challenge, and firms need to weigh the costs and risks of entering these markets when long term growth prospects may be weak.

As we have gone on this global tour I hope you noticed something: most of the opportunity markets lie around the Pacific Ocean. That does not automatically mean that the Seattle area and its ports will be able to capture that opportunity. The region still needs to compete with Los Angeles and its huge local markets and business service base, as well as

San Francisco and Vancouver, Canada, with their strong historic ties to the Pacific Rim. But Seattle has enough going for it that if the region cannot cash in on the opportunities presented by Asia in the coming decades, it will have only itself to blame.

Innovation

In the WEF model, innovation drives growth in advanced economies. This fact has become clear over the past 20 years or so, as the "efficiency" and "quality" phases ran their course through Western economies. Manufacturers in Europe and the U.S. learned from Japanese practices and greatly improved their processes and output. But while doing the same thing better improves productivity and short and mid-term growth, it cannot lead to long term industry leadership. The improved efficiency and quality that proved necessary to save industries still fell into Drucker's category of "problems." The opportunities would start to emerge from places like Silicon Valley, Route 128 and . . .Redmond.

The development and introduction of innovative new technologies drove growth in the American economy in the late 1980s through the 1990s, and integration of those technologies into business processes drove growth and productivity in the 2000s. The fact that this innovation came out of just a handful of places did not go unnoticed, and, as described in Chapter 1, regions around the world began to chase the model they thought they saw in Silicon Valley. These efforts mostly produced scant results, and high level innovation remains concentrated in just a few places, with the Seattle area, fortunately, among them.

In his 2012 book *The New Geography of Jobs*, University of California, Berkeley, economist Enrico Moretti sums up the innovation landscape:

> *A growing body of research suggests that cities are not just a collection of individuals, but complex, interrelated environments that foster the generation of new ideas and new ways of doing business. For example, social interactions among workers tend to generate learning opportunities that enhance innovation and productivity. Being around smart people makes us smarter and more innovative. By clustering near each other, innovators foster each other's creative*

spirit and become more successful. Thus, once a city attracts some innovative workers and innovative companies its economy changes in ways that make it even more attractive to other innovators.[5]

Knowing what we now know about the Seattle area economy, innovation will be central to growth going forward. Right now the region has the assets to remain a center of innovation and to sustain that status well into the future. We need to protect and renew those assets so they keep delivering benefits and fueling the virtuous cycle that Moretti describes. This will not happen entirely by itself. Let's consider some related groups of assets that are particular strengths in the region.

Research institutions serve as the seedbed for innovative technologies. The University of Washington has been central to the region's position as a leader in innovation, and can continue to be. The impact of state education funding cutbacks on the UW's research mission is not at all clear, and needs to be better understood. Alongside the UW is the constellation of independent research organizations, most in the life sciences, that form the "research industry" of the region. And I suspect that there are helpful spillover effects emanating from the massive brain trust that is Microsoft Research, whether they like it or not.

Studies in both Germany and Sweden have shown that the spillover effects of academic research diminish sharply with distance from the institutions, so even if the results of research get published in globally-available academic journals, the region still benefits from the fact that the researchers work and live in the area.[6] The borders between universities, non-profit research institutions and technology businesses can be quite porous, with individuals moving fluidly among all three, sharing knowledge and insights. It is these agglomeration effects, aided by the physical proximity of different players in a place like South Lake Union, that produce real economic benefits over time.

We have an opportunity to build on existing institutions and foster creation of new ones. The expansion of global health activity has attracted local offices of major international relief organizations, demonstrating the power of having a critical mass of institutions and activity. The strength of cross-sectoral alliances in life sciences and global health, as described in Chapter 7, indicate that leaders understand the opportunities these institutions present.

The second asset group consists of people. As this book has repeated to the point of nausea, there is nothing more important for the Seattle region's future than nurturing, attracting and retaining highly talented people. And there are few things more dismaying than the haphazard way we think about talent recruitment and retention. If the economic development establishment finds out that a business is thinking of bringing a factory to the region, the alarm is sounded and it's all hands on deck. But if a bunch of big brains are thinking of moving here, we generally have no idea about their intention and few tools with which to recruit them. We understand how to attract physical capital, but not how to recruit intellectual capital.

We have an opportunity to build far better awareness of the benefits that a target individual would enjoy by bringing their big brain to Seattle. We like to imagine that everyone knows all about the wonderfulness of the career opportunities and the lifestyle of Seattle, but I suspect that people know less than we think, especially the farther away they are. What I am suggesting is a pretty straightforward marketing exercise, that begins with research, such as the work on amenities discussed in Chapter 5, and produces a communications strategy meant to lure people who might otherwise not consider the Seattle area a good place to settle down for a long and satisfying career.

Another set of assets, not nearly as strong in the region, consists of the various intermediaries involved in the process of turning research into products and services. Scientists are notoriously bad businesspeople, and most businesspeople lack the patience to move science out of the lab and into product development. Bridging this gap is the collection of technology transfer officials, entrepreneurs, funders, lawyers and other denizens of the innovation ecosystem who, collectively, absorb and manage the risks inherent in the early stages of innovation.[7] And for absorbing those risks, of course, they expect ample rewards in the form of ownership and fat fees (with the expectation they will get little or nothing if the venture falls apart). In any case, innovation does not happen at all without them, and the Seattle area has never had as deep a base of intermediaries as Silicon Valley or Boston.

Yes, the region does have successful entrepreneurs, and ventures do get local funding, but all too often innovators find themselves on planes heading to those other centers. The region has an opportunity to build a more complete set of intermediaries within its innovation ecosystems to leverage the strong research institutions and their highly capable scientists and engineers.

Innovation is not a generic activity, however, but occurs within specific industries and disciplines. Any region can have only a limited number of functioning innovation ecosystems at a time. Seattle has well established ecosystems in aerospace, software, internet commerce, gaming and some life sciences fields. Is this enough? Can we create new ones out of whole cloth? As noted, many regions have attempted to do this, pumping up academic departments at universities, building science parks, using public money for venture funding and providing a host of other services. Should leaders in the Seattle area put on a big push to develop new innovation ecosystems in other sectors?

If so, it is not immediately apparent what sector would have the most promise. Quite a number of people have been pursuing the clean technology cluster, which includes alternative energy, resource recovery, energy conservation and other related disciplines. Given the need to transform the nation's energy profile and improve the efficiency of resource use, these fields certainly have huge growth potential. The question is, does the Seattle area have any unique characteristics and assets that would give it an advantage over other regions. Like the life sciences, nearly every economic development plan in the world targets clean technology, and only a few will become major innovation centers in it.

On the other hand, maybe this does not matter at all. We have a limited ability to target successful clusters, and in the end need to rely on the serendipity with which our current clusters took shape. By taking care of our major research institutions, having a good collection of intermediaries and making sure that smart, innovative, adventurous people want to live and work here, we can heed Pasteur's observation that chance favors the well prepared.

We need to heed Schumpeter as well. Technology industries face the same dynamic of creative destruction as heavy industries. Recall that WordPerfect was the industry standard word processing software in the 1980s, but the company stuck with its old DOS version far too long and ended up eclipsed by Microsoft Word. WordPerfect refused embrace the innovation of graphic user interface and, in the process, destroy its old, highly successful product. Now, touch screens mark the first major interface change since Windows, and Microsoft does seem willing, with Windows 8, to destroy its old interface in order to adapt to the new. This is a huge risk—potentially ticking off hundreds of millions of users who will have to learn a new system—but, at least from an economic development perspective, also a heartening development.

Fifty years ago, as I have pointed out, Seattle did not have industries subject to much in the way of creative destruction, and so avoided that trauma. Well, it has them now, and Seattle's future as a center of innovation rests, in large part, on their willingness to embrace change.

Energy and climate change

A few politicians may have lost their jobs because of the Great Recession, but no political force got smashed flatter by the economic train wreck than the issue of climate change. Before the economy went off the rails in 2007, we could see the country gradually coming to grips with the impact of greenhouse gasses on the global climate and the need to make major changes in the way we use energy. And even as the science remained uncertain, policies began to take effect that would have implications for businesses, households and communities.

Then, as a larger, much more definite emergency took over the national consciousness, the climate crisis moved well down the political agenda. Cap and trade legislation died in Congress, and individual state efforts languished. A few concrete elements, like renewable portfolio standards that require utilities to use renewable energy, did come into play, and automakers came out with a slew of electric and hybrid cars. But given the magnitude of the pre-recession rhetoric, the entire issue has gone very quiet.

It will come back, though, as the economy improves and opinion makers get around to thinking about other things. The problem of climate change may be global, but the impact of change itself and our response to it will vary widely across the planet. We can imagine several impacts on the Seattle area, each of which presents both opportunities and risks. Let's look at some of them, starting with proposed actions to reduce the use of fossil fuels, and then moving on to the implications of the climate change that seems inevitable.

Serious reductions in net carbon output will require a substantial cut in the amount of energy used by households, businesses and governments. Alternative, carbon-neutral renewable energy sources are the obvious long-run requirement, but those energy technologies and the infrastructure to produce and deliver them reliably will not get to scale for many years, so we need to cut back on energy use in the interim. Not surprisingly, this means different things in different parts of the country: some areas are more carbon-intensive than others. It turns out that the Seattle area has a relatively low individual carbon footprint.

The region's hydropower capacity provides the most obvious source of our climate friendliness, courtesy of the dams on the Columbia, Snake, Skagit and other rivers. Beyond that, the region does have a somewhat greater tendency toward using transit and other alternative modes of transportation and to have shorter commutes than in many Western cities. But we can also thank geography, once again. The region's mild climate means moderate use of winter heating and low use of summer air conditioning. The least climate-friendly regions, in contrast, use more heat in winter and/or large amounts of summer air conditioning plugged into coal-fired power plants.

In general, the coastal areas of the West have the most climate-friendly weather patterns in the country and relatively high use of public transportation. If West Coast metropolitan areas begin absorbing a larger share of the nation's growth, more Americans could lower their household carbon footprint while minimizing the impact on their lifestyles. As a number of observers have pointed out, however, West Coast metro areas have among the nation's most restrictive policies on housing development, while places with much higher per capita carbon output make it very easy to develop housing.[8]

I realize that I will not win friends by suggesting that Seattle should invite more development and growth, but the truth is, the Pacific Coast does offer a climate friendly alternative. To pat ourselves on the back about all our environmental virtues but, at the same time, restrict growth and push it to the Sunbelt, smacks of hypocrisy. To take advantage of the opportunity to attract more residents who want to lower their household carbon footprint we do not need to weaken our own standards for environmentally responsible development. We just need to get used to the idea that as the nation moves away from the need for lengthy car commutes and air conditioning, we may find ourselves unexpectedly popular.

As for becoming a center for energy saving or alternative energy technologies, quite a number of people in the region have been hard at work on everything from the energy efficiency of buildings to algae-based biofuels and tide power. These are exciting possibilities, enabled by the life science, engineering and information technology innovation ecosystems operating in the region. But as noted above, these activities are underway all over the country and the world, and as much as I would like to think that the big breakthroughs will come from the Seattle area, I am aware that only a few big winners will emerge. Cautious optimism is perhaps the best place to land on these opportunities.

One area of the overall energy space that presents both risk and opportunity to the region involves air travel. We can figure out how to convert lots of energy consuming devices to clean electricity, but not airplanes. Liquid fuels have very high energy densities and given the range and weight restriction of aircraft, there really are no substitutes. The region has the opportunity to build on its expertise in aerospace and become the center of aviation biofuels. This process is already underway, spearheaded by Boeing, along with participation by Alaska Airlines and the Navy. The risk is that we don't solve the fuel problem and, either by price or policy, the world cuts back on air travel, thereby reducing the demand for aircraft.[9]

Another opportunity comes from building on the region's existing leadership in creating innovative communities and homes. Seattle area architects and homebuilders have made great strides in developing home and neighborhood styles that use less land and energy while meeting diverse housing needs. These ideas grew out of a desire to rein in sprawl, but they adapt perfectly to the new imperative to cut back on home energy use and commutes.

But if even the more moderate predictions about climate change are in the ballpark, we can expect real shifts in weather patterns to emerge in the coming decades, in spite of all our efforts to reduce fossil fuel use. And as much as I try to remain optimistic, the impacts of climate change on the Seattle area do not inspire confidence. Sure, this will be a cooler place to live year-round than much of the country, but some impacts cause concern.

The region's hydropower advantage rests on the ability of the mountains of the Pacific Northwest and British Columbia to hold vast amounts of water at high altitudes in the form of snow, and then release that water into rivers gradually over the spring, summer and fall. Some climate modeling shows that in the future the Northwest will get as much or more precipitation during the year, but that less of it will fall as snow and more as rain. A smaller snowpack and earlier melt-off would make the hydropower system less productive, as it churns out more power during the rainy season, and less during the summer, when air conditioning loads peak.

Another area of concern surrounds the possibility of a rise in ocean levels. Most of the region's waterfront areas are reasonably steep, so the loss of property would not be too extensive. The larger concern is waterfront industrial and port infrastructure and the ability of these facilities to withstand higher water. Estimates of water level changes vary widely, but some models suggest dangerous levels at high tide. Fortunately, this change does not happen overnight, and businesses and ports can rebuild docks as needed. The cost will not be insignificant, however.

Climate change could also have an impact on the state's agricultural producers, especially in the form of new pests that might migrate from other areas as the climate changes. Washington products have a reputation for high quality and safety, and the introduction of new pests could threaten that reputation. While few products from the immediate Seattle area make it overseas, much of the state's output flows through the ports of Seattle and Tacoma. Moreover, agricultural exporters add a very important component to the region's overall global reach.

In his book *Climatopolis*, economist Matthew Kahn sketches out the many ways that markets will respond to the realities of climate change and how new products, services and land uses will help the world adjust. Kahn makes a sort of ideological leap that puts mitigation of climate change impacts on par with, or maybe even ahead of, prevention measures.[10] I sense that environmental and civic leaders in the Seattle region have not yet made that leap and still focus mostly on reducing energy use. But when they do realize that climate change is coming, the region should be poised to capture opportunities as the world adjusts.

Global networks and relationships

The overwhelming tragedy of World War II gave rise to a set of international institutions designed to manage global tensions and prevent future major conflicts. This array of multilateral institutions included the United Nations, the World Bank and the entire Bretton Woods system of global trade and financial arrangements. As long as the industrialized countries dominated these organizations, especially the economic ones, they operated relatively smoothly. But in recent decades they have come under severe strain, and the world has become a far more complicated place. The National Intelligence Council's report *Global Trends 2025* indicates that:

> *The trend toward greater diffusion of authority and power occurring for a couple of decades is likely to accelerate because of the emergence of new global players, increasingly ineffective institutions, growth in regional blocs, advanced communications technologies, and enhanced strength of non-state actors and networks. . . . Recent trends suggest that existing multilateral institutions—which are large and cumbersome—will have difficulty adapting quickly enough to undertake new missions, accommodate changing memberships, and obtain necessary resources. NGOs and philanthropist foundations—concentrating on specific issues—increasingly will be a part of the landscape. . .[11]*

The international political environment, once dominated by national governments and international organizations, has become far more open to new actors. Metropolitan regions are among those actors, and the networks that these cities create will form an important part of the geopolitical framework going forward. Perhaps the biggest opportunity that Seattle has in the coming decades will be to position itself as a critical node in these metropolitan networks. Given Seattle's relatively small size and current position with respect to Los Angeles, San Francisco and, to some extent, Vancouver, this will be a major challenge. But the rewards will be substantial. The region has a number of opportunities.

Most obviously, Seattle and Tacoma must continue to position their ports as major gateways for North American trade. Not only is it symbolically important to have large ships coming in and out of the harbors, the movement of goods provides an excellent layer of jobs that help pre-serve the all-important middle of the earning scale.

Next, we can leverage the strengths of the ports. Going back to the idea expressed in Chapter 1, the region needs to expand its array of international business services so that it becomes a center for transac-tions, and not just movement of cargo. Firms from across the country should come to Seattle for expertise in conducting business overseas, and then use the ports to complete that business. Seattle and Tacoma need to aim for "world port city" status.

The region is already a center of ideas, but much of the world does not know that. Leadership in software and global health brings people from all over the world to Seattle, and we can extend this convening role, dusting off the goal of becoming "the Geneva of the Pacific Rim." Ag-glomeration economics teaches us that idea generation needs face-to-face communications, and Seattle should be the place where that happens in a wide variety of fields. And in this role Seattle's geographic position, once such a liability, becomes a huge asset, with the region positioned equidistant by air between Europe, Asia and Latin America.

I recall back in the 1980s, Chamber president George Duff said that, as he saw the global economy taking shape, only a few cities would gain what he termed an "international franchise." By this he meant exactly what I am talking about here: an important and central position in the networks of regions that, working together, will fill in the spaces vacated by national governments and international organizations.

In 1999 many of us thought Seattle had achieved all this. The WTO meetings would put the icing on the cake, confirming Seattle's status as a major global center. It did not work out quite that way. The bruising of the WTO experience set things back a bit. Not that the international community blamed the Seattle hosts for the debacle—worlds were about to collide and we just happened to be the spot where that collision hap-pened—but it caused local leaders to question our direction. But in hindsight, perhaps Seattle had hitched itself to the wrong wagon. WTO would continue to fail, protestors or no protestors, and the future ap-pears to be heading other directions entirely.

One of those new directions had been taking shape for some time, and has become the global network of metropolitan areas. This, I would contend, is the place that Seattle can show real leadership. The idea of global urban networks is still evolving, and Seattle can help define this new form of connectivity. Saskia Sassen writes:

> *The growth of global markets for finance and specialized services, the need for transnational servicing networks in response to sharp increases in international investment, the reduced role of the government in the regulation of international economic activity and the corresponding ascendance of other institutional arenas, notably global markets and corporate headquarters—all these point to the existence of transnational economic arrangements with multiple urban locations in more than one country. Here is the formation, at least incipiently, of a transnational urban system.[12]*

Earlier, I noted my concern about the ability of regions like Seattle to compete in a world dominated by places like Tokyo, Los Angeles and Shanghai. How do we avoid getting stomped on? The key, I think, is forming common cause and building networks with similar cities around the world that also do not want to get stomped on. Seattle has begun this, with the International Regions Benchmarking Consortium, and should continue to build that network. Zipf's Law, from way back in Chapter 1 says that places like Seattle will never become places like Los Angeles and will continue to fill roles appropriate for their size. Other mid-sized regions around the world face the same limitations and opportunities and have plenty to learn from each other and business to do together.

The idea of Seattle as a global center is not a new one. *Seattle: World City that Had To Be*, a boosterish pamphlet published in 1930, touts the city's superior port facilities, steamship service and location closest to "700 million people living in China, Japan, the Philippines and the rest of the Orient, all with real money to spend."[13] Sound familiar?

Finding Century 21 City

I began this book with an optimistic view of the future of Seattle and I think I have backed up that optimism. Data and trends indicate that few mid-sized regions in the country are better positioned to succeed in the twenty-first century.

If it's all about being smart and globally connected, we've come a long way and have opportunities in front of us to go much farther. Fifty years ago, when Seattle hosted the Century 21 Exhibition, the region had already become reasonably smart and connected, especially for a remote, provincial city with sawdust in its hair and fish guts between its toes. But we needed a way to get out of our geographic corner. Eddie Carlson and the gang found a way out, advancing a vision that has proved remarkably durable: celebrate science and embrace the world. The ride has been bumpy, but worthwhile for those who've stuck it out.

Roger Sale ended his book about Seattle with a description of naked, stoned hippies jumping into Lake Washington off the abandoned freeway ramps in the Arboretum. From his perspective in the early 1970s this would have been a compelling image for Seattle: free spirits cavorting on structures, the abandonment of which symbolized the changing of the political guard and the emergence of a new environmental and community consciousness.

I am going to end this book in a very different place: the Tully's Coffee shop in Lincoln Square in downtown Bellevue, where I am sitting at this very moment. The things that count about the twenty-first century city are all around. The office tower above me swarms with Microsoft employees who cycle through this shop daily, listening to sales pitches, giving informational interviews or catching up with colleagues and partners. I have no idea which of the many tentacles of Microsoft operates up there, but I like to think they are busy inventing some piece of the future.

The other half of the office tower contains the corporate headquarters of Eddie Bauer, the retailer that first created the image of the Northwest outdoor lifestyle around which we still build our identity. And next door, at the Hyatt, Brooks Sports, the Bothell-based running gear company, is holding a major international sales conference.

If I burst through the back wall of the coffee shop I would end up in front of the headquarters of Paccar. Long a part of the industrial bedrock of the region, Paccar builds the finest Class 8 trucks in the world, taking advantage of new technologies at every turn. If I took a slight shift to the right, I would end up at the headquarters of Expedia, Microsoft's most successful spin-off. A few blocks north of Expedia I would come to the Bellevue library, outside of which stands a statue of Mohandas Gandhi, a gift from the Indian government in recognition of the

Eastside's large Indian population.

But even with all that, you might ask, will I really find Century 21 City in a suburb? Yes, you will. Downtown Seattle, with its lovely harbor and skyline, forms just one part of a region alive with activity. I could have written this coda at a sidewalk table in South Lake Union, surrounded by life sciences researchers, Amazonians and cool loft apartments. Or I could have sat on the grass at Sixty Acres park in Redmond on a Saturday afternoon, in Alfred Marshall mode, listening to the buzz of ideas floating through the air while a United Nations of techie parents watch their kids play soccer. Or, maybe I could just sit by the fence at Renton Airport and watch the daily maiden flight of another brand new Boeing 737, sporting the livery of some exotic airline—a beautiful reminder of what has gone right for the past fifty years.

I would not, however, bring this story to a close with the free spirits. Yes, we really need them to keep us honest, and God bless their unchained souls in all their fixed-gear, inked, pierced, ear-gauged splendor. But at its core, Seattle has never been about the free spirits. It has always been about the very people in this coffee shop right now: smart, creative, hard working, risk-seeking. People like the Denny party that set up camp in the November rains of 1851. Or my grandparents, who dug for gold in Nome and later helped carve a community out of the stumps a couple of miles from where I sit right now. Or the Balatico family, whose Mercer Slough farm provided me with my first paid employment. Or Nellie Cornish or Mark Tobey and the Northwest School, or Jim Whitaker, first American to climb Mount Everest. . .

I am sitting just a few yards from the spot where my mother's childhood friend, Peter Bishop, had his travel agency, a paragon of mid-twentieth century small town commerce: idyllic and local. I now find myself surrounded by the ingredients of metropolitan success in our era. I come to this coffee shop often because I like the energy and diversity and the sense I get that Seattle has lived up to the dreams of the World's Fair and become Century 21 City.

Acknowledgements

This book started out as a sort of brain dump that allowed me to spill out a quarter century's worth of accumulated random data and thoughts and pull it all into a coherent story. But as fun as that was, I always ran two risks. Would I get the story right? And would it be readable and make a useful contribution to the historical record of the Seattle area and, I hope, the larger understanding of urban economic geography?

Fortunately, I had many wonderful people who helped on both counts, and I was able to launch the book out into the world with reasonable confidence. When I finished my first draft I recruited a number of friends and colleagues to read it and provide their unvarnished opinions. These reviewers offered advice, corrections, new and valuable details and, most importantly, encouragement.

Two of the reviewers, George Duff and Dick Ford, have been in the middle of the action for most of the fifty years covered in the book, and their general imprimatur gave me great comfort. Bob Drewel, Stu Elway and John Howell have been around almost as long, each offering unique perspectives. Rick Olson and Tayloe Washburn helped me think about how to connect with audiences in ways I had not considered.

Catherine Hardy and Rebecca Johnston scoured the text for typos, missing words and all those little infelicities that creep in after a while.

On the technical side, two professors helped keep me out of trouble. Kriss Sjoblom, a bona fide urban economist, smoothed out the rough theoretical edges and provided corrections and details on core trends and events. Bill Barnes, at the National League of Cities, who has written extensively on metropolitan development, asked tough questions and helped tighten some of my loose thinking.

During my twenty-five years working on public affairs around Seattle, Bill Stafford has guided, mentored, harassed and supported me in ways too numerous to count. His generosity with his time and energy as I worked on this book is greatly appreciated.

I also need to acknowledge the many friends, neighbors and colleagues who put up with my incessant interrogations. A central thread of the book is the question of why people come to Seattle and why they stay, and since I am surrounded by highly talented transplants, I never miss an opportunity to grill them. Their stories and impressions have expanded my own parochial view of the region and helped me understand what it looks like from the outside.

Finally, my family has been a source of encouragement and, most importantly, patience, so thank you to Maryann and to Sean, Melanie and Andrea.

About the Author

Michael Luis is a consultant in public affairs and communications, and serves as a councilmember and mayor in the city of Medina, Washington. His consulting practice, which he has operated since 1998, centers on economic development, housing and development issues. He has also spent considerable time working on issues related to taxes and public finance, higher education and local government. Clients have included Fortune 500 companies, state and local governments, economic development agencies and regional businesses.

Prior to starting his consulting practice, Mr. Luis spent ten years working for the Greater Seattle Chamber of Commerce, first as a public affairs manager and later as Vice President for Public Affairs. In this capacity he managed a wide range of issues and served as lead staff for the Intercity Visit and Leadership Conference programs.

Mr. Luis began his career serving as Director of the Export Task Force, a bipartisan pro-free trade caucus of the U.S. House of Representatives.

He holds a bachelor's degree in history from the University of Washington and a Masters Degree in International Affairs from the George Washington University.

In a volunteer capacity, Mr. Luis has served as Treasurer and President of the Eastside Heritage Center, the organization dedicated to the stewardship of the history of East King County.

He is married and lives in Medina, Washington, where his three children are now the fourth generation to live in the family home on Evergreen Point Road.

Notes

Introduction

[1] To learn more about this quintessentially Seattle sport, visit the website of the Hydroplane and Raceboat Museum, at http://thunderboats.ning.com/, or, better yet, go to the museum itself in Kent, Washington

[2] Nevermind became number 1 on Billboard's charts on January 11, 1992; Microsoft released Windows 3.1 on April 6, 1992; Boeing began final assembly of the first 777 on January 4, 1993 from subassemblies created in 1992; Starbucks held its IPO on June 26, 1992.

Chapter 1

[1] For a discussion on early twentieth century thinking on the evolution of cities, see: Witold Rybczynski, Makeshift Metropolis (New York: Scribner, 2010)

2. Jane Jacobs, *The Death and Life of Great American Cities* (New York: Random House, 1961); David Riesman, *The Lonely Crowd* (New Haven: Yale University Press, 1953); William Whyte, *The Organization Man* (New York, Simon and Schuster, 1956)

[3] Seaside, Florida, illustrates the basic problem of the New Urbanist movement, which tries to impose a very rigid vision of a romanticized past. The only way to do this at any scale has been to create brand new communities like Seaside or Disney's Celebration, where the developer can control everything, down to the smallest detail. This, in turn, requires large, attractive tracts of land which can only be found at a reasonable price in remote areas. The towns being emulated were entirely organic, but these places are not. Check out www.seasidefl.com.

[4] Neal R. Peirce, *Citistates* (Washington, D.C., Seven Locks Press, 1993); William Barnes, Larry Ledebur, *The New Regional Economies: The U.S. Common Market and the Global Economy* (Thousand Oaks: Sage Publications, 1998)

[5] This point is made most succinctly in: Edward Glaeser, *Triumph of the City: How Our Greatest Invention Makes Us Richer, Smarter, Greener, Healthier and Happier* (New York: Penguin Press, 2011)

[6] Bruce Katz, "Global Cities: The Drivers of Economic Growth," www.brookings.edu/upfront/posts/2011/10/20-global-cities-katz

[7] 1900 data from: U.S. Census Bureau, Special Reports, Occupations at the 12th Census, 1900. Found at: www.census.gov/prod/www/abs/decennial/1900.html. 2010 data from U.S. Department of Labor.

[8] U.S. Bureau of Economic Analysis (BEA), National Income and Product Accounts (NIPA). Found at www.bea.gov.

[9] U.S. Department of Agriculture, *Rural Poverty at a Glance*, (Rural Development Research Report Number 100, July 2004)

[10] U.S. Census Bureau (Census), Population Estimates. Found at www.census.gov/popest/

[11] Luis M.A. Bettencourt, Jose Lobo, Dirk Helbing, Christian Kuhnert, Geoffrey B. West, "Growth, Innovation and Scaling and the Pace of Life in Cities," *Proceedings of the National Academy of Sciences* 104 (2007).

[12] For vivid descriptions of population trends in developing countries, watch the various video presentations by Hans Roebling, professor of global health at Sweden's Karolinska Institute. Many of these can be found at www.ted.com, or on YouTube.

[13] "Majority of Chinese Now Live in Cities," *New York Times*, January 17, 2012

[14] Jane Jacobs, Cities and the Wealth of Nations, (New York: Viking, 1985)

[15] Peirce, *Citistates;* Saskia Sassen, *Cities in a World Economy,* Third Ed (Thousand Oaks, Pine Forge Press, 2006); Barnes and Ledebur, *The New Regional Economies;* Allen J. Scott, *Regions and the World Economy,* (Oxford: Oxford University Press, 1998)

[16] Thomas L. Friedman, *The World is Flat: A Brief History of the Twenty-First Century* (New York: Farrar, Straus and Giroux, 2005)

[17] Richard Florida, "The World is Spiky," *Atlantic Monthly*, October, 2005

[18] BEA, Regional Economic Accounts.

[19] Census, 2010 American Community Survey. Accessed in the American Factfinder, found at http://factfinder2.census.gov/faces/nav/jsf/pages/index.xhtml

[20] U.S. Bureau of Labor Statistics (BLS), Local Area Unemployment Statistics, found at www.bls.gov/lau/

[21] Peter Ganong, Daniel Shoag, "Why Has Regional Convergence in the U.S. Stopped?" Social Sciences Research Network working paper series..

[22] E.F. Schumacher, *Small is Beautiful: Economics as if People Mattered* (London : Blond and Briggs, 1973)

[23] BLS, Current Employment Statistics, found at: www.bls.gov/data/

[24] WardsAuto, Data Center, found at http://wardsauto.com/data-center

[25] Many books have been written about the magic of Silicon Valley. One of the earlier attempts to figure out what made Silicon Valley work, and still among the more useful, are: AnnaLee Saxenian, *Regional Advantage: Culture and Competition in Silicon Valley and Route 128* (Cambridge, Harvard University Press, 1996); and Margaret Pugh O'Mara, *Cities of Knowledge: Cold War Science and the Search for the Next Silicon Valley* (Princeton, Princeton University Press, 2004)

[26] A list of Siliconia names can be found in the archives of the now-defunct newsletter Tasty Bits from the Technology Front: http://tbtf.com/siliconia.html

[27] Margaret Pugh O'Mara, *Cities of Knowledge*

[28] Census, Population Estimates. Found at www.census.gov/popest/

[29] Xavier Gabaix, "Zipf's Law for Cities: An Explanation," *Quarterly Journal of Economics* 114 (1999)

[30] Internal Revenue Service (IRS), U.S. Population Migration Data, found at: www.irs.gov/taxstats/index.html

[31] Rosen, Sherwin. 1979. "Wage-based indexes of urban quality of life." In Peter Miezkowski and Mahlon R. Straszheim, eds., *Current Issues in Urban Economics*. (Baltimore: Johns HopkinsUniversity Press 1979). Roback, Jennifer. "Wages, Rents and the Quality of Life." *Journal of Political Economy* 90(1982

[32] Adapted from a slightly more complex formula in: Edward Glaeser, "The Economics Approach to Cities," National Bureau of Economic Research Working Paper No. 13696, 2007

[33] Charles Tiebout, "A Pure Theory of Local Expenditures," *Journal of Political Economy* 64 (1956)

[34] Bill Bishop, The Big Sort: Why the Clustering of Like-Minded America is Tearing Us Apart, (New York: Mariner Books, 2009).

[35] William Alonso, *Location and Land Use*, (Cambridge: Harvard University Press, 1964). Edwin Mills, "An Aggregative Model of Resource Allocation in a Metropolitan Area," *American Economic Review* 57(1967). Richard Muth, *Cities and Housing*, (Chicago: University of Chicago Press, 1969).

[36] Edward L. Glaeser, Jed Kolko, Albert Saiz, "Consumer City," Harvard Institute for Economic Research Discussion Paper No. 1901, 2000

[37] The Des Moines-Do More campaign can be found at www.desmoinesmetro.com/

[38] Joseph Gyourko, Christopher Mayer, Todd Sinai, "Superstar Cities," National Bureau of Economic Research working paper # 12355, 2006

[39] The cosmopolitan-local distinction has been described in several places. A helpful guide is found in: Daniel Elazar, *Building Cities in America* (Lanham, MD, Hamilton Press, 1987)

[40] Richard Florida, *The Rise of the Creative Class And How It's Transforming Work, Leisure, Community and Everyday Life*, (New York: Basic Books, 2002)

[41] Friedman, *The World is Flat*

Chapter 2

[1] Census, Population Estimates

[2] Washington State Office of Financial Management (OFM), Population, Population Change, Births, Deaths, and Residual Migration 1960 to 2010 by year by County, found at: http://www.ofm.wa.gov/pop/migration/default.asp

[3] Census, Population Estimates

[4] National death rate taken from the Centers for Disease Control and Prevention, National Vital Statistics System, found at: www.cdc.gov/nchs/nvss.htm. Regional death rate taken from OFM, Population, Population Change, Births, Deaths, and Residual Migration 1960 to 2010 by year by County.

[5] OFM, Population, Population Change, Births, Deaths, and Residual Migration 1960 to 2010 by year by County.

[6] OFM, Decennial population counts for the state, counties, and cities: 1890 to 2000

[7] Ibid.

[8] OFM, Population, Population Change, Births, Deaths, and Residual Migration 1960 to 2010 by year by County.

[9] IRS, U.S. Population Migration Data.

[10] Jordan Rappaport, "Moving to Nice Weather," *Regional Science and Urban Economics* 37 (2007)

[11] Census, American Community Survey, 2005-2009 5-year estimates.

[12] Census, American Community Survey, 2010.

[13] Ibid.

[14] U.S. Department of Education, National Center for Education Statistics (NCES), 2008 Integrated Postsecondary Education Data System, 2010, found at: http://nces.ed.gov/ipeds/

[15] Ibid.

[16] Census, American Community Survey, 2008-2010 3-year estimates.

[17] Alfred A. Marshall, *Principles of Economics* (London: Macmillan, 1920).

[18] IRS, U.S. Population Migration Data

[19] BEA, Regional Economic Accounts

[20] Ibid.

[21] From analysis of data from BEA Regional Economic Accounts and Census Bureau Population Estimates.

[22] From an interview by Katie Couric on CBS Evening News, December 8, 2008.

[23] James Lyons, *Selling Seattle: Representing Contemporary Urban America* (London: Wallflower Press, 2004)

[24] David Albouy, "What are cities worth? Land rents, local productivity, and the capitalization of amenity values," National Bureau of Economic Research, working paper # 14981, 2009.

[25] Rappaport, "Moving to Nice Weather."

[26] Yong Chen, Stuart Rosenthal, "Local amenities and life-cycle migration: Do people move for jobs or fun?" *Journal of Urban Economics* 64 (2008).

[27] The National Association of Homebuilders Housing Opportunity Index can be found at: www.nahb.com.

[28] Data from the Texas Transportation Institute can be found at: http://tti.tamu.edu/group/mobility/

[29] Data from 2000 Census and 2010 American Community Survey.

[30] Puget Sound Regional Council (PSRC), Covered Employment Estimates, found at: www.psrc.org/data/employment.

[31] Data from 1990 Census and 2010 American Community Survey.

[32] Rappaport, "Moving to Nice Weather."

[33] Robert Frank, *The Winner-Take-All Society: Why the Few at the Top Get So Much More Than the Rest of Us*, (New York: Penguin, 1996)

Chapter 3

[1] This section is based on the general, well-known narrative of Seattle's early history. I drew from a number of sources, most notably: Murray Morgan, *Skid Road* (New York: Viking Press, 1951); William C. Speidel, *Sons of the Profits* (Seattle: Nettle Creek Publishing, 1967); Roger Sale, *Seattle, Past to Present* (Seattle: University of Washington Press, 1976).

[2] The full quote, as reported in HistoryLink, reads: "If I were a member of this community, really I should get weary of being looked on as a sort of aesthetic dust-bin." The remarks were delivered to an British-American War Relief Association benefit event at audience at the Washington Athletic Club.

[3] OFM, Decennial population counts for the state, counties, and cities: 1890 to 2000.

[4] Fred T. Haley, "The Pacific Northwest: America's Most Important Colony," speech to the Seattle Rotary Club, January 23, 1957, mimeograph.

[5] Edwin Cohn, Jr., *Industry in the Pacific Northwest and the Location Theory* (New York: Columbia University Press, 1954)

[6] Seattle Area Industrial Council, "Seattle-Tacoma-Everett Metropolitan Area Economy," mimeograph, 1967.

[7] OFM, Decennial population counts for the state, counties, and cities: 1890 to 2000; Seattle Annexation List, found at: http://clerk.ci.seattle.wa.us/~public/annexations/annex_list.htm.

[8] The most commonly used multiplier for Boeing, 3.96, was originally found in: Glenn Pascall, Douglas H. Pedersen and Richard S. Conway, Jr., "The Boeing Company Economic Impact Study," prepared for The Boeing Company, 1989.

[9] Sale, *Seattle, Past to Present.*

[10] Boeing Company, Orders and Deliveries. Details on every Boeing plane ordered and delivered, since the first 707 in 1958, are found at: http://active.boeing.com/commercial/orders/index.cfm.

[11] OFM, Population, Population Change, Births, Deaths, and Residual Migration 1960 to 2010 by year by County.

[12] BEA, Regional Economic Accounts.

[13] Seafirst Corporation, "Pacific Northwest Industries Annual Review," 1984, statistical supplement.

[14] BEA, Regional Economic Accounts.

[15] BLS, Local Area Unemployment Statistics.

[16] OFM, Population, Population Change, Births, Deaths, and Residual Migration 1960 to 2010 by year by County; BEA, Regional Economic Accounts.

[17] BEA, Regional Economic Accounts.

[18] Washington State Economic Development Board, "Washington Works Worldwide: Positioning Ourselves to Compete in the New Global Economy," Report, 1988.

[19] Information about the National Bureau of Economic Research's Business Cycle Dating Committee can be found at: http://www.nber.org/cycles/recessions.html

[20] Boeing Company, Orders and Deliveries.

[21] Washington State Department of Employment Security (DES), Historical Employment Estimates, found at: https://fortress.wa.gov/esd/employmentdata/reports-publications/economic-reports/washington-employment-estimates.

[22] Ibid

[23] Lyons, *Selling Seattle.*

[24] David Brooks, *Bobos in Paradise: The New Upper Class and How They Got There* (New York: Simon and Schuster, 2000)

[25] OFM, Population, Population Change, Births, Deaths, and Residual Migration 1960 to 2010 by year by County.

[26] Ibid

[27] BEA, Regional Economic Accounts.

[28] DES, Historical Employment Estimates.

[29] Richard S. Conway, "The Microsoft Economic Impact Study," privately published, 1996; Theo S. Eicher, "The Microsoft Economic Impact Study," privately published, 2010.

[30] As of 2012, Boeing's board of directors does not have a single individual with any recognizable ties to Washington State or companies headquartered within the state.

[31] Bureau of Transportation Statistics, found at www.bts.gov.

[32] DES, Historical Employment Estimates.

[33] Ibid.

[34] Ibid.

[35] PSRC, Covered Employment Estimates.

[36] DES, Historical Employment Estimates.

Chapter 4

[1] Washington State Department of Natural Resources (DNR), Washington Timber Harvest Report, available at: http://www.dnr.wa.gov/BusinessPermits/Topics/EconomicReports /Pages/obe_washington_timber_harvest_reports.aspx

[2] A typical refrigerator weighs about 200 pounds and costs about $500, for a value of $2.50 per pound. Chevrolet's website lists a ¾ ton Suburban at $43,830 and a curb weight of 5,824 pounds for a value of $7.52 per pound. According to information on Boeing's website, a 777 weighs about 300,000 pounds empty, and sells for about $275 million, for a value of $909 per pound.

[3] Washington State Department of Agriculture, Export Statistics, found at: http://agr.wa.gov/Marketing/International/Statistics.aspx

[4] Boeing Company, Orders and Deliveries; The Boeing Company, Current Market Outlook, 2012-2031, found at: http://www.boeing.com/commercial/cmo/

[5] Census, American Community Survey, 2005-2009 5-year estimates.

[6] BEA, Foreign Direct Investment in the U.S.: Balance of Payments and Direct Investment Position Data, found at: www.bea.gov/international/di1fdibal.htm.

[7] Sassen, *Cities in a World Economy.*

[8] Michael Luis & Associates, Report of the Foreign Direct Investment Task Force, Prosperity Partnership, 2008. Unpublished.

[9] OFM, Decennial population counts for the state, counties, and cities: 1890 to 2000; OFM April 1, 2012 population of cities, towns, and counties.

[10] Ibid.

[11] Seattle Annexation List.

[12] OFM, Decennial population counts for the state, counties, and cities: 1890 to 2000.

[13] This idea became very public during a speech by Christopher Leinberger at the 2012 Annual Meeting of the Bellevue Downtown Association.

[14] Alan Ehrenhalt, *The Great Inversion and the Future of the American City* (New York: Knopf, 2012)

[15] See Beecham note in chapter 3, above.

[16] Jim Bouton, *Ball Four* (New York: Macmillan, 1970)

[17] Ibid.

[18] Rachel Carson, *Silent Spring* (New York: Houghton Mifflin, 1962). This book, about the impact of pesticides on wildlife, is frequently credited with launching the modern environmental movement.

[19] DNR, Washington Timber Harvest Report.

[20] BEA, Regional Economic Accounts; DES, Historical Employment Estimates.

[21] DES, Historical Employment Estimates.

[22] Frank Shrontz, "Boeing: Our Vision for the Future," delivered to the annual meeting of the Greater Seattle Chamber of Commerce, September 20, 1991.

[23] Data compiled by Barry T. Hirsch, David A. Macpherson, and Wayne G. Vroman, and available at: http://unionstats.gsu.edu/MonthlyLaborReviewArticle.htm

[24] Detailed descriptions of Beck and other union activists in Seattle can be found in Morgan's *Skid Road.*

[25] Data compiled by Hirsch et al.

[26] Ibid.

[27] Robert Chase, "Ties that Bind: The Enduring Economic Impact of Alaska on the Puget Sound Region," prepared for the Tacoma-Pierce County Chamber of Commerce and the Greater Seattle Chamber of Commerce, 2004.

[28] Berk & Associates, "Washington's Defense Economy: Measuring and Growing its Impact, prepared for the Washington Economic Development Commission, 2010.

[29] IRS, U.S. Population Migration Data.

[30] Census, 1990 Census; Census, American Community Survey, 2010.

Chapter 5

[1] Texas Transportation Institute, "Performance Measure Summary, Seattle, WA," found at: http://mobility.tamu.edu/ums/congestion-data/

[2] Anthony Downs, *Stuck in Traffic* (Washington D.C.: The Brookings Institution, 1992)

[3] Cambridge Systematics, "PSRC 2006 Household Activity Survey Analysis Report," prepared for the Puget Sound Regional Council, 2007.

[4] Ibid.

[5] Ibid.

[6] An exhaustive description of Seattle's efforts to gain control of the Cedar River watershed can be found in: Matthew Klingle, Emerald City: An Environmental History of Seattle (New Haven: Yale University Press, 2007)

[7] Federal Aviation Administration, "Primary Airports based on Preliminary CY2011 Enplanements," found at: http://www.faa.gov/airports/planning_capacity/passenger_allcargo_stats/passenger/

[8] C. Northcote Parkinson, *Parkinson's Law* (Boston: Houghton Mifflin Co., 1957)

[9] This remark by Farley is quote and re-quoted frequently, but the origins remain unclear.

[10] Ernst & Young, "Total State and Local Business Taxes," prepared for the Council on State Taxation, 2011.

[11] Ernst & Young, "Competitiveness of State and Local Business Taxes on New Investment," Prepared for the Council on State Taxation, 2011.

[12] The 2002 final report of the Washington State Tax Structure Study Committee, known as the Gates Committee, reviews and documents the regressive nature of Washington's tax system. The report can be found at: http://dor.wa.gov/Content/AboutUs/StatisticsAndReports/WAtaxstudy/Final_Report.htm

[13] The Washington Governor's Office has an Office of Regulatory Assistance that works on high profile projects, but resources only make this service available to a fraction of businesses that run into regulatory issues.

[14] Jeffrey Groen, "The Effect of College Location on Migration of College-Educated Labor," *Journal of Econometrics* 121 (2004); John Bound, et al, "Trade in University Training: Cross-state Variation in the Production and Stock of College-Educated Labor," Journal of Econometrics 121 (2004).

[15] A list of businesses spun out of UW-developed research can be found at the UW Center for Commercialization: http://depts.washington.edu/uwc4c/start-ups/uw-start-ups/

[16] NCES, 2008 Integrated Postsecondary Education Data System.

[17] Census, American Community Survey, 2005-2009 5-year estimates.

[18] Ibid.

[19] The Washington State Department of Licensing (DOL) tracks the trade-in of out-of-state drivers licenses, and reports new licenses by county. Unfortunately, other states do not do the same thing, so accurate data is available only for in-migrants. Also, this data does not cover most military relocations, since service personnel are not required to get a new license for the state they are posted to. This data can be found at: www.dol.wa.gov/about/driversreports.html

[20] Manzer J. Griswold, *Newcomers to King County 1870-1990*, United Good Neighbors of Seattle and King County, 1965

[21] Census, American Community Survey, 2005-2009 5-year estimates.

[22] A discussion of the "thickness" of jobs markets can be found in: Enrico Moretti, *The New Geography of Jobs*, (Boston: Houghton Mifflin Harcourt, 2012)

[23] Chen and Rosenthal, "Local amenities and life-cycle migration."

[24] Census, American Community Survey, 2010.

[25] Gerald B. Nelson, *Seattle: the Life and Times of an American City* (New York: Alfred A. Knopf, 1977)

[26] Michael Luis & Associates, "Research Universities and the Knowledge Region," prepared for the International Regions Benchmarking Consortium, 2010.

[27] Atkinson and Andes, *2010 State New Economy Index*

Chapter 6

[1] Washington State Office of Financial Management (OFM), 2002 Washington Input-Output Model, found at: http://www.ofm.wa.gov/economy/io/

[2] Calculated by author from the 2002 Washington Input-Output model.

[3] Prosperity Partnership, "Regional Economic Strategy for the Central Puget Sound Region," found at: http://www.psrc.org/econdev/res

[4] Boeing, Current Market Outlook; Airbus, "Global Market Forecast 2011-2030," found at: http://www.airbus.com/company/market/forecast/

[5] DES, Historical Employment Estimates.

[6] The information in this section, covering the market for commercial aircraft, is mostly taken from unpublished research I performed while serving as aerospace advisor to the Washington Governor's Office. It came from a wide variety of sources, mostly the websites and publications of the Boeing, Airbus and the other airframe producers.

[7] Timothy Bartik, *Who Benefits from State and Local Economic Development Policies* (Kalamazoo: Upjohn Institute, 1991)

[8] Port of Seattle, Centennial Map and Timeline, found at: http://portseattle100.org/map-and-timeline/

[9] The Puget Sound ports have a natural advantage in the depth of the waters in their harbors – up to 300 feet. Unlike many U.S. ports, the Puget Sound ports do not need to be dredged to maintain safe depths. The fact that shippers through the Puget Sound ports still pay the Harbor Maintenance Tax, none of which goes to maintain those ports, is an ongoing sore point.

[10] Martin Associates, "The Economic Impact of the Port of Tacoma;" Martin Associates, "The 2007 Economic Impact of the Port of Seattle."

[11] Wouter Jacobs, Cesar DuCruet, Peter de Langen, "Integrating World Cities into Production Networks: the Case of Port Cities," *Global Networks* 10 (2010).

[12] DES, Historical Employment Estimates.

[13] Eicher, "The Microsoft Economic Impact Study."

[14] Ibid. Eicher makes this point with respect to 2008. Figures advancing the data to 2011 taken from Eicher and DES, Historical Employment Estimates.

[15] BEA, National Income and Product Accounts.

[16] Washington Research Council, "Trends in Washington's Life Sciences Industry," 2011, found at: www.researchcouncil.org.

[17] Ibid.

[18] Ibid.

[19] DES, Historical Employment Estimates.

[20] Ibid

[21] OFM, 2002 Washington Input-Output Model.

[22] U.S. Department of Commerce, Office of Travel & Tourism Industries, found at: http://tinet.ita.doc.gov/outreachpages/inbound.general_information.inbound_overview.html

[23] Dean Runyan Associates, "Washington State Travel Impacts 1991-2010," prepared for the Washington State Department of Commerce, 2011.

[24] Port of Seattle, Cruise Statistics, found at: www.portseattle.org/About/Publications/Statistics/Seaport/Pages/Cruise.aspx

[25] Berk, Washington's Defense Economy.

[26] Ibid.

[27] Ibid.

Chapter 7

[1] Clinton v Cedar Rapids and the Missouri River Railroad, (24 Iowa 455; 1868).

[2] Census, 2007 Census of Governments, found at: www.census.gov/govs/cog/

[3] Ibid.

[4] Elazar, *Building Cities in America.*

[5] Not In My Back Yard

[6] Tiebout, "A Pure Theory of Local Expenditures."

[7] Robert Dahl, *Who Governs? Democracy and Power in an American City,* (New Haven: Yale University Press, 1961); Edward C. Banfield, *Political Influence* (Glencoe, IL: The Free Press of Glencoe, 1961); Edward C. Banfield and James Q Wilson, *City Politics* (Cambridge: Harvard University Press, 1963)

[8] A basic description of the evolution of elite theory is found in: Alan Harding, "Elite Theory and Growth Machines," in David Judge, Gerry Stoker, Harlod Wolman, eds, *Theories of Urban Politics,* (London: Sage Publications, 1995).

[9] Overviews of urban regime theory can be found in: Gerry Stoker, "Regime Theory and Urban Politics," in Judge, et al, *Theories of Urban Politics*; and Clarence N. Stone, "Urban Regimes and the Capacity to Govern," *Journal of Urban Affairs* 15 (1993). A longer case study is found in: Clarence N. Stone, *Regime Politics: Governing Atlanta, 1946-1988* (Lawrence: University Press of Kansas, 1989).

[10] Harvey Molotch, "The Political Economy of Growth Machines," *Journal of Urban Affairs* 15 (1993).

[11] This narrative of mayoral leadership in Seattle is drawn from a number of sources, including Sale's book, articles in History Link, occasional dips into Wikipedia and, especially for the period since the mid-1980s, my own personal recollections.

[12] Barnes and Ledebur, *The New Regional Economies:*

[13] Original enabling legislation is found in Revised Code of Washington (RCW) 35.58.

[14] Peirce, *Citistates.*

[15] *The Seattle Times*, "Who Runs Seattle: Facts and Opinions about People, Politics and Power in the City," April 12, 1987.

[16] David Birch, Job Creation in America: How our Smallest Companies Put the Most People to Work, (New York: Free Press, 1987)

[17] The domestic Intercity Visit and North American Study Mission program has taken delegations to: Baltimore (1983); San Francisco (1984); Minneapolis/St. Paul (1985); Toronto (1986); Tampa (1987); Boston (1988); San Diego (1989); Pittsburgh (1990); Atlanta (1991); Cleveland (1993); Toronto (1994); Silicon Valley (1995); Research Triangle (1996); Boston (1997); Washington D.C. (1988); Minneapolis/St. Paul (1999); San Diego (2000); Washington D.C. (2001); Chicago (2002); Washington D.C. (2003); Denver (2004); San Diego (2005); Philadelphia (2006); Washington D.C. (2007); Austin (2008); Montreal (2009); Boston (2010); Silicon Valley (2011);Atlanta, Savannah (2012).

[18] The International Study Mission program has taken delegations to: Amsterdam, Rotterdam, Stuttgart (1992); Kansai (1994); London, Bristol (1996); Singapore (1998); Sidney (1999); Berlin (2000); Stockholm (2002); Barcelona (2003); Shanghai (2004); Munich (2005); Dublin, Belfast (2006); Melbourne (2007); Fukuoka (2008); Helsinki (2009); Persian Gulf (2010); Scotland, London (2011); Chile (2012).

Chapter 8

[1] Joseph Schumpeter, *Capitalism, Socialism and Democracy* (New York: Harper, 1942)

[2] Daron Acemoglu, James Robinson, *Why Nations Fail* (New York: Crown Business, 2012)

[3] For a discussion on the merits of place-based policies, see: Moretti, *The New Geography of Jobs.*

[4] Rosabeth Moss Kanter, *World Class: Thriving Locally in the Global Economy* (New York: Simon and Schuster, 1995).

[5] Philip Carlow, *Seattle Spirit*, published in the *Seattle Post-Intelligencer*, 1909.

[6] Peter F. Drucker, "The Five Deadly Business Sins," *Wall Street Journal*, October 21, 1993.

[7] Klaus Schwab, ed, *The Global Competitiveness Report 2011-2012* (Geneva: World Economic Forum, 2011)

[8] Gyourko et al, "Superstar Cities."

[9] Florida, *The Rise of the Creative Class.*

[10] Found in: Daniel J. Hughes, ed, *Moltke on the Art of War: Selected Writings.* (New York: Presidio Press, 1993).

[11] Charles E. Lindblom, "The Science of 'Muddling Through,'" *Public Administration Review* 14 (1959)

[12] Kenichi Ohmae, The Borderless World: Power and Strategy in the Interlinked Economy (New York: Harper Business, 1999-revised ed)

[13] IRS, U.S. Population Migration Data.

[14] Barnes and Ledebur, *The New Regional Economies.*

Chapter 9

[1] Richard S. Conway, Jr., "Foreign Exports and the Washington Economy," prepared for the Washington State Department of Trade and Economic Development, 1987; Richard S. Conway, Jr., "Foreign Exports and the Washington Economy," prepared for the Washington State Department of Community, Trade and Economic Development, 1997; Robert Chase, "Washington State Foreign Imports," prepared for the Washington State Department of Community, Trade and Economic Development, 1999.

[2] Trade Development Alliance of Greater Seattle, Washington Council on International Trade, "An International Competitiveness Strategy for Washington State," 2012.

[3] International Monetary Fund (IMF), *World Economic Outlook, April 2012*, (Washington D.C.: International Monetary Fund Publication Services, 2012).

[4] Transparency International (TI), "Corruption Perceptions Index 2011," found at: www.transparency.org.

[5] Moretti, *The New Geography of Jobs*.

[6] David B. Audretsch, Erik E. Lehmann, Susanne Warning, "University Spillovers and New Firm Location," *Research Policy* 34 (2005); Roland Andersson, John M. Quigley, Mats Wilhelmsson. "Urbanization, Productivity and Innovation: Evidence From Investment in Higher Education," *Journal of Urban Economics* 66 (2009).

[7] Luis & Associates, "Research Universities and the Knowledge Region."

[8] See discussion in Glaeser, *Triumph of the City*.

[9] The Boeing Company, "Aviation Policy and Geopolitics 2012."

[10] Matthew Kahn, *Climatopolis* (New York: Basic Books, 2010)

[11] National Intelligence Council, *Global Trends 2025: A Transformed World* (Washington D.C.: Superintendent of Documents, 2008)

[12] Sassen, *Cities in a World Economy*.

[13] Carl W. Art, R.A. Wegner, *Seattle: World City that Had to Be!* (Seattle: Metropolitan Press, 1930)

Index

Made in the USA
San Bernardino, CA
19 February 2014